"The night before I left for Peru I sat and meditated. I was beginning to see I could take control of my destiny in every way. My work would not only be person to person now, but person to humanity. It was now important for me to take complete responsibility and to be aware of what was going on around me, but not afraid. I recognized and acknowledged that I had prepared for my trip to Peru for a very long time; that the first time I went I decided to use that trip as a vision quest, and knew then that I would write the book that would become a film that would take me back again."

—from *It's All in the Playing*

Shirley MacLaine

It's All in the Playing

BANTAM BOOKS
TORONTO · NEW YORK · LONDON · SYDNEY · AUCKLAND

IT'S ALL IN THE PLAYING

A Bantam Book
Bantam hardcover edition / September 1987
4 printings through September 1987
Bantam paperback edition / September 1988

Library of Congress Cataloging-in-Publication Data

MacLaine, Shirley, 1934-
  It's all in the playing.

  1. MacLaine, Shirley, 1934-   . 2. Entertainers—
United States—Biography.   3. Spiritualists—United
States—Biography.   I. Title.
PN2287.M18A3   1987   791.43'028'0924 [B]   87-47560
ISBN 0-553-27299-3

Published simultaneously in the United States and Canada

Bantam Books are published by Bantam Books, a division of
Bantam Doubleday Dell Publishing Group, Inc. Its trade-
mark, consisting of the words ''Bantam Books'' and the por-
trayal of a rooster, is Registered in U.S. Patent and Trademark
Office and in other countries. Marca Registrada. Bantam
Books, 666 Fifth Avenue, New York, New York 10103.

PRINTED IN THE UNITED STATES OF AMERICA

KR   0 9 8 7 6 5 4 3 2

I would like to thank

    Colin Higgins
    Bella Abzug
    Stan Margulies
    Thomas Sharkey
    John of Zebedee
    Tom McPherson
    Lazaris
    Charles Dance
       and
    John Heard

each of whom helped me to
realize an aspect of myself

When the eagle of the North
flies with the condor of the South—
the spirit of the land she will awaken

Peruvian Inca prophecy

It's All in the Playing

Chapter 1

I stretched upright, lifted my arms to the sky, and breathed deeply. I needed the oxygen. The altitude of the surrounding Cordillera Blanca mountain range, high in the Andes of Peru, was 22,205 feet. I was standing at only 12,000 feet and could still feel my heart pounding and thumping. It occurred to me that it would be worth the discipline of coming here just to get in shape for a new show. Returning to two shows a night at sea level would be a breeze.

From where I stood I could see straight across the valley of Rio Santa, known among the Andeans as the Callejón de Huaylas. The Rio Santa valley is one of those places so stunningly beautiful as to be literally breath-taking—in fact, its impact on me might have been the real reason I was short of breath. To attempt a description can give only a hint of the meadows of waving corn, silent turquoise lakes, and luminescent waterfalls tumbling into the rich and fertile valley below, backed by unending vistas of ice-covered peaks marching in glacial splendor to their high horizon. I have always loved mountains, always felt a sense of peace and elation being there, a glowing feeling that something wonderful is going to happen just around the corner—and even if it doesn't it won't matter because every present moment is so magical. I wondered what Gerry would think of this ancient Inca land, of its secretive, mystical quality. I reached out and peeled the soft skin from a quenuales tree. It was more like fabric than bark. Gerry said that all of his happiest moments had been connected to nature, yet he never had too much time for it. The smell of Scotch broom and eucalyptus mingled in the glacial mountain air. God, it was so strange how I missed him, particularly since there hadn't been any personal involvement for so long.

It had been ten years since our troubled love affair had sparked the self-search that pushed me into writing *Out on a Limb,* which, in turn, first brought me to these mountains. Long enough, I thought, for me to be objective about Gerry in the film I was now making of the book. And I had good cause to be grateful to Gerry, whose rigidly skeptical attitude about spiritual values had provoked me into further explorations both on my own and with my friend David—David ... who had been a composite of so many people acting as spiritual guides for me, condensed into a character who would become real on the screen. I wondered about all the people whose various realities I had combined to crystalize in David. Would they see the film in far-flung areas of the world? Would they even know, from distant mountaintops, that it existed? David—my creation, a marvelous, quirky, gentle, strong friend who led me into the labyrinth of my self and left me to find my own way. I had created David. I had created myself. Was life like the movies, only a dream?

I felt a crisp, cold, yet mellow warmth flow together like a textured elixir over my bare arms. I could see sugar-cane fields far down in the valley. The air was so clear I could make out where sheep and cattle dotted the craggy mountains, and where molle (red pepper) trees provided shade for the mountain people in their brilliantly colored ponchos. Brilliantly colored so as to permit people to distinguish one another in the mountain distances, each village subscribing to its own color.

The peasants took great care of their sheep, the most highly prized of animals, for their perennial gift of wool. Often the Andeans used pigs as watch animals to tend children—animals and peasants all participating fully in family life. When I asked why I never saw llamas or alpacas or vicuñas in this part of the Andes, no one seemed to know except that "they had just never come over here."

I sat down under the quenuales tree and bit into an apple I had brought with me. I focused on the irony of the stunning countryside, remembering how deeply affecting the natural disasters of the area had been in scarring the memories of the people who lived here just recently. It would be impossible to understand the culture of the people here without recognizing the accepting, fatalistic undercurrent that made it possible for them to live under the threat of storm, earthquake, and volcano.

Huarás, the central commercial and cultural mountain city of the region, with a population now of 50,000, suffered a massive earthquake on the afternoon of May 31, 1970. Measuring 7.8 on the Richter scale, it killed about 67,000 people, leveling almost every town in the Callejón de Huaylas. In terms of lives lost it was the worst disaster in the history of the Americas. The quake lasted about fifty seconds and was followed by aftershocks all through the night. It was so severe that two days later helicopters were still unable to land in some places, because the dust was so thick. The death toll would have been greater had it not struck on a Sunday when children were out of school.

Not long after, in 1972, the shocking avalanche landslide occurred which buried the beautiful mountain city of Yungay, killing 18,000 of its inhabitants. The people still speak of the massive slabs of granite that broke loose from the west face of the north peak of Nevado Huascarán. Three million cubic meters of ice and mud rode a cushion of air down to Yungay and the Santa River in only three minutes, at a speed of 300 kilometers an hour. The only survivors were 240 people watching a circus outside the avalanche path who managed to scramble to a high knoll.

Way back when, Gerry had been shocked that I was going to Peru. He and I had talked of the destiny of those 240 people. Why were they different? He said it was coincidence. I said it was karmic.

As I sat munching my apple I wondered what I'd do if I found myself caught in an event of that magnitude. And worse, how would I feel if I survived? Would I know why? As soon as the thought struck me I was reminded that I *had* been through such disasters many times—not in this life, but in others. Even today I have a haunting terror of tidal waves. I "knew" I had watched, transfixed in horror, as a mountainous wall of water bore down on me, curling me into it. The terror of my memory was not associated with being inundated by the weight of the water, but more by the pull of the giant undertow as it sucked me out to sea again. I remembered dying then, almost relieved that earthly panic and pain had ceased.

I was convinced that I had lived before, "died" before, and would live and "die" again.

As I sat thinking I reflected on what I had just been through. I was exhausted from shooting a five-hour miniseries based on my book *Out on a Limb* in which I played myself. It was that original experience in Peru that led me to search out the possibility that life was more multi-dimensional in its reality than what I could see or prove. Having lived and "died" before was only part of it. Life was ongoing and eternal. I was sure of that.

But now I was beginning to explore the concept that everything that happened in my life was occurring because *I* was creating it in order to learn about myself. The uniqueness of filming *Out on a Limb* was that it was a metaphor and a constant daily reminder of that truth.

I looked out across the mountains and asked myself what I had learned from the experience. If I acknowledged that I created my own reality on every level, then I had been totally responsible for everything that had gone on. That would be something to write about, I thought. But dare I go back to the well of my Peruvian adventure in order to peer into the illusion within the illusion of my life? Would that be the ultimate self-centeredness? Yes. The more I understood self, the more centered I became. And the more I understood others. That was the point. It all starts with self.

Truly, life is a stage and each of us players upon it. We choose our parts, but how we play them is the real issue. Sometimes we complain about the parts we have written for ourselves; sometimes we wish we had someone else's part. But more important than anything, we so harshly judge the manner in which we play ourselves, as well as how someone else is playing his or her part. We all know there is a need for protagonists and antagonists in a "play" in order to have color and dramatic, or even comedic, tension. Without the polarity of tension and points of view in a play, there is no interest. So why is it that we are so unwilling to be tolerant of those very values that give us the color and tension and differences in the grander play called *life*?

That is what this book is about. Life was becoming like a play to me. A play that I was not only writing for myself every day of my life, but acting in as well. So, necessarily, all the characters were characters of my own creation, on the screen and off; apparently necessary because I found them either amusing, intriguing, infuriating, upsetting, repulsive, entertaining, loving, or uplifting. Characters who failed to hook me emotionally were not in my play. They didn't need to be. I noticed that only characters who enabled me to learn and touch more of myself were in my play. I barely knew the others existed. In fact the characters in my life's play seemed to exist in direct ratio to what I needed or wanted to learn about the world and myself. And when I learned whatever it was, the characters that had acted as mirrors for me subtly disappeared, somehow replaced by new players who offered entirely new themes and perspectives. Not all my characters were in for the run-of-the-play contract. I didn't want them to be. Did that seem cruel and unfeeling? No, not really. It was just simply true. I did that to players in my drama and *they did that to me in theirs*. We existed on several separate levels of reality simultaneously. Or to put it another way, the creatures, persons, events of my reality, as in the activity of all creation, took on a life of their own.

I remembered a dream I used to have as a child—a rather prophetically sophisticated dream as I look back on it now.

I dreamed I was being chased by a gorilla. I ran until I came to the edge of an abyss. Then I had a choice. I could confront the gorilla or jump, out of fear, into the abyss. I turned to the gorilla and said, "What do I do now?" The gorilla threw up his hands and answered, "I don't know, kid. It's your dream."

That's just about how I look at things now. It's all my dream. I'm making all of it happen—good *and* bad—and I have the choice of how I'll relate to it and what I'll do about it.

Other people are creating their dreams, too, with their own casts of characters. These realities intersect in ways so involved that the dynamics of the outcome ultimately drive one in upon one's own reality. The question then becomes: "What do *I* do about this, or what do *I* want from this?" which, of course, was the question in the first place. The lesson? Perhaps we are all telling the truth—our truth as we see it. (Or hiding from it, of course.) Perhaps everyone has his own truth, and truth as an objective reality simply does not exist.

There's nothing like making a movie to bring home that point, because you can make the truth anything you want it to be. Particularly if what you're dealing with is your own life. I have been accused by some of "remarkable" hubris in making *Out on a Limb,* but because of the experience of playing myself in a film, I was able to look closely at the illusion within the illusion. It began in Peru ten years ago and ended in Peru ten years later. But the stops along the way were the real story.

Chapter 2

ABC Television approached me to consider making a miniseries film of my book *Out on a Limb*. They spoke of metaphysical searching being popular now and extraterrestrials and UFOs as something the public was genuinely interested in. Witness *Cocoon, E.T., Star Wars, Close Encounters, Starman,* and so on. For a long time I didn't take their suggestion seriously. Somehow in my mind, my writing speculations were separate from my performing career. It wasn't until later that I realized that each was an aspect of the individual creativity, coming from the same source and returning to the same source.

About the same time, I found myself "accidentally" in a restaurant in the San Fernando Valley talking with my friend Roddy McDowall, who said that writer-director Colin Higgins (*Harold and Maude, Nine to Five, Foul Play, Best Little Whorehouse*) thought that *Out on a Limb* would make a good movie. A movie? Or a television miniseries? A captive audience shelling out $5.50 per person for the privilege or a living-room audience getting up for a beer? Then I thought: Two hours isn't enough time to tell the story, and besides, every American household has at least one member of the family who has had a mystical experience, felt *déjà vu*, seen a UFO, or experienced an inexplicable "coincidence" of one sort or another.

I decided to call Colin.

"Listen," I began. "TV seems to me to be a natural medium (no pun intended) for a real-life drama about my reincarnated love affair with a British M.P., and a Peruvian encounter with a man who claimed to have a relationship with an extraterrestrial from the Pleiades. What do you think?"

"Well," said Colin, "I see a lot of entertainment value either way. What you just outlined is already funny."

God knows Colin Higgins knew comedy, irrespective of the fact that he spent his childhood in Australia. I wondered how funny he would think TV salaries were. Or more to the point, how funny would his high-powered Hollywood agent feel if Colin was slumming in television.

It didn't matter. Colin, as it turned out, was a fellow searcher. He had attended as many metaphysical seminars as I had, and even introduced me to a transmedium I had never previously heard of. He also began to reveal to me a set of personal values of the highest human priorities I had run into in twenty years of successful artistic encounters. The litmus test for me then was, as it is now: do people apply their spiritual and metaphysical knowledge to the roles they play in life? Colin does—in spades, as they say.

So we began a creative and personal friendship which challenged us both and which I'm sure will also stand the test of time and artistic trauma. It was evident to both of us that spiritual material, if honestly perceived, tended simultaneously to keep the working and personal relationship free of contaminating influences such as power grabs, ego trips, temperamental fury, writer's block, and fear of what the audience thinks and feels.

Colin is about five eleven, storybook handsome,

with a brown mane of hair so luxuriously rich that on first meeting him I had the impulse to run my fingers through it but hesitated for fear the tresses would come unglued in my hand. A baseless fear. The hair was real. I emphasize the hair of the man because somewhere under there I felt that it was the gift wrapping for his creativity. I was right.

Now, Colin has an interesting way of walking. I can always tell what mood he's in by the way he walks. If he's been hurt and is feeling vulnerable, his arms hang from his sides and his steps seem as though they are moving in place. His chin juts out as though he expects a jab, and a smile of ironic resignation plays on his lips. When he's in centered spirits his eyes flash, he speaks much faster, with clarity and force, and when he walks, his arms move more enthusiastically. Sometimes he even holds a cigarette "to seem grown-up," and always he cuts right through the comedy chicken fat until the bone of humor is pristine and sparkling. I've noticed that really creative comedy scientists never feel the need to perform. They are too busy observing and analyzing why something or someone else is truly comic—as opposed to "hostile" comic. But when their own funny bone is tickled they let go with uncontrollable abandon. Every once in a while that happens with Colin and he becomes an incisive, mischievous brat; the essence of comedy bite. That's when I started calling him Harold after the character he conceived in *Harold and Maude*. In fact I sometimes see myself as Maude (the eighty-year-old fun-loving Auntie Mame character) and him as Harold. Anyway, that's my way of referring to him when I love him the most or when I feel he should listen harder.

So Harold and I began to interview prospective writers for *Out on a Limb*. He would oversee and supervise and I would keep it real and honest, since it was my life.

To make a very long one-year story short, we decided to write the screenplay ourselves. We knew the material better than anyone else. Even though I had never written a screenplay before, and Colin, an experienced screenplay writer, had no idea about writing a five-hour film with commercial breaks, we proceeded with courage. A regular two-hour screenplay usually took a year. So were we talking a two and one-half-year job here? Well, we both knew the UFOs would have landed already if we took that long.

I had attempted a kind of detailed screen treatment of five hundred pages on another subject I had shown Colin some months before. He was impressed with the fact that I "worked hard." Now I pulled out the screenplays for *Terms of Endearment* and *Being There* (two that I admired a great deal) and began to study them as a writer, not as an actress. I began to see and understand the subtlety of the craft a bit more. I wrote the first three hours of *Out on a Limb* as an exercise in on-the-job training. Colin said, "Now at least we know it can work."

So then we wrote a "treatment"—that is, a brief plot rundown with high-point scenes and a fleshing-out of the chief characters—for a five-hour screen scenario based on the book. There were really going to be only four major protagonists: Gerry, my British M.P. lover; Bella Abzug, whose life and friendship speak for themselves; my precious David, who introduced me to spiritual matters and guided me in Peru; and myself. Colin and I worked with our proposed producer, Stan Margulies, who was an experienced television miniseries producer (*Roots, The Thorn Birds*) until Stan said we were ready to present our outline to Brandon Stoddard, head of entertainment at ABC.

I was leery of television executives, feeling that you could put their collective intelligence on the head of a pin and, as Oscar Levant once said, still have some room left over. But Mike Nichols had told me that Brandon

Stoddard was different. Mike had made *Silkwood* for
ABC. He was right.

Brandon ushered us into his office with an informal
flourish. (He looks like a shrewd child-man with intensely intelligent eyes and a skin of scrubbed freckles.)
He listened politely as Colin and I blue-skyed our presentation. (We embellished as we went along.)

Stan sat quietly, reminding me of an inscrutable
Talmudic scholar who, in calm shrewd silence, knows he
will always get his way. Stan had earned the respect of so
many people, he didn't need to do anything that even
hinted at pulling rank. He knew the show would be
good.

One of ABC's female executives was present as
Brandon's co-decision-maker. She was a pants-suited "I've
come a long way, baby" female. She must have seen her
job as one of being the devil's advocate (again, no pun
intended) in a sea of mystical spiritualistic ecstasy. On an
earlier occasion she had literally auditioned Colin and
made some sterling suggestions for Shirley's character,
such as: "She is too successful, too much in command of
her life, and doesn't have any problems the TV audience
can identify with. Maybe you should give her a serious
leg injury so she can't dance, or maybe make the love
affair with Gerry really agonizing to the point of suicide
and *that's* why Shirley goes on her spiritual search."
When I pointed out that neither of these suggestions was
even remotely true and hence hardly relevant to my life
story, she countered with: "But we need to pull a rat-
ing." I felt doubly awkward because she was a woman in
an important job, but her need to prove her "executivi-
bility" was earnest, so we simply had to cope with it as
well as we could.

Brandon fortunately turned out to be his own
decision-maker. He caught the drift of my remarks in
response to further suggestions from the lady and sent
Colin and me away to come up with whatever script we

thought would work. He said ABC had been attempting a metaphysical story for years and could never arrive at anything personally dramatic and involving. He was well aware of the growing spiritual hunger in the American culture and wanted to be the one who had the courage to okay the nourishment.

Colin and I left extremely impressed. Thus began the collaboration of Harold and a slighter, younger Maude.

In June of 1985, Colin came up to my house in the Pacific Northwest. His agent did not know what he was doing there. If he hadn't known better, he could have explained it away as a Hollywood fling or something. But Harold and I never thought of each other in those terms. He had a kind of a girlfriend anyway and I had sworn off men for a while. Or rather the "feeling" gave me up—I didn't give it up. The two of us were to make the gossip columns quite frequently, but that only made us laugh.

Anyway, there we were in my home. It is a place of beauty and a joy forever, surrounded by trees and located on a mountaintop looking straight across at Mount Rainier, and with a full-fledged tumbling river below us. There is a swimming pool with warm water and a hot tub of hotter water, all of which one enjoys with the surrounding 360-degree view.

This house is my personal paradise which I bought by dancing two shows a night—the leg action that the female executive had wanted me to sabotage for "ratings"! (I always have felt that telling the truth is the wisest course, as well as explaining my feeling that one definitely deserves everything one has earned.)

Anyway, my assistant, Thomas Sharkey, endearingly known to me and my friends as Simo (because of a past-life connection), runs the house for me. He takes care of the dogs (a handsome chocolate-brown Lab named Hot Fudge Sultan and, a later arrival, a snow-white American Eskimo named Shinook). We have a large vegetable garden, which Simo tends and nurtures, along with flowers abounding in rainbow colors, and chickens and birds that the dogs delight in pestering. Simo also cooks, which is important to this story, because Harold and I love to eat. Plain, regular eating is one thing, but eating as a kind of artistic reward is quite another. It's difficult to articulate the joy of eating half a coconut cake *after* you know you've written a good scene. And conversely, it is probably hard for anyone to believe that we sometimes wrote good scenes because we knew there was coconut cake in the oven at the other end of the tunnel. But that's the way it was with Harold and me.

We wrote in the kitchen den. We could have chosen any room in the house, but we chose to write near the food. It kept us going. And when Simo went into his act in the kitchen, it was up for grabs which of us was the most entertaining. The smell of barbecued shrimp, steaming homemade lentil vegetable garlic soup, hot homemade bread, and fresh apple pie was enough to motivate us to write *Citizen Kane Revisited*.

Colin began as an actor. He has exquisite sensitivity regarding the problems of actors. So before we committed a scene to paper, we acted it out. Sometimes I took the part of "Shirley" and sometimes he did, and sometimes we switched roles in midstream. In any case, Simo had no idea that we worked that way. He had heard that writers *write*. So most of the time he would discreetly baste the roast, with his head in the oven so as not to overhear our artistic arguments. Then, in the middle of tempers flaring and insults screaming, Colin and I would stop cold and say: "No, that doesn't work. Let's try this." And we'd be at it again. For a while Simo thought we were conducting a New Age relationship where we'd let it all hang out and comment as we went. What pleased Simo the most, however, was that in the first few days Harold and I devoured three cakes, pounds of shrimp and scallops, a couple of chickens, enough salad for an army of rabbits, and several quarts of ice cream.

Both the screenplay and our bodies were getting fatter. We worked and ate thirteen hours a day, sometimes taking a break to swim or walk. We didn't answer the phone, and thought and breathed nothing but our story. In ten days we felt we had completed the first draft of the first three hours.

At this point I should elaborate more on what it means to have a professional association with an individual who is himself seriously involved in spiritual meaning and metaphysical perspectives. The cornerstone of such values is the understanding that each of us creates our own reality. Blaming whatever happens to us on someone or something else went out with high-button shoes—it's old-fashioned. Colin and I both understood that each of us was responsible for whatever positive and negative events were flowing in our lives. With that kind of clear perspective, it was possible for each of us to be honest about ourselves and each other. And when you can be honest with the person you're working with, all sorts of blockages fall away, because you discuss them openly, and as soon as they are acknowledged, they seem to disappear almost as though "once what is to be learned from them is learned," there is no need for them to exist anymore.

Colin and I had the view that life itself is a situation comedy, where we play the same scripts over and over, learning something different each time; each of us devising a script for ourselves that enables us to know ourselves better. We saw creativity as a necessary expression in life; almost as though to be alive is to be obligated to create. We also felt that to be creative was to be closer to the meaning of God or the Universal Mind or whatever one wishes to call it. We felt we were drawing on forces beyond our reach, beyond our own empirical understanding.

Colin and I were both totally familiar with the process of trance channeling: that is, using a talented psychic (medium) as a channel of communication with entities who acted as guides and consultants—and, indeed, as friends. It was a process I had first written about in *Out on a Limb,* and it would be, of course, one of the main subjects of the movie. In that context we both felt it was something that had to be handled with careful authenticity.

Channeling is one of the most controversial and popular processes of the New Age. There are pure channels (mediums) and there are channels who have so much emotional static of their own that the teachings from "the other side" are quite garbled and even inaccurate. I have observed both forms and find both fascinating.

But there are many people who feel that all of the mediums are acting; that through some process of self-hypnosis they can put themselves into a trance state and pretend that they are teaching complicated revelations in metaphysical truth.

And so I had studied meticulously and rigorously the emotional language that occurred during channeling. That was one reason I had sessions with so many. I had, by now, met and had sessions with more than twenty trance channeling mediums around the country. All the channelers had originally experienced the same thing. During meditation or in some other relaxed mind state, a spiritual guide would begin speaking, usually first inside their own minds (causing them to believe they were crazy at first) and then, as an adjustment occurred, the spiritual entity used the bodies and facilities of the channelers themselves to convey information. In every case, the trance channelers experienced a shift in perceptions relating to objective reality and, of course, a change in the way they led their lives. In each case there was an adjustment to the curiosity that others evidenced, but also they all told me they became happier in their personal lives because they had "proof" that death was not the final end—that life was eternal as evidenced by their guides, who now resided in a spiritual dimension with personalities and emotions and even involvements in the progress of spiritual understanding and development here on the earth plane.

I was more interested in *how* the spiritual guides actually used the medium's body. Each one of them explained the same thing. They don't "possess" the body of the trance channeling medium. They "overshadow" it. The medium puts his own "self" consciousness into a trance state, and gives permission for the spiritual entity to overshadow him, imbuing him with the energy that accesses the larynx, the hands, the face, the body, and so on.

Some trance channeling mediums actually have the experience of leaving their bodies (out-of-body experience) and some simply put their "self" consciousness into an unaware state. All of them say they cannot remember what occurred while in trance, and most of them are concerned that the spiritual entity did not humiliate them or otherwise act without social appropriateness. Some channelers whom I have talked to have been profoundly shocked (while listening to tape recordings later) by the information that came through them, and others have totally rejected some of the knowledge channeled. Often there was *no* agreement at all between the beliefs of the channeler and the beliefs of the spiritual entity. But always there was an agreement that the entity had permission to use the body of the channeler.

Colin had by now introduced me to his spiritual teacher, an entity named Lazaris. Lazaris is an entity who channels through a trance medium named Jach Pursel, who lives in San Francisco. Jach is a quiet, affable, unassuming man. He lives and works around the Illuminarium Art Gallery in San Francisco. He is an appreciator of beauty and good food, which we often enjoy together, and is a delightful man just to spend quiet times with. Lazaris came through one day when Jach was deep in meditation. At first Jach was uncomfortable and perplexed as to what had happened to him, but in due time his close friends assured him that the information coming from Lazaris was beneficial and loving. Lazaris as a spiritual guide and teacher spoke about the unseen divine reality which is at our disposal and available to us if we'd make ourselves aware of it. He taught that the universe is an extremely successful place—it is man whose perceptions have veiled the truth. Lazaris taught that mankind's natural proclivity was to be in harmony—just as plants, animals, fish, and birds were in harmony—that just to *be* was the goal and the secret to happiness. That was why nature was the ultimate teacher.

Colin and I were both coming to understand that struggle and strife were not necessary to the creative process. In fact, the notion of needing to overcome adversity in life itself was rapidly becoming passé to us. Adversity is not a requirement anymore. It never comes from outside of us, anyway. It is self-generated, because we believe we need it. So why continue to generate obstacles and impediments in our lives when by now we should know better?

All of this brings me to what happened after Colin and I finished our first three hours and turned it in to Stan Margulies and ABC.

The reaction was lukewarm. I knew we had more fine-tuning to do, but I also knew we had a very good script, so I couldn't understand why ABC wasn't more positive.

I called Jach Pursel. He went into trance and Lazaris came through. (Jach often channels on the telephone for his clients.) I asked what had happened. Lazaris was simple and to the point. "Unconsciously," he said, "you are not certain you want to expose yourself in front of fifty million people who might potentially see your show, contrasted to a few million who have *read* the same material. As a result, you are preventing the project from flowing smoothly."

I was astonished, as yet another fine point in creating my own reality hit me. I had *intellectually* understood the profundity of such a concept but in my gut I hadn't really felt it. Lazaris brought it home to me.

"You mean," I said, "that *I* caused the lukewarm reaction to what I worked so hard on?"

"Precisely," said Lazaris. "You have a hidden agenda of fear of public judgment on a mass-consciousness level. Recognize that truth, and if you desire to overcome the fear, the energy of the project will be cleared and you will find it going forward rather smoothly."

"Why didn't I recognize my own fear?" I asked.

"Because," said Lazaris, "you don't realize yet that you create your own reality every moment of your day."

To make sure of what he was saying, I repeated, "Then you're saying that *I* created the lukewarm reaction to my script?"

"That's correct. It happened in your dream, did it not?"

"Yes. But so is this 'conversation.' "

"Exactly. You also created me to point it out to you."

"So that's what you mean by all knowledge being available if we just make ourselves open to it?"

"That is correct. In the spiritual dimension, one can sometimes see more clearly because we don't have the density of physical life blocking us. However, we also are not experiencing the rich adventure of life as you in the body are."

"Do you wish you were in the physical dimension sometimes?" I asked.

"If I wished it deeply enough it would be my reality. I would do it. For now, I am happy and fulfilled counseling you and others who allow us to be of service and to love you."

I thought a long time before I asked the last question. "So you're saying that if *I* overcome my fear, ABC

and Stan will do a turnaround on their opinion of our
script?"

"We believe so," he answered. "Yes, try it."

I hung up. Talking to a disembodied spiritual entity,
even on the telephone, was no longer novel to me. I had
learned to enjoy the give and take of a phone chat as I
would with a friend who still had a body! And after
hanging up I always looked into my own heart for a
correct assessment of the conversation. I had long since
learned that I was my own best evaluator.

Unseen spiritual guides speaking through transmediums are not always correct, particularly when it
comes to matters of time and mathematical figures. From
their plane of consciousness time does not exist in a
linear measurement (past, present, and future). All life
and experience is occurring for them simultaneously in a
hologram. To paraphrase Einstein, "There is no such
thing as time as a linear reality. Time is an invention of
man."

I have been fortunate to "create" and attract accred-
ited transmediums in my life who have been correct a
great deal of the "time." But the test for me has always
been how *I felt* about their advice and projections of the
future. The transmedium's behavior is as important to
me as the information coming through: which brings me
to the subject of trance mediums charging money. This
issue has of course been of primary concern not only for
people involved with the New Age awakening of the
spirit but for the press as well.

Materialism itself is a subject that everyone in this
society, affluent, middle-class, or poverty-ridden, has to
confront, whether the confrontation involves spirituality
or not. We see material greed everywhere: in the churches,
in the government, on the stock exchanges. We might
each ask ourselves what role money plays in our lives.
We may understand that greed is wrong and not spiritual, but can we also accept the truth that to be abundant

is a spiritual act? The question of spirituality and materialism is full of complexities.

Should spiritual counselors receive remuneration? Jesus and his disciples come to mind. Their remuneration came in the form of food, housing, and the supply of basic human needs required for their happiness, comfort, and well-being during their travels. Money was barely a medium of exchange then in regard to spiritual matters. But money is the system of barter today in almost all matters. In whatever work we do (acting, medicine, psychiatry, and so on) we charge what we believe we're worth and we pay for services in the same way. If each exchange is mutually agreed upon, it becomes an equal exchange of energy. The services are energy put out. The money is energy earned.

In my opinion, when metaphysical practitioners render a service of spiritual value they should receive remuneration just as anyone does who renders a service of value. If the price is too high, the demand for services will diminish. And if excessive materialistic greed motivates a transchanneler, the information coming through the medium can actually be distorted. If a medium isn't free of static the message won't be clear.

So I have concluded for myself that I need, as each individual needs, to determine what I feel about the value of the material and the spiritual in a broad sense, and to judge from that evaluation the meaning of a spiritual-material exchange.

Those in metaphysical circles who conduct their lives with excessive materialistic motivation act as negative reminders that there but for the grace of GOD go the rest of us. Because to be truly aligned with the God-Force makes greed and excessive profit motivation unnecessary. True abundance is co-creating one's reality with the grace of divine energy, and utterly without fear. To me greed comes from the fear of poverty and the lack of self-esteem.

*   *   *

When I hung up from Lazaris I took stock of my own feelings relating to the reaction to our script. Somewhere deep in the darkness of my own heart I wasn't certain I wanted to expose my spiritual search to the American television audience. I guess playing myself had something to do with it, also. Anyone who went to the trouble and expense of buying my book presumably had an interest in what they were about to read; that was not necessarily true of simply switching on the TV.

I relaxed into my self, letting my mind drift clear and remote, allowing it to observe the real sources of its power, to really examine the feelings (the old saw "look into your heart" says it very well). It had been a struggle to learn to be guided by feelings after all the years of school and societal conditioning that one should never allow oneself to be ruled by the heart. My mind had accepted the risk, but could my heart? Perhaps the heart wasn't more impulsive and spontaneous than the intellect after all. Perhaps in some instances I *thought* I was prepared for much more than was true.

I talked it over with Colin. He understood immediately. He had had some of the same qualms himself. Although his face wasn't going to be earnestly smiling through the TV screens of middle America, his name would be on the credits. Until now he had pursued his spiritual search in a private and confidential manner. There was no question that activities such as spiritual channeling, alternative medical approaches, food combining, metaphysical seminars, past life regressions, rebirthing, fire-walking, and spiritual mastery programs relating to human insight had become more and more popular, and Colin had attended many, many sessions with deep interest. Yet to go public with one's newly assessed spiritual approach in areas which heretofore had been confined to the Church or the privacy of an intimate relationship was a big step in personal communication. And of course he agreed complétely that "the universal energy" was respecting our reluctance in creating a reality that might just prevent our script from being accepted. There was no discussion about what we would have written differently. We *knew* we were programming the turndown.

That understood, we discussed the nature of communicating what we found to be true and real in our lives even if it sounded spaced out. We knew better, and if we were to contribute to the consciousness of the society in even the entertainment industry, what better way than to do a show that would be something besides rape, car chases, cops, street people, and low morals in high places?

After not too extensive a discussion, there was clearly no point in putting up unconscious personal resistance for very much longer. I knew my task was to extend emotionally to television what I had already done in my books, and Colin's was to begin his initial foray into a public declaration. That resolved, it was, unsurprisingly, only a few days before ABC called and said they'd like us to go ahead with writing the script for the second night. Lesson? Release and resolve fear, and what you want flows freely.

We wrote the second night in the same way—fast and full of food. Five days, to be exact. Any more than that and we'd have to shoot from the Fat Farm.

We turned in the final two hours and waited for Brandon Stoddard to read them, which would most likely occur on an airplane between New York and L.A. That's where most creative thinking is done in TV land—the solitary office in the sky.

Brandon called Stan Margulies about a week later.

"Be in my office at ten o'clock," he said.

Stan gulped, notified Colin and me, and we prepared for what we had by that time come to expect—the best, not the worst.

We were all there at ten except for Colin. He was not a fashionably late individual, so I wondered what was up. Well into the social breakfast amenities, he arrived. He made no remarks about his tardiness. Brandon probably expected that from a hot "feature hyphenate" (writer-director).

Brandon cleared his throat, put one leg over the other, and began. "I felt wonderful when I finished reading your script. I want to do it."

We smiled confidently and waited for more instructions.

"All I ask," Brandon went on, "is that you make sure the audience understands cosmic justice and that we each are responsible for our own reality. That's what the viewers will *want* to respond to."

An important issue in the show was the exploration of karma. The concept that states: "What we cause, good or bad, will have an effect—on *us*" is karma. Karmic justice is the extension of cause and effect, so that the seeds we sow in one lifetime may not be reaped until a much later lifetime. Hence, Karmic Cosmic Justice. Brandon, ever vigilant regarding the American consciousness, wanted to contribute somehow to making the world make more sense.

"And," he commanded, "I want you on the floor [to begin shooting] November fifteenth, because I want the option of having it on the air May '86 for sweeps week."

Stan choked on a piece of Danish.

"Brandon," he said in his best Talmudic experiential tone, "we're late already for that date. This means twenty-two-hour days."

Brandon smiled and tapped his feet. "Right. I still want it. Now make up a budget. Twelve, fifteen million, whatever it is. Hopefully, we've got an Event here. I like what these guys have written. Besides, my sister would kill me if she heard I turned it down. There are more people into this stuff than you think. And I want ABC to be first."

Stan and Colin and I looked at one another. It was best to quit while we were ahead. Brandon continued.

"I know you have work to do on the script, casting, production, location hunting, and all that—so leave now. Whatever you need—you've got. I'm going on vacation."

Brandon stood up, shook hands with us, smiled, winked, and left.

Stan hitched up his belt, threw up his hands, looked into an imaginary place above his head, and said, "Entities, we are going to need all the help we can get."

He walked out, throwing over his shoulder a parting shot: "What kind of reality have we created for ourselves, stress-wise!?!"

I gathered my stuff, stood up, and looked into Colin's eyes. I somehow was not surprised to see tears.

"My real Maude, Ruth Gordon, died this morning," he said. "That's why I was late. I guess she decided to go so she could oversee this whole thing comedy-wise."

"Oh, Harold," I said, knowing what her passing meant to him symbolically, particularly on this day. "She probably wants you to get on with integrating your spiritual talents. She can help you much more from where she is now."

Colin nodded, giving a lopsided smile. Knowing friends are around in spirit is all very well, but the grief of loss still hurts.

I took his hand and we left together.

Chapter 3

It was the end of August and we were to begin principal photography in eight and a half weeks. We had no cast or director. Colin was leery of the directorial speed required in television. Seventeen setups (camera angles) a day, and usually more, leave the creative artist in a dust whirl of artistic frustration. There would be no time for reflection, or even for learning from mistakes. The clock would tick ominously as network "spies" reported artistic indecision and temperamental differences. Colin would need to shoot in half the time allotted a feature film.

With that kind of pressure he concluded he couldn't handle directing five hours of screen time. The luxury of feature film-making was pressurized enough.

I had to agree with Colin when he passed on being the director, so we shelved that problem for the time being and went back to work to improve our first draft. We got a kick out of seeing our white pages turn the color of the rainbow (for every rewritten scene there is a new color so as to make rewrites clear).

In L.A. we worked at Colin's house off Benedict Canyon. His office was comfortable, homey, with wood paneling, plush couches, and a picture over the fireplace of the cosmos. Somewhere in the galaxy of millions and billions of stars there was a speck with an arrow and the directive YOU ARE HERE. That about said it all. That picture always put our working sessions into proper perspective.

Colin had a housekeeper named Alice who called me "Honey" and Colin "Mr. Higgins." I'm still not sure what I did to create that reality. (Of course I'm sure. I like to be just one of the people.) Anyway, Alice made good roast chicken and could really shop for cookies and ice cream.

She never answered the phone because she knew "Mr. Higgins" would pick it up out of insatiable curiosity anyway. That's when I'd go bananas. He was always so polite and generous with his friends. While I was trying to hold a thought in my head that had to do with making a trance medium funny, I'd sharpen a pencil really loud until he hung up and I could make my point. He'd just laugh and say "Okayyyyy," as though he'd been finished with that scene anyway.

I had never collaborated with anyone before and neither had he. My rhythm was faster and more disciplined and driving. His was thorough and ploddingly specific. I was more demanding. He was more free-flowing. And both of us were focused. As we worked on the final draft, we continued our improvisational arguments.

Colin had a real problem with some dialogue which had to do with looking up at the stars and calling them "zircon plums close enough to pluck."

"The words are too elaborate," Colin said. "It sounds too poetic for a cold night in the Andes. How would Shirley say that?"

I shrugged. "Simple," I said, "since I'm an actress. It's all in the playing."

Colin grunted sarcastically. "That's your answer to everything."

"Yeah," I agreed. "Just like life."

Addressing the director problem, Brandon Stoddard had suggested his number one choice to be Robert Butler. Butler had directed the pilot films for *Hill Street Blues* and *Moonlighting* and if we were lucky enough to find him available, we should grab him.

Butler was available, but that didn't mean he'd want to do the show. How many directors could feel conversant with extraterrestrials, spiritual entities, and reincarnated love affairs? Well, we soon found out.

My daughter Sachi's birthday was September 1. I decided to throw a little party for her in Malibu and invite Kevin Ryerson, who was the trance channeler I wrote about in *Out on a Limb*. The question now was: Should he play himself in the film or should we get an actor who could *act* that he was channeling entities from the spiritual dimension? To witness Kevin channeling, along with the proposed director, Robert Butler, I invited producer Stan Margulies, Colin, my agent Mort Viner, and some of Sachi's best friends. Aside from Colin, none of the people involved in the show had seen the phenomenon of trance channeling. Sachi had, of course, and was longing to speak to several of the entities she hadn't had contact with for some time. So for everyone it would be useful.

But several of the friends present were not working on the film and didn't know a spiritual entity from the Exorcist—and frankly couldn't have cared less. But because I don't feel anything is an accident, I was comfortable with the thought that everyone there was present for a reason. I would have a chance to see the level and quality of skepticism, so that I'd have an idea of what to expect from a wide television audience which would almost certainly include many individuals who would think we were not playing with a full deck of cards.

So, after dinner and the cake and presents, we turned down the lights (spiritual entities say they can see our vibrational light-frequencies better when electricity doesn't interfere with the medium's own eyes), and settled into a channeling session. The waves gently lapped outside as I turned on the tape recorder and waited for Kevin to go into trance. Everyone in the room watched intently. It was the transition into the trance state that usually told the story. If they believed the medium was "acting," it would be during that transition. I, on the other hand, was checking the process in a professional sense, knowing that we should not allow the film editor to cut away from Kevin going into trance because such a cut would give the impression that a trick was being played on the audience.

In about four minutes the first entity, John, came through. Was four minutes going to sustain itself on the screen? Could we even afford such a length of time?

"Hail!" he said—as usual. "Greetings and state purpose of gathering."

Everyone leaned forward. What was this strange Biblical dialect? Sachi returned John's greeting. She said we were all gathered for her birthday and even though there were people present whom John would consider strangers, we were in fact all friends.

John responded immediately. "There is no such thing as 'strangers,'" he said. "There are only friends one has not yet met." Several people blinked and sat back to digest this remark.

"Oh," said Sachi. "Excuse me." She hesitated. At once John offered cordial birthday wishes and congratulated her for deciding to come into an incarnation on the earth plane at this period of time. She thanked him. He then asked for questions. No one said anything. Subtle body movements, the odd uneasy glance indicated that some of those present were busy adjusting to a new method of communication, or were simply uncomfortable with the whole scene, or possibly were afraid to speak up in "public"— even though this was not a large audience of strangers. We all knew one another more or less. Still, I suppose no one had quite figured the way through to an actual confrontation with a nonsolid person. . . .

I could sense Bob Butler and Stan pondering this disembodied spiritual entity named John, who would be playing himself in the film—should we decide to use Kevin as the actual trance medium. They needed to be professional in their attitude, but I could feel their personal curiosity as well. I decided to break the silence and get on with it. I asked John if he would be able to rehearse and stick to the script we'd write for him.

He answered succinctly. "If I can speak lines that match the philosophic framework of myself and that will also be reminiscent of the original lines spoken in our first meetings, that is agreeable, yes."

Stan and Bob looked over at me. Mort coughed politely—but really wanted to say something witty like "But do you do windows?" Sometimes Mort would joke and wisecrack to relieve his own tensions and break up stress in others. Still, I decided to continue with practical questions.

"No, John," I said. "I mean, if I ask you to do a scene over again and make it faster, will you be able to do it?"

"Correct," he answered.

"Okay. Now tell me: Will there be a problem with the camera equipment in relation to your electromagnetic frequencies?"

"That could present a difficulty," said John. "However, I will endeavor to lower my frequencies through the instruments, thereby avoiding problems with your sensitive camera equipment."

Stan's eyes lit up with a fascinated grin. Bob Butler just squinted. Mort looked as though he were in a trance himself. "Lower frequencies" to match camera equipment? He was having enough trouble adjusting to the fact that someone was going to play him in the movie. (He was holding out for Paul Newman.)

I moved right ahead with my questions.

"John?" I continued. "Will there be some problems with crew members who have never been exposed to this stuff before?"

John cocked his head. "No. We sense there will be a mutually respectful working relationship with everyone involved. There will be conscious and unconscious cooperation. Each will make his own personal adjustment."

Stan smiled and leaned forward. "I would like to say that in film-making we often need to repeat a scene time after time. Will you be able to say your words accurately, or will you improvise when you do it again?"

John seemed to smile to himself. "I have been repeating the same teachings for thousands of years. The duration of a film scene should not make that much difference."

Everyone laughed.

"There may be mild differences in languaging, but in the main it will be an exact parallel."

"Differences in languaging?" I turned the phrase over in my mind, reflecting on how prejudicial words could be in describing metaphysical phenomena and spiritual dimensions. I was having a kind of *déjà vu* flash on the time when I first encountered words with "kook" connotations. But Stan was quite unfazed, pursuing practicalities. He leaned farther forward.

"John, as you know, we will be shooting in Peru, where a lot of the story took place. The altitude will be difficult on everyone, and as Shirley has suggested, there will be many crew members who will be exposed to these issues for the first time, including extraterrestrial life. Are we to expect an extraordinarily difficult time, or will it go smoothly?"

John turned his head and Kevin shuddered slightly.

"Pause," said John. "Entity desiring to speak."

A tiny susurration of surprise rippled through the room. One could feel new energy surge through Kevin's body. Then everyone realized what had happened. Kevin's facial expression altered completely.

"Hello, out there," said a new personality. "Mc-Pherson here. Tom McPherson. How are the lot of you doing?"

"We're doing fine, Tom," I greeted him.

"Now then, I believe there was a spot of an inquiry about difficulties you might encounter creatively and in high altitude. Is that correct?"

"That's correct," said Stan.

"First of all, you would do well to continue to handpick your crew. You already understand that no one is a part of your venture by accident. You might want to double-check the medical records of several of your crew in regard to heart trouble and blood pressures. Other than those minor conditions, I believe you will find it adventurous but no more strenuous than what you would find in regular location conditions."

I wondered which crew members would have trouble.

"What about weather?" I asked.

"First of all, you can regulate the weather by your own consciousness. But of course you already know that."

Several people self-consciously cleared their throats.

"I would say, though," Tom continued breezily, "that the best filming dates would fall between January eleventh and as late as February twenty-fourth."

I saw Stan do a swift calculation on his pocket calendar. He smiled to himself.

"Well, Tom," I inquired, "what about the need for security relating to that leftist guerrilla group called The Shining Path?"

Tom paused for a moment.

"As I scan the area you will be working in, I don't

see that harassing you would be to their advantage. It would be best to keep your publicity at a minimum. But document the making of the film for future publicities."

"Why? Because things might happen beyond what we anticipate?"

"Oh," he said, "there will be a few surprises. I won't unravel them right now. Look for unusual phenomena in a spiritual vein while you're working."

Stan sat up straight and scratched his head. I laughed.

"Are you talking about UFOs, Tom?" asked Stan.

Tom cocked his head. "That would be pleasing, wouldn't it?"

"Yes, it would," Stan answered, smiling and twitching his nose as he thought of the attendant publicity.

"I wouldn't put it outside the realm of chance—let me put it that way," Tom went on.

Bob Butler chuckled to himself, as though this spiritual film-making might prove to be more intriguing than he had originally thought.

I took a deep breath, thinking of how we'd have to rewrite the script should Tom's suggestion materialize.

"Tom," I said, "you have a whole room full of witnesses here. Are you really serious with what you're saying?"

"Most definitely," he answered.

"Why?"

"Because it would be a marvelous demonstration of the collective karma vibration that each of you have individually with this type of phenomenon. There could be cooperation with these entities who may desire to stimulate it. Also, the earth is due for another wave of information; another UFO flap, as you call it. Such sightings would be in the collective receptivity."

Everyone looked at one another. No one knew what to make of such an outrageous semi-prediction. Stan and Bob shrugged. Colin and I smiled. Mort blinked enigmatically. Sachi's face was full of wonder, and the rest of the people in the room shifted their positions, indicating that this was without a doubt one of the most unlikely birthday parties they had ever attended.

"You must remember," Tom continued, "that the collective consciousness of the crew will be the deciding factor. Each individual is capable of experiencing an event such as UFOs. The collective is only as receptive as the sum of its parts. If the human soul is troubled or deprived, it affects the whole, not only for simple things like sighting UFOs, but for world-shaking events in your lives. If you study the dynamics of human history, this is indeed the story of the human race, isn't it?"

We all nodded solemnly, as though we understood what that meant. Bob Butler took a long sip of water. I could see he wanted to ground the conversation into practicalities.

"Tom," Bob said, "how many takes can we do with you? I mean, should we use multiple cameras during the scenes with you and Kevin's other entities? Can you say your lines twenty or twenty-five times like most actors?"

Tom hesitated. I jumped in to clarify.

"I think he wonders," I said, "how long you spiritual guides can stay in Kevin's body without draining his energies and tiring him out. We wouldn't like production to be held up because of it."

"I see," said Tom. "The instrument, Kevin, can usually stay in trance for about two hours, three or four times a day. However, much depends on which personality is speaking through him. If it's John exclusively, he may stay out easily for two hours because John's vibration is higher and less taxing on the instrument than the rest of us. Allow the instrument about thirty minutes of recoupment period, and he will be able to go out again for a two-hour block. Does that sound favorable to your shooting?"

We all looked at one another and nodded.

"Yes. Yes, that would be fine."

I asked another scientific question. "If we have three or four cameras going, would that amount of electromagnetic frequency harm Kevin or anyone?"

"No, not at all," replied Tom. "If anything, *we* must keep our vibrations down so we don't harm your equipment. However, the instrument, Kevin, may be bothered by the heat levels of your lights and is sometimes subject to heat exhaustion, but that usually occurs in sunlight rather than under electronic conditions."

Tom paused between answers, waiting for the next question in that peculiarly distancing way the spiritual entities have of communicating through sound and light vibrations. Stan asked if we should take any particular medical precautions in Peru. Tom advised bringing as much of our own food and water as we could. Again he cautioned against people with blood-pressure problems and cardiac difficulties. Since the location reconnaissance trip had not yet taken place, we asked if we should base out of Huancayo, where the action of my real-life adventure took place. Tom recommended a careful look because of potential accommodation problems.

Returning to a more metaphysical note, Butler asked once again what type of spiritual phenomena we could expect during shooting. Peru and Kevin's entities were not the only potential adventures. We were also to shoot with a Swedish medium in Stockholm who channeled an entity named Ambres, who in fact was the first trance channeler I had ever witnessed. Tom now explained that during the shooting with Ambres we could expect some interesting developments because of the mediumistic tendencies of some of the people involved (including myself) and said that the energies we would all be running would be high. I put it on the back burner of my mind. Sachi then asked some personal questions about her life and the pain she had been experiencing in her neck and back. Tom answered in his humorously profound manner, explaining the karmic blockages as he saw them.

Sachi and Tom had been fast and trusting karmic friends
during his incarnation as a Scotch-Irish pickpocket. They
had both been involved with street theater during the
Elizabethan time period, and coming from poverty-stricken
backgrounds, they augmented their income by "rifling
the pokes of people who were much better off." Tom
was working off some of the karma he had incurred for
himself in that incarnation by helping and counseling
people now—Sachi in particular, because he had taught
her to steal! She adored talking to him and usually
followed his advice.

I begged everyone's indulgence and asked Tom what
I could expect with the publication of *Dancing in the
Light*. He said some of those "whose art was interview-
ing" had found metaphysical and spiritual subjects more
accessible since I had first plunged in where "fools"
feared to tread with *Out on a Limb*. He said *"Light"* was
a more controversial book because it was so personal,
thereby placing the reader in the position of having to
decide whether I was indeed crazy or perhaps (because
of my unwavering belief) there was actually something to
this spiritual-dimension stuff that I seemed to have made
a part of my life. He went on to say that I had been
around publicly long enough for them to know I wasn't
crazy, so they were in the uncomfortable position of
either walking away, insisting on retaining their own
prejudices, or opening up to take a look at what I was
saying. Either election would contribute to their discom-
fort until they were ready to recognize and integrate their
own spiritual awareness. In other words, the condition of
spiritual awareness would be a gradually escalating process which would be ultimately regarded as socially
transformative.

I looked around my living room. Those who had
never heard of spiritual channeling before were beginning to look slightly glassy-eyed or defensively suspicious. There were also individuals, fresh to this experience,

who were looking for answers to conflicting dilemmas in their own lives. Nearly all of them were grappling with some kind of pain, disappointment, anger, or self-esteem problem. The questions that followed centered around those personal issues. The answers seemed to alleviate some anxiety. Then someone asked about AIDS and what was really causing it. Tom was circumspect.

"If you want the spiritual reason," he began, "which is of course at the bottom of all there is, let me begin by saying that it is fairly black and white. This disease preys predominantly upon those individuals who are socially disinvested—those who find themselves isolated from the mainstream of society. AIDS, if you will notice, has become more prevalent and in direct ratio to the homophobia in your social order. It is a social consciousness illness."

"What can we do about it?" asked a young man whose friends were afraid.

"There can be a reversal of the karma here. If all of you citizens were to embrace each other and through that spiritual alignment become more demanding of AIDS research, you would find the karma decreasing. Ask not for whom the bell tolls. It tolls for each of you. Death is not prejudiced. Your administration is involved with footdragging on the issue because they regard it as a gay pestilence. But when it begins to cut across all boundaries, they will intensify the research allotment."

"Well, are there any positive aspects to this disease?" I asked.

"Indeed there are," answered Tom. "You see, this disease is serving to *AID* the understanding that all disease is a question of human consciousness. Body follows mind. When the spirit is low or unaligned or unhappy or disinvested (as we were saying), the body manifests that spiritual state of mind. Such severe diseasements aid the society in this fundamental understanding. Your doctors and psychiatrists are already beginning to see the role consciousness plays in disease. The word *dis-ease* says it all, does it not?"

"Are you saying disease, or health, is a question of attitude then?"

"Yes. Pure energy relating to attitude stimulates the healing process. This disease has appeared, in your social order, to focus on the problems of stress upon the immune system. An immune system which is not spiritually aligned with the positive universal forces will break down. It is difficult for a socially disinvested individual to feel aligned. Eliminate your prejudice. You will decrease the disease."

There was silence at the implications of this sweeping statement.

"I must be going soon," Tom said finally. "I don't want to tax the instrument's energies. I can take one more question."

Stan leaned forward.

"Mr. McPherson," he began, "there will be a great deal of energy put into this production. My question is: Have any of us shared this creative energy in the past? Are we going to be re-creating an experience we may have already had together in a past life?"

I never expected the producer of *Roots* and *Thorn Birds* to ask such a question. But then, there were producers—and producers. Tom's answer was even more astounding.

"Absolutely," he said. "This entire group was together in the Amarna period of Egyptian history, when there was the first radical breakthrough in art and culture in two thousand years. It occurred under the reign of Akhenaton. You were innovative in your visual arts then, as you will be now."

I watched Stan as he listened. Tears sprang to his eyes. I didn't know why.

"I must be going now," said Tom. "May the saints be looking after ya. God bless you."

A shudder went through Kevin's body. John's energy returned.

"Hail," he said. "Seek to be at peace with those things you receive in spirit, for you will find they are to further thy fathers' works, and indeed you are that work. You will find that just as you may have many thoughts, yet you have only one mind. In turn, there are many souls, but only one God. Each of you is a thought and creation within the universal mind which you call God. Walk in this the father-mother God's light. God bless you. Amen."

John left Kevin's body. There was a moment when no one seemed to be in there, least of all Kevin. Then slowly he began to regain consciousness. He rubbed his eyes. Then he stretched.

"Hello? Hello?"

He held his hands outward in front of himself.

"We're here," I reassured him.

Kevin opened his eyes. "Well, how was it?" he asked.

Stan got up. "Thank you, Kevin," he said.

He didn't seem to want to say much more. I looked around the room. No one said much. Obviously some would be wondering whether this had all been some kind of magic parlor trick. Others were considering the ramifications if, indeed, Kevin's entities were for real. The party broke up. I thanked Kevin and drifted toward the leftover birthday cake. Stan walked up to me.

"This is astonishing to me," he began. "I was passionately committed, and worked for two years on a miniseries based on the life of Akhenaton. I never understood the depth of my passion until today. I believe Tom when he says we've all been together."

I looked into his eyes. "Really?" I asked.

He pushed in his solar plexus. "I just feel it here."

"What do you think we're getting into, Stan?" I asked.

"As far as I'm concerned," he answered, "we're already in it."

Stan walked over to Butler, who shrugged his shoulders at me from across the room. (His deal hadn't been made yet. I wondered what effect this might have on it.)

Colin sidled up to me.

"So do you think Kevin can play himself?" he asked. "And what about the entities? Tom says he used to act, eh? Do you think he's Abbey Players quality or just temperamental?"

I laughed. His question was so valid I dared not think of the implications. If the audience didn't believe the channeling sessions were real, we had no movie. And most people had enough of a problem believing the medium himself wasn't acting. Now we were going to say, "Yes, he's *playing* himself but he's not pretending—it's real. . . ." I was going to be "acting" myself. And he was going to be "acting" himself. On top of that, the *entities* were going to be "acting" themselves. A person within a play, playing himself in a play. Yes, that was the perspective from which to view this whole multidimensional experience. Pirandello was born too soon.

So the decision of who would play Kevin would probably be made according to who would come off as the most believable. Wasn't that the way it was in life too? Was art imitating life, life imitating art, or was life actually the art form we were each creating for ourselves?

Mort whispered in my ear between cake bites. "I never really understood what you were into before tonight. Now that I get it, I'm not so sure I like it. I'm glad I have my orchid plants to talk to. Am I to expect they will soon talk back? Should I be their agent?"

I laughed and pummeled him on the shoulder.

"Listen," he said, "never mind who plays Kevin. Who's going to play me? Newman isn't available. How about Clint Eastwood? The character shouldn't have many lines."

Mort hugged Sachi, wished her happy birthday, and told her to stay out of miniskirts on Sunset Boulevard. Stan said he was going home to tell his wife he was really an Egyptian pharaoh, while Harold stared into his tea-cup, probably thinking about Ruth Gordon.

Bob Butler walked around muttering, "I'll sign anything."

I went to the window and looked out over the waves below. I took a deep breath and tried to assimilate the implications of what I was doing in making *Out on a Limb* for public scrutiny.

Regardless of how artfully we crafted the story and the shooting, would basic human skeptical prejudice over-whelm the potential of moving an audience? People were touched by what they could identify with. How many could identify with disembodied spiritual entities who helped "Shirley" along her spiritual path? How many even cared about spiritual questions anyway?

For me personally, the existence of disembodied spiritual guides proved that we never die, that we just change form and go into other dimensions; that all souls exist somewhere guiding and helping others. That made sense to me both scientifically and spiritually. I knew many others who felt the same way. But on a mass-consciousness level—to which television speaks? I wasn't so sure.

I opened the sliding glass door and walked out onto the balcony. And what about the critics? Most people seemed to think television critics didn't matter much anyway. But how would those arbiters of public taste feel about exposing their own attitudes and beliefs when it came to reviewing a real person's autobiographical spiri-tual experience? Sixty-seven percent of the American public—according to recent polls—have had an "other-worldly" experience themselves. If the critics hadn't, how could they evaluate whether I had crafted it artistically or not? There would be no basis for identification, only a basis for ridicule. And if a critic *had* had a spiritual experience, would he be afraid of expressing it in his review?

I thought of how I would review a show based on material that I believed was twilight-zone mumbo jumbo. I concluded that I would dismiss it as frivolous and silly if I had never thought about such things. However, if I had my own entrenched religious beliefs relating to spiritual matters, and found metaphysics offensive, I would probably find it impossible to separate being offended from artistic objectivity. And finally, if I was a left-brained, eloquently cynical skeptic who was convinced that God and Cosmic Justice were myths and that man was involved in a spiral of tragically negative proportions, ready to blow himself up out of conflict and despair, I would probably attack a karmically spiritual point of view with violent anger because it would offer an explanation of the human condition that would leave me without an identity—an identity defined by limitations and anger and despair rather than by idealistic hope and positive individual responsibility based on the law of cause and effect (karma).

I looked for a long time at the ocean. Did any of my qualms really matter? Was I going to keep who I was in a closet? Did it matter what anybody else thought? Conviction and personal principle weren't based on public or critical acceptance.

I leaned over the balcony, and as I focused on the foam-capped waves of the rising tide below, I heard myself say: "You've lived your life in public. Why stop now?" I walked back inside.

Chapter 4

*T*he following week we did a rehearsal with Kevin and his entities. I had given Kevin the screenplay so he could learn his lines. The entities, Tom and John, would scan Kevin's subconscious so that they could study their lines also.

Colin and I met Kevin at my apartment in Malibu.

Kevin put Colin and me through a meditation that entailed isolated focusing of the seven chakkras (energy centers along the spine). With each focusing we hummed the corresponding note on the scale. There are seven notes on the scale, seven colors in the color spectrum, and seven chakkras to the human body. Each note on the scale has a vibrational frequency that matches the corresponding color in the spectrum. When one hums "OM" (considered in Hindu scripture to be the first original sound of language) along with visualizing the color that matches each chakkra, the energy in the human body becomes perfectly aligned. Kevin said three people in a meditation were easy to balance because each represents mind, body, and spirit.

After the meditation we prepared for our first informal rehearsal with Kevin and his entities. Colin and I decided I should go right into the scene when the entities came through, as though we were reenacting our first meeting.

Kevin went into trance. We waited. Pretty soon, John came in as he always does and said, "Hail. Please state the purpose of your gathering."

Word for word, as Colin and I had written the script, I introduced myself as though we had never met before and we proceeded to rehearse the scene of our first meeting. I had the script in front of me. John was accessing Kevin's subconscious and was letter-perfect in the scene, with even an added touch of biblical dignity. At exactly the correct point, per script, John said, "Pause. Entity desiring to speak."

I waited just as the script called for and in a moment Tom McPherson was in.

"Tip of the hat to you. How are you doing out there?" he said perfectly.

I acted a laugh, behaving as I had the first time Tom showed up, and he said—as he had then—"I hadn't expected a reaction like that quite so soon."

As the script indicated, I laughed again. Tom began to cough, per script. He asked for a mug, which I fetched for him. I placed it in his hand and he put it to his lips, then said, "There will be something in this to drink when we actually play the scene, will there not?"

I cracked up. He had broken character just like a regular actor.

"Sorry," he then added quickly. "I don't mean to pad my part, even though I can see that the instrument [Kevin] has padded his body!" (Kevin had put on fifteen pounds.)

I laughed again. By now I was completely out of character—well, out of phase, anyway. I was in my own present-day character rather than the person I was ten years ago. It's really weird passing back and forth between one's selves, as it were.

"I hope," said Tom, "that you will play your part more authentically during the screen test. You were nothing like this when we first met."

"Neither were you," I countered.

"Quite right," said Tom.

I waited for him to take his imaginary sip from the mug so I could say my next line referring to it. He didn't.

"Sip your tea, Tom, so I can say my line."

"There's no stage direction," he said, "that says I should sip my tea here."

"Yes, there is. Read the script."

"I couldn't. I could only scan the instrument's mind. He's not much for stage directions or for anybody telling him what to do."

"Okay," I said, "let's go on."

I went on to the next line of dialogue and Tom performed the rest of the scene perfectly. He hit the high points and the low points and even embellished his part a bit. When the scene was over, Colin and I applauded. Tom thanked us and reminded us that he had done a great deal of Shakespearean street theater in his day, in between picking pockets, but these days he much preferred to pick the brains of people than pick their pockets, much better for him karmic-wise, too. After the rehearsal we sat and chatted.

"Listen, Tom," said Colin, "will you stick to the script even if you get bored doing it over and over?"

"Yes," said Tom. "Besides, I have my new accent to keep my interest. How did you like it?" Colin and I looked at each other and winked. Tom was behaving like any actor eager to do his best, yet conscious that he was laying himself on the line, risking public humiliation if he bombed.

"I used this accent," Tom went on, "when I was twenty-five years of age. It has a more joyful frequency to it. I would prefer to be joyful in this show of yours rather than the thirty-five-year-old attitude which I usually use when we speak. Would that be all right?"

"That's okay," said Colin. "Just don't make it too Abbey Players. Okay?"

"Quite right," said Tom. "They came much later."

"Any more ideas?" I asked. "We don't want you to feel restricted."

"Well," said Tom, "would you like me to get up out of the chair and use the instrument's body? I could perform a slight Irish jig for ya. Ya know. As a matter of fact, you and I used to perform our jigs together on shipboard during my pickpocket incarnation. You wouldn't be remembering it, but we had some rather wild and woolly times together."

"I was a friend of yours then?"

"Yes."

"Why didn't you tell me before?"

"You never asked," said Tom.

"Oh, yes. That's right," I remembered. "You only answer what we ask."

"Quite right," said Tom. I smiled mischievously at him, wishing I could "see" him through Kevin's body.

"Okay," I said. "Can you use Kevin's body all right to do a jig?"

"Oh, yes," said Tom.

Then he leaned down and looked at my carpet.

"However," he added, "a hard deck is much easier than this carpet. I'll miss some of the footwork. Would that be all right?"

"Yes. That's all right. Let's see what you have in mind."

Tom moved his head from side to side. Then slowly he rose from the chair. "Allow me," he said, "to adjust my vibrational frequencies to that of the instrument a bit more closely."

He walked away from the chair.

"Would you have a blindfold about, please? The sunlight in here is interfering with my capacity to see the light frequency of the floor."

Tom stood still. I ran to get a scarf. I returned with it and tied it around Kevin's eyes.

"Oh," said Tom happily, "this is infinitely better."

Tom then proceeded to take Kevin's body across the floor of my living room. He put his hands on his hips and jumped up and down, crossing his feet and performing an impeccable Irish jig. And all the while he was dancing, he told stories about incarnations that Sachi and I had had with him. He described how we were pirates, how he had taken Sachi in one incarnation as a ward of his, how I had saved his life in another, and so on. He jigged and jagged and laughed and dramatized until he ended the whole display with the final line in my new book *Dancing in the Light* (which Kevin had *not* read!).

"Oh, *yes,*" he exclaimed. "The dance and the dancer are one!"

Tom really tickled me. When the jig and the drama were over, he went back to his chair and sat down.

"Well, now," he said quite breathlessly, "what did ya think? Could ya use a bit of any of that?"

Colin and I applauded.

"Well," I said, "I guess a lot of that will be up to Bob Butler." (In fact, when the scene was filmed, it was shot as it had originally happened—without Tom's shenanigans.)

"Oh, of course," said Tom. "You know your Mr. Butler is certain he's the only sane one on the project. He was an English magistrate when I was a pickpocket. By the by," he added, "did I effectively point out the Akhenaton influence with your Stan man? I thought that might make him pay attention. Did it?"

I laughed ironically. "Of course it did, Tom, and you know it. Why are you even asking?"

"Quite right," he answered. "I like compliments. Will there be any inquiries before I take my leave?"

"No, thank you," I answered.

Then something did occur to me that had been bothering me for weeks. It had to do with a feeling that I was being guided to include a certain scene in the screenplay because the "guide" (whoever it was) felt the screenplay needed more suspense. I explained that to Tom and asked if I really was feeling a guide or was it all just coming from me.

"Well," said Tom, "if you really want to know, what you were feeling was your old friend Alfred Hitchcock."

"Hitch?" I said excitedly.

"Quite right," said Tom. "He's decided to help you now, remembering that he was not what would be considered pleasant in certain areas when you worked together. Correct?"

"That's right, Tom. In some ways he was very hard on me."

"Yes. Well, he's trying to make up for that by helping you with suspense in this spiritual screenplay. He has worked in thirty-year cycles with you. He was present at a critical turning point in your life thirty years ago when you began, and he is returning as you enter a new phase of expression with your TV miniseries now. Though he is having a bit of a teeth-gnashing time over here at the moment."

"Why?" I asked.

"Because, the law of karma being perfect, some of the actors he abused when he was in the body are now directing some of his old classics for the new Hitchcock television series—and not very well in his opinion. If he had any hair left he'd be pulling it out by now."

Colin and I slapped our thighs, Hitchcock stories being familiar to both of us. He had nothing but contempt for actors, said we were nothing but cattle. And now look: Tony Perkins and Burt Reynolds, among others, were directing Hitchcock remakes. Evidently Hitch wasn't turning over in his grave—he was gnashing his teeth on the astral plane as he was working out karma with actors!

"But he sees the humor in it all," said Tom. "He was, after all, one of your great practical jokers who loved elaborate pranks. Well, now God has done him one better—prank-wise."

"Well," I said, "tell Hitch I'm sorry I couldn't make it to his funeral."

"Oh," said Tom, "he wouldn't have noticed. He wasn't there either. You know how he felt about funerals."

By now I was calculating how I could include what was occurring in our channeling session on the screen. I didn't want to waste it. But a thought occurred to me.

"Before you go, Tom, I assume you'll be wanting billing and credit on the show?"

"Quite right," said Tom. "I am a professional. Shouldn't everyone be included?"

"Yes."

"Well, then," said Tom with commanding dignity, "I would like my billing to say 'Tom McPherson appearing as Tom McPherson.' "

"Oh," I said. "Okay. What about John?"

"One moment, please," said Tom.

He returned in a moment.

"John," he said, "would like to be called John, son of Zebedee."

"Oh," I said. "Okay."

Then it occurred to me.

"Wasn't John of Zebedee, John the Beloved?"

"Quite right."

"Well, isn't that the same guy who wrote Revelations?"

"Quite right," said Tom. "You may say that we

entities simply play ourselves, if you must. I must be going now. Saints be looking after you."

And he was gone. Kevin returned to consciousness and the three of us went out onto the balcony to watch the waves. Kevin wondered why the calves of his legs were sore. I told him he had been doing an Irish jig.

The following day I parked my car in the parking lot attached to ABC Circle Films. As I stepped out of it I noticed a man walking by with a pink script under his arm. The face was familiar. The man was Tom Hulce, who had just lost the Academy Award to his co-star, F. Murray Abraham, in *Amadeus*.

"Hey, Tom," I heard myself say, "you'll win some other time." Tom smiled and hugged me. "What are you doing with that pink script?" (When Stan had asked me what color I wanted our script to be, I had said pink.)

"It's yours, dear girl. Don't you even recognize your own script?"

I was perplexed.

"But why do you have it, Tom?"

"Because I read it and liked it and my agent asked if I'd like to come in and do a reading with other actors just for the fun of it. Don't you want to see how it plays?"

Well, indeed I did. But I never expected an actor of Tom Hulce's stature to do a reading for the fun of it.

Arm in arm we walked into the ABC building. Then I experienced one of the genuinely thrilling moments of my life. On a par with having my baby, winning the Oscar, and meeting Clark Gable! I saw SCRIPT READING: OUT ON A LIMB on the rehearsal-hall door. I opened the door, walked in, and found Colin, Stan, Dean O'Brien (production manager), two assistant directors, and a long table surrounded by actors who would re-create what I had lived and written about. The past five years flooded back. No one who hasn't experienced such an evolution in expression could possibly understand the impact of seeing your life and its characters about to spring to life in a professional environment. For a moment I felt like Sally Field. "You take me seriously—you like me. You like me," I wanted to blurt out. But it was much more than that. This room was full of people about to rehearse a script that seriously and respectfully treated trance-mediums, extraterrestrials, disembodied spiritual entities, and UFOs as an alternative reality to traditional reality. It wasn't a Spielberg fantasy. It was real. It was happening to me. And suddenly it hit me. Brandon Stoddard and ABC had thirteen million dollars' worth of faith and belief invested in the credibility of my spiritual search.

We took our seats. We all introduced ourselves. Tom was the only actor I knew, but each of the others was an experienced "working" professional.

For me the reading was an event, the personal satisfaction notwithstanding. For the first time Colin and I heard the rhythm, the hidden comedy, the tension of the love story, and whether the interpersonalization of the characters worked. It did. There was more work to be done—but in the main it was all there. For me to play a love scene with an actor who was depicting a real man whom I had loved was an exercise in double vision. It was then that I knew I'd have no trouble re-creating myself or allowing another actor to portray a real-life character in my life with freedom. From that day on I began to come to work and get into the character of who I had been ten years earlier. That was the separation I needed. It was essential that I play "Shirley" with the skepticism and confused disbelief that had been part of my early spiritual learning process ten years previously.

Soon after that realization, I did the screen test with Kevin—except that I stepped out of character with very unpleasant results as a consequence.

Chapter 5

*K*evin and I arrived at the taping studio soon after lunch. There were several arrangements of flowers waiting for us from Stan and company.

Kevin sat in the makeup chair. The makeup artist didn't realize she was making up a trance medium until fifteen minutes into the procedure. I think that was because Kevin mentioned that Tom McPherson might smear his eye makeup with a blindfold. When she asked who Tom McPherson was, Kevin actually told her. She was so fascinated she took three hours to "complete" his makeup. And all it consisted of was base color!

The entire taping crew was prepared for visitors from outer space or, at the very least, a tap-in from *Poltergeist*. It was the first of many times that I'd notice a kind of respectful silence prevail on the set whenever the presence of beings from the other side was expected. It was endearingly humorous, because as jaded as some of them were, each of them had a healthy respect for the possibility that it just might be true. Either that or it was Hollywood people doing what they do best—covering their bases. Knowing how the butter for their bread spreads . . . "stay with the money."

The crew was ready. So was Kevin. He had been studying his lines diligently and so (according to him) had Tom and John. The crew, of course, didn't know what to expect.

Bob Butler seemed quite comfortable on the taping floor. I wondered how he'd be with a film crew instead. He directed from the booth, and fairly soon Kevin became accustomed to the voice above him instead of an actual face in front of him.

Everyone was set. Kevin went through some motions with his hat and coat, since he had an entrance to make through my door in Malibu. It was funny and dear to observe the vanity of even so unassuming an individual as a medium who allowed other beings to use his body without regard for how it looked.

Bob gave the countdown to tape rolling and then we began. Kevin walked through the door and began his lines. He was nervous. I in turn became immediately supportive. With my prompting he acted out his lines. He told "Shirley" what to expect, explaining that he was really acting as a telephone for disincarnate beings to speak through. I snuck a peek at the dumbfounded crew. No one blinked. (Hollywood crews have seen it all.)

Then I forgot my lines. Someone handed me a script. By now I was definitely out of character.

Kevin went into trance, as per script. The crew didn't know what was going on. They waited. A few of them adjusted the lights.

John of Zebedee came through and said, "Hail. Greetings. State purpose of gathering."

Several members of the crew very gently backed up. I chuckled to myself. John proceeded to play his lines letter-perfect—not with any great dramatic flair, mind you, but with precision. When he paused and said, "Pause. There is another entity desiring to speak," there was another almost palpable reaction from the crew. I heard one of them murmur, "Should this guy get the Academy Award or is this real?" I found myself whipping between playing the scene and watching the crew react to an honest-to-God channeling. It was really difficult for me to get the concentration I needed.

Tom McPherson, in all the glory of his Irish brogue, came through. "Tip o' the hat to you," he began and proceeded to introduce himself and launch into *his* portion of the scene. He was as letter-perfect as John. Kevin had had trouble remembering his lines—the entities had no problem. "Earth plane anxiety," Tom would explain later. "When the director yells the word *action,* the aura of every person on the set goes muddy. What are they so worried about? All of life is a movie, not just the one you're making." Sure, Tom, and we all wear IT'S ONLY A MOVIE buttons, too.

Tom then proceeded to pad his part a little by turning to the crew and saying, "I'd like to encourage all of you out there to enjoy having a body. I haven't had one for four hundred years. I miss it. When you're floatin' around up here you're like a saint or somethin'. All you can be is good, gooder, and goodest." Some of the crew laughed.

Tom explained his identity per script, Irish pickpocket and all. The crew gaped. How could a pickpocket be a spiritual guide? "He's working off his karma," said one of the guys with long hair and an earring. I made a note of his identity—we should definitely take him to Peru, I thought.

We were well into the scene when Tom suddenly reached over and took my hands. I felt a surge of warm, almost liquid, electricity go up my arms and through me.

"Would you like to do an Irish jig now, lassie?"

"Oh," I said, startled and completely out of character.

"Well," Tom went on, "help an old pickpocket to

his feet. You have an advantage over me up here. Just get me to my feet and I'll be fine, don't ya know."

I helped Tom to his feet. He looked down.

"Good floor," he said. "It's not the hardwood deck of shipboard, but it'll do."

With that, Tom began to direct me in an Irish jig. He held my hands loosely and told me about the incarnations we had had together as pirates. I wondered how much karma he would have to work off before he was done with it.

I was laughing as Tom improvised even more lines. Then I began to be aware that I was becoming nauseated. It wasn't the physical activity. It was something else. I really began to feel terrible, as though I would throw up right on his hardwood floor.

"Tom," I said, "I'm getting really sick. I have to sit down." I looked around at the crew. They thought it was part of the scene. Nobody did anything.

"Yes, lassie," said Tom. "We must be sittin' then." He guided me to my chair. The crew was mesmerized. I started to hyperventilate. I heard a crew member say, "These two are really good."

Tom sat down opposite me.

"How're ya feelin' now, lassie?" he inquired, quite concerned.

"I'm really ill, honestly. Why? What's happened here?"

"Well," he said, "if you really want to know the truth, I thought you'd be playing your part from the emotional frame of reference of ten years ago. That carried with it a lower frequency in your being. You've been out of character for the last fifteen minutes and I didn't pull back my frequencies in time. I thought you'd snap into character when we danced. But you didn't, so when you came into physical contact with my frequencies it was too much for you. I'm sorry."

The crew shook their heads in disbelief.

"Oh," I said, understanding what he meant. "I'm sorry too."

"Yes, lassie," he added. "I thought we were dealing with professional acting here. Forgive me, but if you had stayed in character this wouldn't have happened."

One of the guys in the crew lit a cigar.

"Okay," I said. "I get it. You don't have to humiliate me in front of the crew."

"Oh," replied Tom, "a little humility never hurt anybody. Keeps your feet on the ground, as I am constantly reminded myself."

I pushed him in the shoulder and retracted my hand quickly. I didn't want to risk any more contact just now.

"Shall I be goin' then?" said Tom. "Or will ya want to be doing it all again?"

I was really nauseous now. "I think we'd better quit for a while, Tom. If we need to do it again, I'll talk it over with Kevin."

"Saints be lookin' after ya, then," said Tom. And he was gone.

The lights went off on the set. The crew just stood there. Kevin rolled around to consciousness. "How'd it go?" he asked with his familiar curiosity.

The guy with the cigar walked up to him and very politely said, "Excuse me, mister, but where were you during all this?"

"Where was I?" asked Kevin ingenuously.

"Yeah."

"I was asleep, I think you'd say."

"Asleep?"

"Yes. That's what it feels like anyway. My own personality moves out of the way for other personalities to come through me. That's why they call me a medium."

The guy puffed seriously on his cigar.

"Yes," Kevin went on. "I'm one of the few people in the world who gets paid for falling asleep on the job."

Kevin and I left the taping studio. Everyone adjourned until another day when I would rehearse in character. We had a quick dinner together. I didn't feel like eating much and discussed matters in relation to what happened to me. When Kevin dropped me off at my car, I forgot and left my flowers behind.

When I walked into my apartment in Malibu a floral smell swept over me. I went to the living room and dining room, wondering where the smell was coming from. There were no flowers to be seen; plenty of plants, but no flowers. I sat down, quietly perplexed. I had heard many tales of floral scents in relation to spiritual visitations, and even from people who claimed to have been in the presence of a UFO. Something about high vibrational frequency causing an identical smell as that of another nature. It made sense, I guess, but I didn't understand how it worked. Then the telephone rang. It was Kevin.

"Listen," he said, "I've been sitting here thinking real hard how I can get your flowers to you. You left them in the trunk of my car. I took them out and watered them, but not knowing when I'd get back out to Malibu, I've been sending them to you telepathically."

"What?" I asked.

Until that moment I had forgotten I'd left the flowers with him.

"Yes," Kevin went on. "I was wondering if anything unusual had transpired in relation to your flowers."

I gulped. "How about there's this pronounced floral smell all through my apartment, and I don't have a flower in here except silk ones."

"Oh," said Kevin calmly. "I'm getting better at it. It's not at all unusual when two people are in tune. This also bears out what McPherson's been saying about your developing mediumistic potential."

A rush of concern went through me.

"I don't want to become a medium, Kevin," I said. "I like knowing what's happening to me all the time."

"Oh, my goodness, of course not," he assured me. "First of all, there has to be an agreement between beings for me to be used as an instrument. I've told you often, it's probably my karma to be a human telephone this time around, and I have certainly given my permission."

I thought a moment about the day's events. I could feel the understandable skepticism of the crew. Was Kevin just acting or might it be something in his own subconscious he was expressing? I finally thought of a question which, if properly answered, would serve as a point of proof for most people regarding the legitimacy of channeling. So I asked him: "Kevin, are you the only medium who channels Tom McPherson?"

To my surprise Kevin replied, "No. Actually I knew about at least one other man, whom I've since met, and probably another whom I haven't checked out yet. Any time you'd like to talk to Tom through somebody else, let me know."

Oh, boy, would I take him up on that. I thanked him for the telepathic flowers and hung up, hoping to get some rest.

The telephone rang. It was Jach Pursel's two partners from San Francisco. Jach was the medium who channeled Lazaris, a high-level entity who, according to him, has never been embodied. Therefore he doesn't speak from earth-plane experience, which he claims doesn't necessarily diminish his physical understanding. Anyway, Michael and Peny and I began to chat. They were interested in how the screen test had gone with Kevin; a little friendly medium rivalry, you might say. I told them what had happened when I danced the jig with Tom: my nausea and so on. There was a long pause.

"Well," said Michael. "We don't feel that that was very advanced of McPherson. I mean, why was it necessary to put you through all that?"

"Well," I answered, slightly taken aback, "I don't

think it was necessary. It was just a mistake—mine as well as his."

"Well, he shouldn't have made that mistake," they insisted.

"Oh, well," I tried to assure them, "it was nothing, really. No harm done."

"What do you mean?" said Peny. "Aren't you angry and outraged about it?"

"Me?" I asked, startled at her intensity. "Why, no. Not at all. For what would I be outraged?"

"Well," she continued, "because McPherson really came on strong and he had no right to do that."

"But, Peny, he didn't mean to. He apologized. And besides, I told you I wasn't rehearsing my part with the emotional frequency of ten years ago."

"No," she said. "You deserve better than that. You should *face* your anger and hostility and allow yourself to feel it."

"But I don't feel any anger."

"Then you are holding it at arm's length. That way you don't experience pain. But you'll prevent your growth that way."

I stopped and thought about what she and Michael were saying. By now they were on two phones. I didn't know where Jach was. What they were saying was a little like the early days of psychoanalysis and *est* training. If you don't feel anger and rage, it's because you're suppressing it.

I tried very hard to conjure something up. But I couldn't get mad at McPherson.

"Listen," I finally said. "I'm really trying to get mad and pissed off, but I can't get it up, so I can only say maybe *you* guys are mad and pissed off. Maybe you have a problem with McPherson, and I can understand that perfectly. After all, I guess everybody wants to believe *their* spiritual entity is the best."

Soon after that we politely hung up. It was my first

taste of what would soon develop into the competition of the entities, or as someone put it more succinctly, "the battle of the Gods." And because I was in the eye of the hurricane of the rapidly developing metaphysical movement, I and my endorsement would be a prized trophy. It was indeed a lot like Hollywood studios. Each was creative, knowledgeable, accomplished, and useful, _and_ each dealt with the stuff dreams are made of. There was no way to choose. I loved them all.

Bob, Colin, Stan, and I had still not decided whether Kevin and his entities should play themselves. We had some trepidation that "talking heads" would become boring. It was fascinating to witness in person, but how would it translate to film? The entity John was of particular concern, because he lacked "a certain comedic or dramatic flair they like to see on TV."

We were sitting in the rehearsal room discussing the problem when, as though on cue, the telephone rang. It was Kevin. (The guy definitely had a hot line to God.)

"Listen," said Kevin with no preliminaries, "John will very likely come through 'on the day,' exuding an energy overtone with more earth-plane personality, which the television audience would find more similar to the vibration of the present day."

I relayed the message to the guys word-for-word, without sarcasm. I hoped they would understand it. They rolled their eyes. I guess they didn't get it either. I went back to Kevin.

"So you're saying John will put some modern-day oomph into his performance?"

"Yeah," said Kevin. "By the way, does Butler still think he's the only sane one on the project?"

I laughed.

"Well, then," said Kevin. "He was just on a location hunt in Peru, was he not?"

"Yes," I answered curiously.

"Get him to tell you what happened to him up there."

Kevin hung up and I looked over at the guys. Stan, Bob, the production manager Dean O'Brien, and the art director had done a location reconnaissance since we last met. We had not yet had time to discuss the results.

"So how was it in Peru?" I asked.

"Sit down," said Stan.

I sat.

"Okay," he began. "The four of us were being driven in a car by our interpreter and scouting organizer. We were looking forward to seeing the UFO CONTACT POINT sign that you described in your book. We had taken pictures of towns, llamas, babies, mountains, and every rock we ran across, so of course the *pièce de résistance* would be the UFO sign."

I didn't know what he was driving at.

"Yeah?" I asked.

"Well, the four of us fell asleep in the car at the same time, like we had lost consciousness or something. And when we woke up an hour or so later, we asked our driver when we were going to get to the sign. He looked at us very strangely and said, 'what do you mean?' I repeated the question and he said, 'But Mr. Margulies, you *did* see it. You all saw it. You got out and took pictures of it. You talked about it among yourselves. Don't you remember?' Well, none of us remembered. It was as though it was wiped from our minds. We still can't remember, *and* there is nothing on the film we took."

I stared at Stan.

"So," he said, "Mr. Butler no longer thinks he's the only sane person on the movie. Apparently either we're all losing it or something else is going on. Didn't Tom McPherson say we would get UFOs on film if the collective consciousness is receptive?"

"Yes," I answered.

Stan and the others exchanged looks.

"Maybe the message was we're not ready."

"Maybe," I said disappointedly.

"But that's not all," Stan said.

"What else?"

"After we got back, we asked for someone in our Peruvian office down there to take pictures of the UFO sign so we could duplicate it."

"Yeah?"

"Only half of the sign is visible in *their* photos. It's as though it doesn't fully exist for us."

I thought a moment.

"Well," I said, "maybe that's true."

"God, Shirley," said Stan. "How could we *all* forget what we *did*?"

"I don't know. I guess somebody is trying to tell you something."

Stan rolled his eyes again. "The question is: *who*?"

Chapter 6

*I*n mid-September, *Dancing in the Light* was published. I had promised my publisher, Bantam Books, that I would do a promotional tour of several cities. So in between preproduction chores for *"Limb"* I once again experienced the hustle of American cities and I freely discussed the evolvement of my spiritual and metaphysical search. It was entirely different from the tour I had done two years previously. I don't know whether newspaper and magazine editors were taking me more seriously or whether the reporters they sent to interview me were chosen for their open-mindedness about spiritual search. I only know I was so pleasantly surprised that most of them had done a great deal of metaphysical reading on their own.

They had evolved into being more aware of past life therapy and past life trauma, chakkra energy sources, the way karma works, and so on. Some of them had sought out their own trance mediums because it was common knowledge that really fine mediums were developing their psychic talents and instrumentality at a greatly accelerated rate. The information coming through was nourishing, knowledgeable, highly sophisticated, and, more often than not, completely accurate. Some of the finest skeptically astute reporters in America were on their own spiritual path of investigation; so much so that our interviews often turned more into shared conversations than interrogative questions and answers. I noticed, however, that *these* reporters found it necessary to evidence the most skepticism in their written articles. That was okay. They had bosses and needed to appear doubly objective.

The call-in TV and radio shows, particularly Larry King's, were truly phenomenal for me. All told, I must have talked spontaneously and live to about three hundred callers, and except for a woman on Phil Donahue's show who said what I was talking about was witchcraft, *not one person* said "this stuff is crazy" or anything even resembling such a point of view. In fact, just the opposite. I wondered myself why I wasn't getting more evidenced adverse reaction. The talk-show hosts couldn't explain it either. Maybe people somehow sensed that there were unseen realities in their lives, too, just as I was experiencing in mine. They called to discuss past-life recall, what happens to them during meditation, how color therapy works in healing, what mediums I could recommend, what other books I suggested, visions they had experienced after a loved one left the body, and, of course, UFO experiences—which were becoming more and more prevalent.

The UFO contacts were coming up in connection with spiritual searching because the callers understood that the basis of the knowledge the extraterrestrials were bringing was both a scientific and a spiritual knowledge of the God-force. In other words, the beings behind the craft had learned to harness the unseen energies in the cosmos and use them in a beneficial manner. That was how they could travel at such high speeds. That was how they defied linear time frames. That was how they could achieve dematerialization and rematerialization. They understood the subatomic molecular structure of every living thing. That was why they were so curious about Earth and the human race. And the reason they didn't announce themselves more publicly was not only because of potential panic (which was actually questionable) but more because mankind would tend to revere them as gods and abdicate personal responsibility for their own human growth.

The basic lesson the extraterrestrials were bringing was that each human being *was* a god, never separated from the God-force, and capable of doing and learning and understanding all that there is: that we were each in possession of the total truth at all times if we *wanted* to recognize it. The difference between us and them was that they *knew* it and we didn't. They accepted that they were gods and we couldn't even say the words. They were therefore reluctant to appear to be our masters, because it was against Cosmic Law to interfere karmically with the pace and growth of another human being. To rob another of the physical body through which to learn his spiritual divinity was incurring a heavy karmic debt. So ... Were UFOs and extraterrestrials to be feared? I guess it depended on how much responsibility we were willing to take in relation to the mastery of our own divinity.

In any case, this was amazing stuff to deal with on talk shows, or by phone with the call-ins—certainly not your usual chitchat-what-d'you-feed-your-cat talk. I took it very seriously—as seriously as did all those interested in discussing the subject with me.

At the same time, as my book tour progressed, I pursued the preproduction work of casting and so forth on the phone.

The role of Gerry was the most pressing to cast because he began shooting first. Gerry, as written, was English, commanding, highly intelligent, ambitious, humanistically motivated to the point of heartbreak, very left-brained, charming, and good-looking, with an unruly shock of hair that continually fell over his forehead.

Irrespective of what the real Gerry was like (composites notwithstanding), Colin and I wrote the part with Albert Finney in mind. But to make a complicated story simple, Albie wasn't available. Soo . . . the search was on.

Richard Harris was a possibility. His agent, who was most eager for him to open up his career to a large TV audience, loved the script and wanted him to do it. Richard, however, declined. He wrote me a letter explaining his own newly formed and deeply felt spiritual beliefs; because of them he had learned to temper his judgment of others. As a result he felt that Gerry's incapacity to understand *my* spiritual searching was an invasion of Gerry's privacy, even though no one really knew who he was.

James Fox was another possibility. But his agent called and said he had become a born-again Christian and wouldn't play an adulterer.

I had seen Gabriel Byrne in *Christopher Columbus* and was very impressed. However, the day before he received our script he had signed for another movie.

Around about then Colin and I had some intriguing talks relating to the dearth of English leading men. Men who could really kiss the girl. Men who would activate in the audience the understanding of *why* Shirley fell for the man in such a big way—knowing he was married.

Since Leslie Howard, some years ago, and Richard Burton in the last fifteen years, who from the British Isles would you want to get into bed with? Because that's what Shirley did—impulsively and without regard for the consequences.

Then I remembered *Jewel in the Crown*. I had been very impressed with Charles Dance. He was new. He had had relatively little film experience. But there was something about his presence that was riveting, particularly when he had the confidence to do nothing.

We inquired about him. Yes, he was available and would like to read the script.

In the meantime, Stan, Colin, and I went to London to "read" other actors, before Charles was available to meet with us.

I was ensconced in the Britannia Hotel with a duplex winding-staircase suite stocked with every kind of booze a good Englishman desires, nuts, chips, chocolates, fruit, flowers, tea, hot scones, and a telephone that always rang on the floor where I wasn't.

I noticed that the room number of my suite had been taken off. When I asked the manager why, he tactfully tried to tell me that they had heard I was adversely affected by "wrong numbers." They didn't know which ones might be the "wrong" ones so he was diplomatically playing it safe by taking them all off.

When I asked him how people were supposed to find my room with no numbers visible, he said typically, "We took the numbers off, madam." That's a British explanation.

I put a cardboard sign up on my door with my room number visible.

All the actors' readings occurred in my suite. I had not often been involved with the pressure and sad humiliation of actors who desperately want and need jobs. I guess I remembered my beginnings, the cruelty of the elimination process, the coldness of "Will you take it from the top and cry?," the faulty self-image that some actors have of themselves, which is clear to all those who will ultimately reject them until that self-image is in alignment with the role.

One by one they crossed my hotel threshold. One by one we sipped tea together as a preliminary icebreaker before launching into a deeply personal love scene witnessed by three other strangers plus a cold-assed casting director. My heart turned over each time; my sensitivity to their anxieties superseded any help I could be as an acting partner. I thought of the preparation exercises they must have put themselves through. I thought of how full of trepidation they must be in playing a character I had not only written, but who was a real character in my life. There was false laughter, a lot of nervous smoking, darting eyes, personal insights shared, and perspiration wiped surreptitiously from the backs of necks.

It went on for days. The unknowns were auditioned in this fashion. The famous or semifamous rated a lunch. Depending on the level of their insecurities, they would read the script beforehand. (The secure had no problem discussing what they thought of it. The insecure wanted an offer before they read.) So I just figured having a meal with someone (with no offer) would give me a pretty good idea of how they'd be to work with, chemistry-wise, whether there was an attraction we could build upon, a sense of commanding intelligence, of looseness, or rigidity, how they'd photograph, how tall they were, and whether I could see myself in bed with them or not.

Of course each one of them had read the script whether they admitted it or not. (Actors don't have lunch to discuss a pending job without knowing how to act.) So somewhere around coffee and dessert we'd segue into what the character "sounded like." By the time the check came (ABC's tab), I usually had my answer. We didn't have our man. I didn't know what to do.

I finally called my friend Albert Finney one more time. He invited me for dinner. It was a dinner that even today I don't understand but will never forget because of its vast theatricality. To be with one of the world's great actors in "real" life sometimes puts "reel" life to shame.

I was walking toward the restaurant when he emerged like a thunderstorm in a black coat from a London cab, his mop of thick brown curls swirling in the London wind. It was like the arrival of Orson Welles in *Jane Eyre*. He gathered me up in his arms.

"Dear girl. How wonderful! We will have a sumptuous dinner, but first we will survey the new fashions."

With that, Finney strongly grasped my elbow and guided me along the shop windows, giving me a running commentary on why certain color combinations were pleasing to the eye and how political attitudes generally followed fashion trends—"A little bare skin showing usually means a more liberal attitude. You *do* see that?"

Anything Albie presented was immensely seeable. He "presented" himself at every moment. As he held my arm I felt attached to a magnetic conduit of powerful energy which he bodily converted into theatrical expression. Yes, he gave new meaning to the concept of "presence."

Soon he ushered me into "his" restaurant—a place he had apparently been frequenting for thirty years. He introduced the wife of the proprietor as his girlfriend, the daughter of the wife as his girlfriend, and every waitress on the way to our table as his girlfriend. Each one of them blushed as though there might have been anticipated truth in every introduction. I thought of the Hollywood heralded playboys I had been around. None of them measured up to this level of the art of theatricalized flirtation. Finney was a show within a show. So later, after ordering several kinds of wine, a seven-course meal, table-hopping with added introductions as he went, I really believed him when he swept his arms in a magnanimous all-embracing gesture around the place and said, "I cast everyone here for your benefit, my dear. This magnificent trio, 'Trio de Paraguay,' came all the way from their native land to serenade you. All of these kind people are here to make a rousing party for you. Now let us enjoy what life has to offer."

Oh, my, he was outrageously appealing with his reckless abandonment of limitation. He ate as though he was portraying a character in *Le Grand Bouffe*—an orgy of epicurean delight and appreciation. He tucked a napkin under his chin and sipped wine (he knew them all) with gusto—proving that one can, in fact, sip in such an exuberant fashion. Between reveling in mountains of food and richly savoring each variety of wine, he gave the distinct impression that anything less would indicate a hopeless lack in appreciation of the good life. The texture of his sensual pleasure was high drama and I a willing audience. Though I wasn't sure we could rewrite the part of Gerry to accommodate these qualities I was being privileged to enjoy, I almost didn't care if they were not in character with the real man.

Then, as the courses came and went, I found that Finney was really interested in metaphysics. I knew he had read *Out on a Limb* and enjoyed it, but delving into the hidden realities I was espousing was another question. Yet indeed he had. First of all he outlined the visitation he had had of a dead relative at night in his bedroom. He leaned forward across the table.

"After that," he said, "I realized there must be another dimension of reality."

Maybe it was meant to happen that he would play Gerry after all—even though the real Gerry would have freaked out at a visitation from a dead relative and certainly wouldn't tell anybody. As I watched Finney eat, I wondered how we could shoot the bathing-suit scenes in Hawaii. Maybe we could play them under a beach blanket.

Finney went on to tell me he had spent magical times in Cuzco and Machu Picchu in Peru. He fantasized about the often-seen spacecraft in the Andes.

"Oh, yes," he suggested, "I believe actors should be allowed to go up in those spacecraft to create their own improvisational drama so that we could study the effects that weightlessness has on human emotions."

Albie rose from the table and improvised a small

scene—around which the National Theatre could have built a play. He then proceeded to hop from table to table thanking the diners for working as extras on their night off—particularly for no pay beyond the food. He gestured to me, obviously indicating that it was a celebration in my honor. I bowed and mock-applauded everyone for welcoming me to their country. Not a soul knew what was going on, but they all seemed charmed and amused.

Finney then strode commandingly to the small trio of Paraguayan guitarists and guided them over to me.

"Play for my lady," he instructed them.

They complied. It was Latin, lovelorn, loud, and long. Albie sat and supped happily through it all. During what I hoped would be the final plaintive love song, I calculated how much time there was left for me to approach him specifically about how much we wanted him for the part. Prior to the evening, Colin and I had agreed that I should have dinner with Albie and that Colin should come afterward for dessert. I had about fifteen minutes left.

The Paraguayan trio left. I leaned forward and prepared to begin my pitch. I saw a flash of panic dart across Albie's face. Reality—hard-nosed, show-business, "what about a deal" reality—was about to rear its ugly truth in the midst of a dining charade. At that very moment Colin came striding into the restaurant and over to our table. I was thrown by the bad timing. I had told Albie he'd be joining us—which hadn't seemed to faze him. Now though, Finney's face registered a mixture of panic and relief. With an opulent flourish he invited Colin to sit and order coffee and a sumptuous dessert. Colin declined.

After a few exchanges of pleasantries—John Huston *Under the Volcano* stories, a discussion of Shakespeare and the "almost culture" of Hollywood—Albie excused himself, got up, made a few more rounds with the diners in the nearby vicinity, and disappeared.

"How'd it go?" asked Colin.

"You can see," I answered. "I wish I had it all on videotape. The man is acting out his life. That could be disturbing, and it could mean he's just rehearsing so he'll know what to do when the red light goes on."

Colin nodded knowingly.

"Well, did you discuss the script?"

"Just as I was about to bring it up, you walked in the room. I mean, talk about colossal ill-timing."

"Yeah," said Colin. "I wonder what that means karmically."

"I don't know," I answered. "It was almost as though you were meant to come in at that moment and squash any discussion. It was really weird. You know what I mean?"

There was no sarcasm on Colin's face.

"Oh, yes," he replied. "I could feel it, too, as though it simply wasn't meant to go on."

"Well, let's see what happens next."

What happened next was that Finney, in a flustered flurry, came back to our table. He didn't sit. He stood and delivered the following lines:

"My friends," he said, "I must take my leave now. I have another friend who desperately needs me."

With a flourish of kisses he left our table, bade dramatic goodbyes to the "hired" extras still lingering in the restaurant, and was gone (an exit by the lord of the manor) into the stormy London night.

Colin and I stared in shock at each other.

"Do you think he thinks this metaphysical stuff is a load of shit?" Colin asked.

I thought about all that had transpired during Albie's extravagant dinner.

"No," I said seriously, "I don't believe it's that. But

I have a feeling he's afraid to go back to work, at least in a film like this one."

"Well, there are no accidents," said Colin.

"Yep. But what does this mean?"

Colin thought a moment. "Well," he finally said, "the guides like McPherson, or Lazaris, would say that Finney has decided he doesn't want to go on in this particular play and that there is someone else dancing in the wings waiting for the chance."

I dropped my fork. "Did you say *dancing*?"

"Yes."

"You think you might mean Charles Dance-ing?"

Colin laughed. "See how it all fits if we can just make ourselves aware of it?"

Even I choked on that one.

The four of us sat in my hotel suite waiting for Charles Dance to arrive. Rose Tobias Shaw, the English casting director, was busy making phone calls. She turned around.

"Charles has been waiting in the lobby for an hour," she said. "I expect there's been a mix-up in scheduling."

I hated to hear that, because I hated that to happen to me.

I got up, having calculated the amount of time it would have taken Charles to emerge from the elevator and walk down the long hall toward my door. Perhaps if *I* greeted him informally, it would take the edge off the mix-up. So I opened the door and leaned out. I saw the tall ginger-haired actor from *Jewel in the Crown* walk determinedly toward me.

"Hi," I shouted in a friendly manner.

He didn't smile. Instead he said, "Why have I been kept waiting for an hour? Couldn't you be more professional than that?"

Whoops, I thought. He comes right to the point. But the point seemed to be overstated.

"Well," I said as he came closer, "I'm sorry. I don't really know what happened. But never mind. You're here now."

As he reached me he blushed.

"Oh," he said. "I didn't realize I was talking to you. I thought you were Rose."

I wanted to ask why Rose warranted being talked to like that, but I was more concerned that his gaffe would make him uncomfortable about our meeting.

"I'm very happy to meet you," I said, ushering him into the room and looking him over as he entered. He was dressed in a corduroy suit and was blushing through his freckles. His skin looked like a peach-and-rose parfait. Even his hair seemed spattered with freckles. He was dazzling. His body movements were awkward, but he was built like a Greek god. I wondered what weights he used to work out with. He turned around and observed me closing the door behind him. I looked hard at him. As a professional, it's always interesting for me to compare what I see in a human face in real life to its translation to the screen. On a small screen (TV), Charles Dance had an entirely different countenance from the one I had seen on the big screen (*Plenty*). I wondered whether the remote look he had had in that film had been his interpretation of the part, because he was playing an insensitive aloof husband who contributed to his wife's insanity. I looked into his face again. He leveled an insecure ogle at me and blinked.

Everyone shook hands all around. Then Charles stood there.

"Well," I began, wanting to break the ice, "how did you enjoy working with my favorite actress Meryl Streep? If there's such a thing as genius, I would have to say she's it."

He blinked again and swallowed. I wondered what was troubling him. Up to then I hadn't known about his interviews on TV relating to working with Meryl.

"Oh," he said, "I didn't enjoy it very much." He hesitated. "It was difficult."

Hmmm, I wondered. He's pissed off at having been kept waiting, and the most cooperative professional in the business he found difficult. He was certainly honest. Maybe he *would* be good for Gerry.

I didn't press the Streep question. Under the circumstances, it would have been unfair.

Charles sat down. He pulled out a package of cigarettes and said, "Well, would you like me to read for you?"

Well, I thought, he's not *that* far off base. Either he's extremely secure or he wants the part very much.

We began. Colin and Stan read other parts while I played myself. Charles had a sensitive command of the character as we went scene by scene. By now I had heard each scene played by about twenty-five actors. It was a pleasure to see and hear an actor who *looked* and *sounded* in character. At the end of the reading, Charles lit a cigarette.

Stan and Colin sat there diplomatically thanking Charles and quietly discussing their reactions. Because *I* had been *acting* with him I was somehow on the other side of the decision-making table at this moment. I felt awkward, because the one question I wanted to ask was whether they felt he was too young to play opposite me. He was thirty-nine. Gerry, as written, was five years older than I when I was forty-five. I decided to voice it anyway.

"What about the age difference, Stan?" I asked.

Stan came right to the point. "Well, Charles," he said, "can you play older?"

Charles came right back. "You've got the wrong man," he answered.

I looked back and forth between the two. Did he really look that much younger than I or was this my own personal concern?

"Shirley," said Stan, "you two look the same age.

It's nothing the audience will even think about. You look really wonderful together."

Charles nodded, but didn't smile. Okay, I thought. If it doesn't bother him or anyone else.

I looked at Charles. "Do you want to play Gerry?" I asked.

"Very much," he answered. "I should have been extremely disappointed had you chosen another actor."

Well, I thought. That's that. We've got our Gerry. I just have to be careful of keeping him waiting. . . .

We had several more rehearsals with Charles so that we could get his input on the script. I liked working democratically, with everyone feeling free to give me an opinion about what I was doing. His input was valuable, particularly in regard to the British class system and the speech Gerry gives in the House of Commons and to the English press relating to Third World poverty. Dance himself came from a needy background and worked his way up, remembering and identifying with those who were disenfranchised. This aspect of Gerry was what motivated him to devote so much of his talent and energy to achieving power so that he could help change people's lives for the better. Up to now Dance hadn't asked about Gerry's true identity. He had the British sensitivity to privacy and anyway probably didn't really care. As for me, I hadn't talked to Gerry in some time and wondered if he had seen that the English papers had announced that Charles Dance was playing him. Dance was scheduled to come to America for wardrobe fittings, makeup tests, and more rehearsals.

I wondered if he would ever want to know who Gerry was.

Chapter 7

Colin, Stan, and I went back to America to find a David, who actually had a larger part than Gerry. And we hadn't even begun to zero in on him. In my thinking about casting for David, I had early decided it had to be someone enormously sensitive with that very particular sensitivity that allows one to find one's own way. Yet he had also to be strong within himself. He was not going to be easy to find, but the leeway we had was that his part didn't begin shooting until January, a good seven weeks into the schedule. We discussed possibilities ad infinitum. Casting David was crucial to me and central to the whole theme of the subject. At last I became semi-settled about it—at least in my head.

John Heard is one of those actors the public doesn't recognize, but within the business we all know he's brilliant. He's an actor's actor. He is not John Hurt, or William Hurt. He is John Heard—a man with a last name that aptly expresses his need to be listened to. His life-style is as legendary as his talent. So is his intelligence. So when he walked into my apartment in New

York only forty-five minutes late, I felt privileged. It was Colin's reaction to John that was the most fun for me. Stan wasn't present.

In real life John looks like a WASP traveling salesman. In "reel" life he can look like anything. He photographs much taller than his five-foot ten-inch frame and more massive than he actually is. He walked in with a growth of beard (to indicate nonchalance?), shuffling along with the thick *"Limb"* script under his arm. He slumped over and glanced at us furtively without settling his gaze on either one of us. He tossed the script on my coffee table and sat down, leaned back, put one leg over the other, and laughed as if we were silly-assed people to want to put him in our movie. Colin bristled, but John tickled me, probably because he was so irreverent.

"Well, John, I really admire your work," I said.

He laughed again, as though that made me a jerk. There was no conventional "thank you," no comment of any kind—he just leaned back and chuckled secretly to himself again.

"Okay," I said. "I see. So what did you think of our script?"

"I didn't read it," he answered. Colin bristled again.

"Why?" I asked.

More chuckles from John. "Because," he said, "I couldn't lift it."

Colin blushed crimson. But I was really warming to this guy.

"Then why are you here?" I asked.

"Because my dentist appointment got canceled," he answered.

Oh, boy, I thought, this is going to be more than amusing.

"I'm fat and bulky," he went on. "You don't want me."

I thought I'd join the game. "Why don't you have your dentist sew up your mouth then?" I asked.

John flashed that childlike shock of one playmate recognizing another playmate sooner than either expected. Colin wasn't sure what was going on.

"John"—Colin decided to participate—"did you come here because you're interested in doing this?"

John chuckled again.

"I mean," said Colin, "do you know what this is about? Do you know anything about David's character? Has your agent read the script?"

"I fired my agent," said John.

"Oh," said Colin. "How about your manager?"

John leaned back on the couch and looked out the window. "If I said there was a flying saucer on the windowsill you wouldn't bother turning around, but if I said there's this funny disc-shaped craft with Donald Duck ears, you'd be up and out of your chair in a flash, right?"

"Not necessarily," I replied.

Colin and I looked at each other. What did he mean? Was our script not funny enough? *Had* he read it?

John did his secret chuckle again. Colin took the bull by the horns.

"Okay," he said. "Let's read. Maybe you'll get the sense out of it as you go."

John shrugged. "Okay, man," he said. "But my teeth hurt."

"I thought your dentist appointment was canceled," I said.

"No," said John. "My girlfriend can't cook. She makes carrot salad for my mother so my family will like her."

Oh, brother, I thought. This is something Woody Allen or maybe Albert Brooks would understand. Or maybe the guy was just scared in an interesting way. . . . It *did* take a certain kind of left-field intelligence which I wasn't sure I possessed to understand him, and Colin apparently didn't even want to—but, as I reminded him later, *he* wasn't the director.

John picked up the script and lifted it slowly to his shoulder as though it were a ten-ton boulder. Then he chuckled and opened it to the first page.

"Some directors say I chuckle like this when I'm insecure."

Yes, I really liked his off-the-wall honesty. Even Colin was disarmed for a second. We turned to John's first scene and he began reading and acting his part. I felt a little premonitory shiver run down my back. I knew some actors were really good at cold readings, but the good ones usually weren't. What we were hearing was an actor reading with in-depth understanding *and* a comprehension of metaphysics and spiritual principles. Had he been kidding us? I said nothing, just kept on going although it was hard for me to concentrate on my own part because he was so unexpectedly brilliant. Finally I couldn't stand it. I stopped the reading and looked at him. I punched him in the arm. He looked at me.

"You're a friggin' liar, John."

"I am?" he said.

"Yes. You've studied the script backward, haven't you? How can you be this good without knowing it beforehand?"

"Oh"—he stopped me—"I'll never be this good again. Don't worry. I'm a fake. You know, I run between the raindrops."

"But did you read it?"

"No," he said, "because I would have told you the truth if I didn't like it and I didn't want to say the wrong thing."

I looked deep into his eyes. He chuckled again.

Just then the doorbell rang. Because John had been late, my appointments were overlapping. It didn't faze him in the least.

"John," I said, "this is Bella Abzug. She is here

because she wants to read for her own part. Can I put you in the den to finish reading this thing?"

John shrugged. He stood up and shifted his weight back and forth and put his hands in his pockets and ran his tongue over his lips. Then he pulled his fingers through his floppy hair and pushed the curls forward as if to make sure their unkempt style would remain intact. *This* was a complicated and spellbinding crazy man. He shuffled back to my den, sat down with the script, and I closed the door in order to give Bella the respect she so richly deserved.

Bella knew we were looking for a "Bella" and had been reading actresses, but she thought *she* should do it. What better way to protect the investment she had made in the character she had invented for herself. I was not enthusiastic, based on how much theatrical discipline I knew it would take for her—or anyone—to do scenes over and over.

Bella had been a close personal friend since the McGovern campaign in 1972. We had had our personal ups and downs, but she has always remained, and I believe she always will, a friend who will be honest with me as I will be with her. She is earthy, witty, more than compassionate, and possessed of an intelligence that blazes with clarity. She is also pragmatic, ambitious, and loves to be the focus of attention. That is precisely why she is so charismatic. Besides all of that, I love her deeply.

She entered my living room dressed in a color-coordinated red-white-and-blue business suit, patriotism being the mood of her day today since she was thinking of running for Congress again.

"So? Why am I here?" she said as she walked toward Colin and me. "You people summoned me, right?"

"Yes," I answered. "We'd love for you to read for us."

She saw the script on the table, picked it up and flipped through it. "So you want me to read this?"

"Well," I said, "we'd like you to audition. You said you were available."

"But I'll blush," she said, "and I'll be awake all night wondering if I get the part."

"That's show business," I said.

Colin smiled at the interplay between the two of us, registering every nuance that might be valuable on the screen.

"My God," said Bella, turning and looking at herself in a wall mirror. "I'll have to read my own lines, right?"

"Right," I said. "And you've already okayed the script, so you can't object to the dialogue."

"God," she laughed, "then I'm going to be more intimidated by you than ever."

I smiled mischievously. "Then you'll know how other people feel about you."

"Be nice now." She paused. "You know how I need you to be sweet to me."

She gave me that pout that she knows always melts my heart. We both knew, but it worked anyway.

The phone rang. It was Stan.

"Hey," I said, "everything's going great. We're reading for Bella now."

"Okay," he said. "When you finish with the Bellas, call me."

"You don't understand," I said. "We're reading the real one."

"You're what?"

From across the room Bella yelled, "Call my agent."

"Shirley"—Stan spoke determinedly into the phone— "you know what discipline this business takes, even for an experienced actress. How would *she* even know how to repeat the same scene over and over and retain the emotional pitch?"

I turned away from Bella. "I don't know, Stan," I said, "but she wants to try."

"Okay. Call me when it's over."

I hung up and Colin and Bella and I went to work.

We picked up the script. I played myself. Bella played herself. And all the while each of us retained the emotional memory of the exact events as they had actually occurred. It was an exercise in recognized illusion. I have never had an experience that so thoroughly brought home to me the truth that we each *act* our lives, we each project the image we really wish to convey—the appearance of spontaneity notwithstanding. There were so many choices for Bella and me to make in expressing ourselves: the choice of wardrobe, hairstyle, makeup, body movement, all vital but relatively finite. But when it came to emotional intent, vocal tone, facial expression, and so on, to say nothing of what we did and said, the choices became literally infinite. I realized that if I were to invent a character like Bella Abzug, I couldn't possibly do as definitive a job as she had done herself. Each movement of the strong hands, each wrinkle of the high-cheekboned experienced face were strokes on a personality canvas that she assuredly painted herself. And as I watched her *acting* lines she had actually spoken and heard myself doing the same thing, I had a kind of double vision in time. Which was the past and which the present? I was aware of how I had said these very same lines years ago. So was Bella. And both of us were also aware that we had been acting them then.

There we were, walking the lines through my kitchen into the dining room. The same dining room. She helped me set my table. The same kitchen, same table. She sat down as I tossed a salad. All the while we read our lines; portraying ourselves, re-creating what we had done so many times together.

And as we indulged in this Pirandello adventure I slowly began to make a professional assessment. Bella in real life was too strong for "reel" life. It was astonishing. She was actually bigger than life—too much for an entertainment piece. For news or documentary coverage she was perfectly in sync with her attuned image. But for a prime-time television entertainment miniseries, I knew it wouldn't work.

The strangest part of it, though, was that she was very convincingly real in playing herself. There wasn't a fake note in her performance—which is saying a lot for a politician! But the truth of the person she conveyed *as* herself was simply too strong for television. In fact I began to assess my own performance of myself in a different light. I had never been faced with this issue before. Was it possible to be too much oneself? *Too real?*

We finished the reading. Colin and I needed to talk together. Bella respected that.

"I know," she said as she straightened her hat and strode toward the door. "Don't call us—we'll call you. I'll see ya later."

She let herself out. Colin went to the window.

"Strangest casting experience I've ever had," he said. "Don't know what to make of how good she was. But will she translate to television? The expression *too much for TV* may be apt here. She's so great as a politician on TV. I've seen her. Strong, sometimes strident, but colorful and riveting."

He thought a moment longer. "I know what it is that's bothering me."

"What?"

"We've written Bella as a friend and foil for Shirley. It's about Bella's reactions to Shirley's metaphysical and spiritual search. And those reactions are earthy and comic. Now it's true that that is how she is. But in real life she is so much more than that. Since we are portraying only *that* reactive comedic aspect of her, essentially the grandness and stature of her political personality overwhelms the limitations of the character we reduced her to be. In other words, she's overqualified for the part."

I looked at him and gulped. "Great," I said. "But how do you tell a person they can't play themselves?"

"Very carefully," he answered with a grin.

I went to my den to retrieve John Heard. I could see he had almost finished the script. He looked up at me with an expression of sheer disbelief on his face. Maybe he hadn't been lying after all. Maybe he was experiencing for the first time the full impact of a script about trance channeling, reincarnation, extraterrestrials, and spacecraft that land. He spoke first.

"I'm supposed to be in love with an extraterrestrial?" he asked.

"Yes," I answered. "Maybe not love in the sexual sense, but certainly in the sense that she changed your life."

John didn't chuckle. He just stared at me.

"But I'm a Catholic," he said finally.

I could think of no sensible response to this and we returned to the living room. We finished reading. He was so uncommonly talented at reading the metaphysical lines, it was as though he understood them. True, they had an Irish Catholic ring to them, but that was what made it human. Colin and I were enthralled. John himself seemed to be enjoying the impossible. He understood that the dialogue was unplayable except by an actor with a profound talent for throwing meaningful platitudes away. He read the stuff as though he were reciting a laundry list, and it worked.

He interspersed some funny sarcastic comments such as "Lake T-I-T-I-C-A-C-A? I'm supposed to say *Titicaca* and not break up? The fathers in the dorm won't like that at all." Then he'd imitate one of the priests right out of Barry Fitzgerald's Hollywood.

Every now and then John would extract a Lucky Strike cigarette from a rumpled pack, light it with ceremony, and take a long comfortable drag. He'd blow tiny little rings while he stared at his feet, tilted his head, and thought. Then he'd say, "I could be down at the bar, or skiing."

I didn't realize it then, but John never said anything that wasn't symbolic. I mean, you had to learn his language even to carry on a conversation with him, but then I had been weaned on Robert Mitchum and Debra Winger. It was basically the language of artful paranoia which provided tidbits of apparently irrelevant remarks slung into the conversational mix and usually relating to something on their minds. If you plucked one of the tidbits and held it close, you might find you had grabbed yourself the brass ring. On the other hand, before you could properly be aware of it, you might be left holding a hot steamy turd. The game was to use human beings as a sounding board against which to experiment with humor, hostility, fear, sadism, and even fun and wit—the intent being to inveigle others into the game but not to divulge the rules. The originators of the game are the only ones who know. That left several options: if the game wasn't proceeding according to their wishes, they could always deny that a game was even in progress. If they got tired of it or felt outclassed, they simply became colorfully incoherent and soon you realized you were playing symbolic Ping-Pong with yourself. The whole exercise was meant to disorient the fellow player so as to expose his weaknesses and insecurities. The result was that the artful paranoiac would be armed with more personal knowledge of his opponent while divulging no such personal information himself.

But when the practitioners of this form of super one-upmanship know you're on to them, it can really be fun. That was the case with John and me. I had sort of learned after rehearsing with Mitchum and Winger how to be honest about the buttons they pushed in me, yet without actually divulging much personal information they could wield against me. (In fact, the personal information was in the public domain, but part of the game is spontaneity, subjective reaction, a kind of dare—to themselves as much as anyone.)

So, after John would say things like "I could be down at the corner bar or skiing" (I don't think he'd ever been on a pair of skis in his life), he'd look at me and say, "Did you really write this stuff?" or "So you think Ronald Reagan is walking in the light?" I'd quickly regroup my reactions and tell him how stunned I was at how skillfully he brought even difficult dialogue "into the light" and "Yes, Ronald Reagan would benefit from that too." He'd do his silent chuckle and blow more smoke rings and tilt his curly head and smile at his black Reeboks.

Colin Higgins had a different reaction. He was a straight person, sensible enough not to bother wasting time with the kind of imaginative child's play that could lead to nothing but overtime and overbudget problems. That was one aspect, and he could cope with that. But the other was the manipulative quality of artful paranoia. Colin was an honest man who deplored insidiousness. Yet I think the irreverent audacity of defying convention with such sleight-of-hand techniques was a method he himself might have secretly admired, yet felt too timid to employ. Whatever—Colin observed John's reading and behavior as a perturbed headmaster would regard an obstreperously canny-shrewd schoolboy.

I felt myself wanting to play with John yet not caring to isolate Colin, which was one of John's pranksterish maneuvers—divide and conquer.

Fortunately the reading came to an end and John was in the position of wondering whether he had gotten the part. Regardless of the labyrinthine lengths to which he would go to be undetected, it still came down to "Do I go to work?"

Colin and I had another appointment, so John ambled out of my apartment, patting the script under his arm as the symbolic signal that he really wanted to play David.

When the door closed, Colin said, "That guy really pushes my buttons. I wonder why. I think I'm supposed to learn a lot from this. . . ."

He gazed out the window and fidgeted. "We come from the same Irish Catholic background." Colin took a stance with his legs far apart and folded his arms in front of him as he counted the available cabs on the street below.

"One thing for sure. The guy can really act. He makes the playing so real."

I stood beside him. A weird sense of perspective came over me. "I get the feeling that all of this is an act right now," I said. "That we're all playing in this play within a play."

Harold got a sly inexplicable smile on his face. "So," he said, "is John Heard just going to help me play myself better?"

I retired to the kitchen for a drink.

"One thing else is for sure," I said. "He'll show us how phony we are."

"What do you mean?" Colin yelled after me.

"I'm not real sure. But I just think he will."

The phone rang. Not more than two and a half minutes could have gone by since John left. It was his manager calling.

"John tells me he doesn't think he gave you what you wanted. Is that true?" asked the manager.

I was shocked. "Are you kidding? He was brilliant. Tell me, had he read the script?"

The manager laughed. "Who knows? You know John."

" 'You know John'? What does that mean?"

"It means: who can figure him out, least of all him?"

That was to become a refrain echoed around North

and South America by a small band of people trying to make a movie about unseen and alternative realities. Then and now, I knew he was what we needed—and what the film needed. Figuring him out was *his* problem.

"Listen, Bill," I said. "He's more terrific than we ever dreamed. He is totally unpredictable, and what he gave us is not what we expected, that's all."

"Well, he just wanted to know."

"Did he call you from a phone booth on the corner?"

"Why?"

"He just left."

"Well, as you probably picked up, he's an anxious fellow."

"Anxious to please?"

Silence on the other end.

"No," said Bill. "I'd say you *will* be pleased, but that's not what he's anxious about."

"What *is* he anxious about?"

"Oh, you know John," he replied.

You might say John had the right manager. . . .

Chapter 8

Colin and I returned to California to inform ABC of our John Heard decision. A deal was made. We also decided that in the interest of legitimate reality, Kevin Ryerson and his entities should play themselves. A real actor could get more out of the scenes but what we'd gain in performance would be lost in credibility. We wanted the show to be as real as possible since we were venturing into such new terrain. Besides, why not have television's first real cinematic trance channeling experience? We then proceeded to read prospective Bellas. Each woman who came to read had something to offer and each woman was understandably pressured by Bella's real-life image, since she was so availably well known.

Anne Jackson, however, was the best. She was funny, earthy, not too broad, and of course an experienced actress who caught Bella's rhythms and punches perfectly for the small living-room screen.

Bella's reaction to Anne's playing her was not so perfect. I heard the Washington politician at work as she lobbied for herself on the telephone.

"Listen," she said. "I know you wrote me as a foil

for you. I have some problems with that anyway," she began.

"What do you mean?" I asked.

"Well, since my full dimension isn't being portrayed—and," she went on, "I know, it's your story, not mine. But since I'm only a foil I want to protect myself by playing the foil *my* way. You can't have it both ways."

Bella was smart and personally self-confident. Everything she was saying made sense from her point of view. I tried to explain that the comedic political lines wouldn't work with her playing herself, because her very presence would demand more than the story could accommodate. Yet, if an *actress* portrayed her, the comedy focus would be acceptable, and as a matter of fact would probably get her votes when she decided to run again.

"When is this thing going to air?" she asked shrewdly.

"Either May or November. Brandon Stoddard is not sure yet."

"But November is after the election if I decide to run for Congress."

"Oh," I said. "I'll tell Brandon it better be May if he knows what's good for him. He'll contact the affiliates and all the advertisers immediately."

I heard her laugh that gutsy no-nonsense rumble that comes from her belly.

"God, it's good to hear that," I said.

"Yeah," she said. "Well, I take this as a personal rejection brought on by the network which is afraid of my political image."

"Oh, Bella. C'mon. That's got nothing to do with it."

"I know you're not telling me because you're not willing to fight them. They're afraid of me and what I represent—*that's* why they don't want to use me and you know it."

This I never expected. "Bella," I protested. "It's *me* who doesn't want to use you. That's the truth. Neither the network or Brandon or any of those guys has interfered with anything I want to do. This is a purely artistic decision. I'm looking for who would be the best to play you, not only for the good of the show but also for the good of your next election. You'll get a lot of votes if this part is played right."

I could have been a lobbyist myself. On the other hand, some part of what I said didn't sound right.

"Are you telling me," she said, "that anybody besides *me* would play me better than *I* would play me? And that somebody else would get more votes than *I* would?"

I gulped. "Yes," I said. "I guess that's what I'm saying."

She hesitated. "Well," she said finally. "You don't know what you're talking about. I've talked to a lot of my friends and they think it is a natural that I play myself."

I really didn't know what to say. We never should have read her in the first place. What would this do to our relationship? We had certainly had our ups and downs, but this time *I* was the cause of her rejection.

"Listen," she said finally. "I know they were thinking of Marilyn Bergman to play me. It's ridiculous. Even though she's a friend of mine, she's a songwriter."

"Yes, Bella," I said. "I know. Marilyn was someone else's idea, not mine. She's not an actress. We'd have the same problem of emotional discipline with anyone who isn't an actress. That's why we're using Anne Jackson."

"Anne Jackson." She said the name as if it were the dog's dinner.

"Yeah," I said. "One of the most brilliant actresses in the American theater. She loves you."

"She's got red hair."

"So do you—*now.*"

"She has blue eyes."

"We'll make her use contacts."

"How can she walk like me?"

"She can't."

"Why not?"

"Because she's much thinner."

Bella began to mock-whimper. "Now you're insulting me. Why are you always right? Why does it have to be your way all the time?"

I sighed deeply into the phone. "Well, my darling, because this is what they call show business."

"Well, why can't I be the star of my own self?"

"Look at it this way, Bellitchka. *You* are going to be the reason that Anne Jackson will be great. And everyone will think you are really that warm and funny."

"Well, aren't I?"

"Yes, of course you are, and much, much more too. But we can't draw attention to the fact that we're not utilizing all of you."

I heard her light a cigarette and blow the smoke into the phone, calculating her next move. "Yeah," she said. "I'm underutilized all the way around. That's my big problem in life. And *you,* my good and best friend, are preventing me too."

I thought I'd let a pregnant pause go by. Maybe she'd think she was going too far. But that's not possible with Bella. What she said next was really hard to answer.

"Listen," she pressed. "Those mediums are playing themselves, right?"

"Right."

"And those ghosts, dead people types are playing themselves, right?"

"Bella, they are not ghosts and they're not dead people. Nobody ever dies. You know that."

"Oh, yeah? You're killin' me!"

"Okay. Go on."

"Well, those spirits then. They're playing themselves."

"Yes, they are."

"Well, why can't I be given the same respect as a spirit?"

"Because," I said flatly, "you've got too much to live for and I don't want you to die in the part."

I could feel her begin to rise to yet another challenge, almost as though combat was her pleasure, not victory. In any case, I begged off as gently as possible and hung up.

Stan poked his head around the corner.

"Slight hitch," he said. "John Heard's manager called. He's decided he can't play the part because it's against his religion." Stan shoved a piece of paper on the desk.

"Here," he said. "These are some other possibilities."

A sledgehammer hit my throat and I suddenly couldn't swallow. My throat closed in a tight squeeze of soreness. I wanted to laugh out loud but it hurt too much. It was clear that I was feeling so constricted in communicating what I wanted and needed that I had instantly given myself a sore throat. It wasn't the first time. Each time I got the flu or a cold, or certainly a sore throat, upon reflection I realized it was tied directly to an emotional disappointment. What made me want to laugh was how fast I could manifest the self-recrimination these days. What used to take a day or two was possible in a few minutes now. A metaphysical sophisticate said to me once: "Isn't it wonderful that you manifest a cold and a runny nose for yourself so that you can release all the pent-up tension and unbalance." As the fly said when he walked over the mirror: "That's one way of lookin' at it."

I sat down and stared at the wall. As far as John Heard was concerned, I wasn't going to take no for an answer. It was too right. As far as I was concerned, he was meant to play the part. That was why I couldn't think seriously of anybody else. The question now was how to handle his insecurity. He wasn't a devout Catholic. He was more like a collapsed Catholic. So what was the real reason? If there *was* one. If he wasn't just game-playing.

After about fifteen minutes of thought, I called Bill, John's manager.

"What's up, Bill?" I asked. "I thought he loved the idea."

"Well, yeah, but you know John," he answered.

"I see," I said prophetically. "But be more specific. What's this about its being against his religion? Didn't he know that when he read it? It's taken a while for the deal to be made. How come he let all that happen?"

"Yeah, well, that's not it."

"What's *it* then?"

"You want to talk to John? To tell you the truth, I don't know."

Bill arranged for John to take my call in about fifteen minutes. John said, "Hi. It's not my religion. It's my dentist."

"Oh, that again," I answered knowingly.

"Yes, and Melissa."

"Melissa?"

"Yes. My girl."

"You mean you'll miss her?"

I could sense his head tilt on the other end of the phone.

"Well, you know. She has real white skin. And she spends a lot of time in balconies."

"Balconies?" I asked. (When in doubt, repeat.)

"Yeah."

"Uh huh," I said.

"Sooo."

"So?"

"Yeah. I mean can you get room service at midnight?"

"Where, John?"

"Well, when I'm hungry."

"I think we can make sure there's always food around."

"I'm bulky. Did you like how I tried to hide my fat stomach with the navy-blue shirt?"

"Yeah. It was pretty clever. But I like you chunky. I think it's cute."

"Melissa doesn't think I'm cute. She thinks I'm a fuck-head."

"Are you?"

"But of course."

"So tell me why you're coolin' on the part, John."

He didn't hesitate. The other was just a preamble both of us understood.

"Because," he said, "I'm not sure I can give you what you want. I mean, you really lived this stuff. How do I know what you're talking about?"

"Well," I said, "I liked the way you *made* it your own. I had not imagined it the way you did it. It was *better*. And you might have noticed I'm not married to anything preconceived."

Somehow during the silence that then prevailed I realized he was thinking about the Catholic Church.

"Listen, John," I said, "if you are worried about the Church's reactions to what we've written, Standards and Practices [the network's clearance department] has already gone through it all and approved it."

"They have?" he asked apprehensively.

"Yes. And my research matches theirs."

"Yeah? Well, that's not really the reason. I mean, the Church fucked me up so bad that I really don't worry about that."

When John spoke with clarity it was indisputable.

"Let me think about it all tonight," he said. "I'll call you in Malibu eleven A.M. your time."

It was another man talking.

"Okay."

"Okay."

He hung up. I walked to Stan's office.

"Listen," he said. "Good news."

"What?"

"Standards and Practices finally concedes the script is correct. They found a turtle that lived to be two hundred and fifty years old."

"Great," I said. "Can he act?"

Charles Dance arrived for his first rehearsal with the director, Bob Butler. Up to then, I think Charles thought Colin Higgins was the director. He did not know that in American television the producer is the creative mind. The director just sort of makes it happen.

Charles sat with a befitting Greek-godlike slouch in slacks and shirt, disturbing his ginger-haired perfection only by not wearing any socks under his businesslike shoes. Butler, in a khaki jacket, glowing with robust health, ruddy complexion, and rugged profile, nevertheless had a nervous scowl on his face. He had never met Charles before. Butler had had little input on casting Charles and John. He was scouting locations, designing sets, assembling the crew, and so on. So he was in the enviable position, should anything go wrong, of saying "What the hell did you pick these guys for?" I couldn't help but remember that he still thought he was the only sane person in the group.

His opening speech to Charles, however, was not exactly Shakespeare.

"As I press forward on this project, Charles," he said, "I'm sure the big 'If' will be the guy in Milwaukee with the beer. Will he say 'Harriet, come in here and look at this,' or will he turn the dial? Is he smarter than all of us or should we worry about him at all?"

Charles blinked several times, stumped as to whether Butler really wanted an answer. I couldn't resist.

"All in all, Bob," I said, "I say, fuck Milwaukee."

Charles shifted his position in the swivel chair.

"Well," replied Butler, unperturbed, "that's certainly an option."

He grimaced and picked at one of his fingers. "But," he continued, "collectively, Milwaukee and Harriet is real smart. You can hate them yelling separately in bars and want to hit them over the head when they tell you individually what they think. But I put them together and there's nobody smarter. So if I'm lookin' up with a confused look on my face, it's because I'm thinking about Milwaukee and Harriet. It's your call. Help."

I clamped my hand over my mouth.

Charles surreptitiously passed me a paper with something written on it. It said: *Is this a television dialect?*

I looked blankly ahead of me.

We proceeded to rehearse. Bob interspersed comments such as: "Well, that scene has zero wiggle in it," or "Let's do it again till we can taste the green." But the best piece of his dialect, which was to become familiar, came when we finished a particularly dramatic scene. Again Bob's comment was "I'll sign anything!"

Charles looked at the director with wary calm, as though he were a restless native. I looked at Butler, remembering that his wife owned a bookstore and hence he knew all about the search for spiritual awareness in the marketplace. Somewhere in between lay the real Bob Butler.

Charles began to acquaint himself with Century City, ABC, the freeways, and room service at his hotel. We were to begin shooting in London in a week, but he had a few weeks later on in Los Angeles.

I took the phone call from John Heard the next morning.

"Yeah," he said. "I remember the day I left the Gonzaga [a Catholic school in Washington, D.C.] dorm. I was supposed to be in the play that week. I overslept— the alarm didn't go off. The fathers said whoever did that would be expelled. So, shit, when I finally woke up and knew I was out anyway, I got in this car and went over to

W-L for the football game. See, I'm from your neck of the woods."

He was right. I had gone to Washington Lee High School in Arlington, Virginia, and except for the age difference would probably have been cheerleading that night.

"So," I said, "I guess this is right karma that we meet again."

"And I don't know what time we got back. It was a dark-blue car."

"I see."

"So," he continued, "I'm expelled."

"Yeah? From what?"

"I can't say the dialogue. I mean, I never could see those flower children walking up to people in airports."

"Listen, John," I said, "I know how arch that dialogue can be. That's why nobody's done a movie like this before. As long as the sense of it remains the same, you can say it like you want to."

"I can rewrite stuff?" he asked.

"Sure," I said. "You've got to make the part your own."

There was a long pause.

"Oh," he said. "I thought you'd want me to say it like it's written."

"No. It doesn't have to be."

"Uh-huh."

"Look," I said finally. "Colin and I are coming to New York on our way to London to begin shooting with Charles Dance. Let's go over the script word-for-word and rewrite it like you want to say it. Okay?"

"Okay."

Another long pause. "I guess," he said, "that I've said yes, haven't I?"

"Yes, John. I guess you have."

We hung up.

I called Stan and told him John was going to be in the picture.

"Sure," said Stan. "I'll believe it when he lands in Peru."

When I called my agent Mort, to tell him John was meeting with us in New York, he said, "First you'll get a phone call saying he can't get a cab, then a follow-up to say he can't find the building, then another to ask where's the elevator. Then the last two will be that he's in the restaurant across the street and finally that he's worked his way to the bar and can't do the part. But stay with it. The guy is *good*."

I was reminded that Mort, bless him, has reason to know about my impatience. But not this time, not this time. Impatient I may be, but also determined and persistent. . . .

It was 10:40 A.M. in New York City.

Colin and I had finished our coffee and were waiting for John. He was twenty minutes late.

"Well, he was forty-five minutes late before," I said upliftingly.

The phone rang. It was John.

"Listen," he said, "I can't get a cab."

I decided to cut through everything.

"Where are you—in the bar across the street?"

As soon as I said it I felt I had been cruel.

There was a silence on the other end.

"John," I continued, "my building is easy to find, you found it before, and the elevator works."

"Okay. I'll be right over."

I met John at the door and put my arms around him.

"I know how nervous you are and how hard this is for you," I said. "I was afraid you wouldn't come."

John sighed deeply and tilted his head.

"Thank you for making it easier."

He walked in.

"I've been skiing all weekend. I'm tired. Excuse the four-day growth of beard."

He ambled into the living room wearing another oversized shirt.

"See?" he remarked immediately, patting his stomach. "I'm covering up my bulk again."

"I like your bulk."

I did. I meant it. John gently placed the script on the coffee table. I could see he had been making notes all over it. He sat down nonchalantly.

"Yeah. That was some weekend," he said exasperatingly. "I'm really tired from defying gravity. I like that downhill racing. Beautiful scenery, though. Those trees— real giants . . . silent snow. God's country."

Colin sipped some cold coffee.

John continued. "So I didn't get much of the script read."

Colin turned red. Then I realized what was going on. John hadn't been skiing at all. Why, he wouldn't know a ski trail from a back alley. He must have seen something in my eye, for he quickly changed the subject.

"You got somethin' to eat?" he asked.

I produced some prepared sandwiches. John picked one up, allowing the lettuce to dangle from the bread as he brought up where Ronald Reagan's politics fit into karma. As he talked he nibbled casually on the sandwich, then another, until, as though Houdini were in the room, all the sandwiches were gone.

"So you say Ronald Reagan is in the light?" he said argumentatively.

I had one for him.

"Certainly," I answered. "Look at how positive he is with his personal attitudes. I think that's why Americans love him."

John lit a cigarette, suddenly very controlled. I saw the first hint of lightning violence in him. But his voice was quiet. "How can you say that when he treats the poor with such disdain?"

John was serious. What he was really trying to ascertain was how genuine I was about my metaphysical-spiritual beliefs. I had told him previously that I didn't believe in evil, that there was no such thing as Hell, and that everyone involved with unpleasant events makes a soul choice to be so involved for the purpose of learning and growing. So the first scene of my third degree was going to be about the participation of the poor in their own karmic dilemma.

I stood up by the mantelpiece. John had a built-in bullshit detector. I had long since learned that in discussing these New Age systems of thought, people who were newly exposed to it responded as much to the quality of emotional conviction as they did to the information. John was looking for my Achilles heel, the chink in my belief structure. He had that pure streak in him when it came to performing material about the destiny of mankind. I chose my words carefully because he was asking for a crash course in karmic philosophy and if he didn't understand, it would be my fault.

"Look, John," I began, "I believe that we have all lived thousands and thousands of lifetimes. We chose each one and we'll choose them in the future. We can choose poverty and the lessons that poverty affords us, or we can choose wealth for the same reasons. Maybe we choose poverty because in a former lifetime we abused wealth and power. Maybe we choose power because we need to learn to wield it humanely. Every person has a soul reason for choosing what he chooses. So, Reagan has chosen power and leadership this time around. Some aspects of it he's handling well. Others he's quite insensitive and blind about. But each person who is experiencing the poverty that Reagan is insensitive to, is also participating in their own destiny. And somewhere way underneath on a soul level they know that."

John watched and listened with acute awareness and sincerity. He was sifting what I said.

"Listen," he said. "What happens to your political activism when you come to the beliefs you have? I mean, if you don't believe anyone is wrong, who are you against?"

"I'm not against anybody anymore," I said. "I'm *for* stuff now. I'm *for* helping the poor to help themselves. I'm *for* a better balance of economics. I'm *for* South African integration. I'm *for* believing this world is going to make it instead of against the turmoil that seems to be causing the disintegration of values. See, I don't believe we're headed for disaster. I believe we're headed for transition."

John crossed one leg over the other as he hugged his waist.

"Are you tellin' me I should just turn the other cheek if someone hits me?"

"Well, you can use your free will to choose what you wish. Just remember you participated in being hit in the first place."

"I want to get slugged?"

"I don't know if you want to, per se, but you choose to have the experience. On some level you have agreed to participate. There are no accidents."

"So should I ignore someone else's misfortune?"

I sat down. I realized he was seeing a glimmer of what I was saying.

"No," I said, "I wouldn't. But that depends too. I mean, if a friend of mine insists on being a coke-head, I'd try to help him to the best of my ability, but, if he continued, I'd finally have to honor his decision to experience self-destruction."

"You mean we aren't our brother's keeper?"

"Yes, we are. But we have to also recognize that sometimes they don't want to be helped."

John flashed a smile and then became deadly serious.

"Your brother is calling one of my girlfriends."

"Oh," I said. "I guess there's some kind of karmic explanation for that too."

He pursed his lips in displeasure.

"Yeah," he said. "Well. So should I leave someone in trouble because they're draggin' me down? Where's the love in that?"

I quickly wrote a scenario in my mind to fit the question. Was Melissa in trouble? Was it an actor friend? Did any of that have to do with his reluctance to film on location? I leaned over and touched his knee. He flinched ever so slightly.

"I think," I said, "if you're a really good friend, you help a person see the best in themselves. If they don't want to, don't sacrifice the best in yourself. You hurt both that way."

John sighed. "The nuns got me early. I like to suffer."

"Well, let's suffer the script, okay? Colin and I have to go to London tomorrow."

"You know," said John, "a cab driver would never think I'm brilliant. He'd think you're brilliant."

"Why do you say that?" I asked.

"Because that's what fame and fortune do."

"Do you want to be famous and rich?"

"No. It doesn't recognize talent."

"Well, I always hear how brilliant you are," I said.

"I know, but it's from people in the business."

"Yes. I think you're right."

"The rest of the people think I'm John Hurt or William Hurt. And maybe they're right."

During this non-sequitur mini-philosophy session Colin remained intriguingly impassive. It was as though he was clocking the subtle rhythms and the not-so-subtle game-playing in order to incorporate them in a future script. He registered every detail, every nuance, while at the same time evaluating his own personal response.

There were no more sandwiches and the coffee was

all gone. John asked what books he should read to educate himself. I told him. Then we read the script. He danced around the part, shadow-boxing in and out of the metaphysical dialogue. He said a friend of his had told him that spiritual language was difficult to write, but Colin and I had done a good job. He said he had been fired from a Royal Court production for "fooling around and being inattentive." When one of his fellow actresses asked if all American actors acted that way, he said, "Fuck ... I guess so." He said that Mike Nichols had told him he was so insecure about a part he was asked to play that Mike felt uncertain about giving it to him. I was amused by John's attempts to blacken his own character, and totally sympathetic with the self-doubts that underlay his efforts. No actor in the world worthy of the name is free of such fears.

As the day drew to a close, John, having made his dragonfly comments on his life and work, sometimes to me, sometimes to the air, finally looked straight at Colin. Colin smiled that quiet smile and said nothing.

John shrugged and said, "Well?"

Colin smiled again and said simply, "You roly-poly insecure fellas get all the women."

John did his secret chuckle.

"Yeah," he said finally. "But look, after all the protestation didn't change one word of dialogue."

John got up, hefted the script to his shoulder, and left.

Colin went to the window. "He'll be wonderful," he said, looking at the headlights of the traffic below. "He's brilliant, he's infuriating, and he'll be so unpredictable in the part that no one will get blown by our spiritual 'know-it-all' dialogue."

"And?" I asked, knowing he wanted to say more.

"And," he went on, "we'll all be a lot older and hopefully a lot wiser about ourselves because of the way he's going to push our buttons." Colin turned to me.

"He's going to create an Irish Catholic 'David' who spouts spiritual dialogue for the viewers in a way they can understand. It's no accident that we will all be working together."

So there it was—the karma providing the tension for our play within a play. But of course it would be weeks before we got to play with John.

Colin had the same thought. "It's going to be a long while before we can work with him," he said. He sounded doubtful.

"But we will," I told him. "We most surely will."

Chapter 9

I arrived in London to an English press that was speculating on whether Charles Dance knew whom he was playing. There were pictures of Charles and me and quotes from my book regarding my "secret affair in the aura of the House of Commons." I was to meet my British M.P. over again, but this time not only in the hidden confines of the bathroom and the bedroom.

I returned to the hotel suite with the winding staircase, defective telephone, and bar set up for twenty. I had the engineers alter the current of my sound machine so that I could sleep. That sound machine was and is the key to my productivity whenever I'm away from Malibu. It's based on the white-sound principle. A turn of the knob produces "rain," "surf," and "waterfalls" from a tape recording that rotates constantly. I lie in bed and picture a genuine ocean outside my hotel window, regardless of the truth. It's called creating my own reality. It has gotten me through Egyptian horn-honking, Manhattan sirens, cable cars in San Francisco, and any number of early-morning celebrations after all-night drinks in the hallways outside my door. It is as precious to me as my passport. Without it I'm afraid I won't sleep even if there is actually quiet.

So, with my machine in fine working order, I thought I would have no problem sleeping. That was not the case.

I was beginning a new film, true. But, much more, for the first time, I was playing my own experience. The prospect of a relived reality overwhelmed me. I had no problem separating my own identity *now* from the person I had been ten years earlier. My problem lay in trying to figure out what really had gone on between Gerry and me and when it actually occurred. I guess we can all look back over relationships and ponder and reflect upon their meaning. But to reenact it was unsettling. So, that first night, I lay awake a lot, fretting at it. No world-shaking insights ensued.

Charles and I took to rehearsing the scenes close to the environment of the actual locations. We would sit at a secluded table in a parkside restaurant having a screen-play argument, while the waiters saw that it was okay to serve us. We walked arm in arm among the trees, doing the scenes over and over. He was trying to grasp the part he was playing. I was trying to grasp the truth I had lived. Both of us discussed the knowledge that we were, in fact, acting every moment of our lives, which inspired Charles to question: "Why is that so difficult for us to admit?" He never asked the identity of Gerry.

We were both gearing up to those first moments when the cameras roll and you know there is no more time for experimentation. You're required to commit to film.

The wardrobe, hair, and makeup help you to become someone else. In my case I had raided my own closets and in some cases chose to wear outfits I had actually worn during scenes I was depicting. I slowly became more aware of my personally idiosyncratic habits, expressions I could feel on my face, attitudes and reactions that must have driven Gerry crazy. The syntax of the phrasing was mine, not that of some "other" character. Usually the first aspect of a character I needed to understand was the way she walked and moved. Trained as a dancer, I worked from the outside in. I would picture the character moving across a room to meet a friend, sitting anxiously to hear bad news, racing to an airplane to greet a lover. As soon as I knew what she was wearing and how she moved in it, I was on my way to understanding the character I was playing. Not only was I dispensing with my usual mental preparation, but this time I was forced to "be" instead of to "act"—a new sensation.

I had had long makeup and wardrobe tests with each behind-the-scenes department. Early into production I found myself referring to Shirley as "she." "She" wouldn't wear this. She is really upset here, so leave off the makeup. All the while remembering that she was me. But then an interesting twist in professional behavior began to happen within me. If I felt that something I had actually done or said did not play, or was dramatically wrong for the "character," I changed it. I felt no allegiance to the truth if it didn't convey what really happened. When Butler, Colin, and Stan saw that taking hold, I think they realized that I could look at myself and my life with a detached professional scrutiny that championed, as its higher priority, entertainment and identification. I surprised myself. It was then that I began to understand the nature of having acted my own life in the first place. I realized that each move I'd made, each decision I'd taken, had been a choice, that my life hadn't just happened, sweeping "me" along with it. I had created the sweep; the sweep, the people, the events, the pitfalls, the triumphs. Every morning I got up, I had created my own reality for yet another day. I could alter the very fiber of my existence by knowing that I had the choice to do it. I could see that now. But ten years back "I" had been too embroiled.

So, as I reenacted the conflict inherent in the relationship with Gerry, it was from a very different perspective. I had decided to experience it all in order to know myself better. Gerry had chosen it, too, probably for the same reasons. Maybe "chemistry" between two people simply accelerated lessons in human learning for us which would otherwise take years to understand. Perhaps falling in love with a married man had as much to do with learning about the wife as it did the husband. One thing was certain: the lessons pertaining to myself indicated that my learning needs were of paramount importance to me only. My behavior had appeared to others to be quite unreasonable. I had flown, at the drop of a hat, to distant and exotic regions of the world just to spend a few days with him, to the detriment of my work and sometimes other relationships. Then, it had been mandatory for me to do it; there was never a question in my mind. I remembered wondering why others couldn't understand.

Then, among the very few who knew his identity, there was the "What does she see in him?" point of view—that age-old comparative judgment we tend to make when we are lovingly prejudiced in favor of one person with no clue whatsoever as to the fundamental reasons for an unexplained attraction to an unsuitable other. We "involved" people certainly couldn't explain it. I couldn't. As though propelled by an unseen force that felt as monumentally irresistible as it did romantically compelling, I had listened to my inner drummer and acted on it. So had Gerry. Now that percussion heartbeat had evolved itself into a full-blown miniseries for television. The acts and the actors were one.

The technological aspects of the first week of principal photography worked remarkably well. Brad May's camera crew was English. He was unused to not having

his own, but he and they were fast and artistic. I was
working for the first time without klieg lights and powerful candlepower. Instead Brad used indirect lighting
bounced off white panels. The result was natural, extremely flattering, and very "docudrama" real.

But I had real trouble at first because I had grown
up in the days of formal Hollywood lighting. I couldn't
even begin to feel the scene until the lights were on. In
the power of the lights lay the permission to emote
freely. Without the protective dome of light I felt my
privacy was being invaded, and conversely I was bathed
and safe and caressed only in the warmth and illumination of the lights. I knew they would magnify my innermost expression, playing on and sculpting my face and
yet simultaneously protecting me from being exposed by
the natural light of day. When the lights went out, my
talent went back under my skin. I couldn't act. I became
anonymous, not wanting to be the center of attention or
even take up anybody's time.

So I had a monumental adjustment to make in the
lighting style. From the first projection-room screen test,
I loved how it made me look. It was how it made me feel
that was the problem.

Along with adjusting to playing myself, not being
brightly lit, and just the advent of what I knew would be
a five-month shoot in which I was in every scene, I found
that I could not sleep. I had my sound machine up full
blast. (The hotel maids thought a hurricane was swirling
from the North.) But it didn't help. I really couldn't
pinpoint what it was. I tossed and turned. I counted
sheep. I did ballet exercises in my head. I chanted man-
tras I had learned. I even had a sleep tape sent over
air-express from San Francisco. It was channeled by
Lazaris. His voice was soothing as it gently reminded me:
"You will feel rested if you believe you are. For every
hour of sleep you will have four hours of rest." The
effect was designed to influence the subconscious.

Instead of allowing that to happen I had a nattering dialogue with myself that I was being brainwashed. Of course I was—that was the point. No, it wasn't brainwashing; it was "motivational suggestion."

As the first week pressed on, I was sleeping only two hours a night. Then the real fear that I would never sleep set in. I tried to construct dreams for myself. I did yoga and meditation in the middle of the night.

I began to get sick and very depressed. After useless attempts at sleep, I'd turn on the television news and register what seemed like nothing but disaster in the world. Northern Ireland just wouldn't quit. A socialized-medical report said there were twelve stroke victims every hour. I wondered why anybody would choose that for a learning experience. Families in the East End of London were hiring "minders" (bodyguards) to protect them from racial crime. I had a "minder" to mind me on the set, too. I'd never had a bodyguard in my life. Why did I need one now? What I needed was a sleepguard. I watched the effects of a Chilean volcano on mud-caked children as they lay, still surviving, for four days. Twenty-five thousand people died. I sat and sobbed on the floor in front of the television set.

The Geneva Summit with Reagan and Gorbachev was a dim hope in the world going mad.

As I cried to myself I thought: This must be a release. It's a good thing. After the depression and sadness is spent I'll be able to sleep and feel more balanced. But what was causing it?

Finally, after one and a half weeks of sleeplessness and depression, I made a decision. I called Gerry. The real Gerry. We had not spoken for some time. I assumed he had seen the papers and knew what I was doing.

"Hello," he said in that breathless, enthusiastic way of his. "Yes. I saw that you were here."

I pictured his tousled hair and the belt around his waist which was never secured in the loops. I could see him turning impatiently in his chair, his private secretary somewhere hovering about.

"How are you, Gerry?" I asked, making a conscious choice to sound gentle and feminine.

"Well," he answered. "I'm very well, but we have these damn budget cuts to contend with. The world does seem to be economically defunct, doesn't it?"

His old priorities were still intact. I wondered if he had changed much in other respects, and what, or whether, he thought of *Out on a Limb*. I avoided what was on my mind.

"Well, maybe the world isn't on the brink of disaster," I said. "Maybe it's on the brink of transition."

"Yes," said Gerry. "Well, it'd better be quick."

I sat up on my bed. As though he heard me do it, he hesitated. I hesitated. Then I thought I'd plunge ahead with what had been on my mind.

"Gerry," I said, "I've wanted to talk to you for some time now, but haven't known how to do it."

I could feel him melt into a smile.

"So have I," he said.

"Have you been getting any flak about us?" I asked.

He laughed good-naturedly. He was not a petty accusatory man.

"Ahh. No, not really," he said with an intake of breath. "Only I have had to learn to eat an apple differently. The way you described it in your book was more than a tip-off. The right-wing faction thought they had me there, but they were too stupid to do anything with it."

"So you didn't really suffer slings and arrows as a result?"

"Ah. No, not really," he said, with a twinge of self-pity manufactured to stimulate guilt in me. I wanted to mention the two women I had heard he had affairs with after me, but I decided to employ class for a little

longer. We talked on about the world situation, about
Reagan. He said all the American President felt comfortable discussing was his tenure as SAG president and his
grade B movies. He talked of Margaret Thatcher's trip to
Moscow ("What a superb marching band they have
there"). He talked of welfare and its attendant problems.
All the while I could see the fire in his eyes through his
voice. I could feel myself attracted to the very same
qualities in him that had been impossible for me to resist
in the first place. Had I not progressed in my own
growth at all? On top of it all, I wanted to see him. But I
said nothing.

"How is your family?" I asked directly.

"Ah. They are doing well. Just as long-suffering as
ever. I would like to see you."

His rhythm was as unpredictable as always.

"Would you?" I asked redundantly.

"Yes, I would," he replied. "Would you?"

"Yes, I would," I replied.

"What are your hours?"

I slumped over on my bed.

"We start at six in the morning and go till eleven at
night sometimes."

"Well, perhaps we could have dinner," he said.

"And how would we arrange that without heralding
the third world war?"

He thought a moment.

"Let me call you later in the week."

"Okay, but I'm leaving on the weekend."

There was a pause.

"Where will you be going?"

"Sweden," I said. "Just like the book."

There was another pause.

"Yes," he said. "I remember very well. . . . Oh,
my . . ."

I melted again. He continued.

"Is Mr. Dance anything like me?"

I could feel my throat ache.

"No, Gerry. Nobody is like you—not even you."

He laughed again.

"Yes," he said. "I see you are still just as persevering."

"Yes," I answered. "I am."

"I will get back to you and we'll arrange something."

We hung up without arranging code names with each other. He was so accomplished with world issues, but with details that derail, he was hopeless.

Nevertheless, I slept that night.

I slept the night after that. Maybe Gerry had been the subconscious problem all along.

The shooting proceeded royally. I began to have fun. I even began to understand Bob Butler's directorial language. When Charles and I weren't sure which way the scene was going, Bob would say, "You're shopping. That's fair enough. I don't see the glitches."

When Charles asked a question, he'd say, "Go with your own tummy." Charles would straighten up, pat his stomach, and come to me for translation.

Once, during dialogue in a love scene, Bob said, "It sounds like it's in the cracks."

I checked the location of the microphone and there was no imminent danger.

Bob would say he was "well" and advise Charles to use "occasional inarticulate enthusiasm."

In between shots downtown, I shopped and reacquainted myself with King's Road. I saw old friends when I had the time and waited for Gerry to call. It occurred to me that even if he had, he wouldn't have used his real name. I felt hurled back in time, with the same clandestine problems we had had during our love affair.

Colin and I had dinner with John Cleese (of *Monty Python* and *Fawlty Towers*). He announced that he was totally opposed to sentimentality in films because it kept the public in the throes of believing that romanticism was reality. "Imagine," he said. "I'd love to do a love story about two people after they finally get together. The story is about who takes out the garbage." He went on to say that he cried when his cat died until he realized that he was being romantic about it. At that point he said, "I blocked the sentimentality and quit crying."

When was love romanticism and when was it love? Did you not grow until *after* you took out the garbage?

Saturday morning rolled around. Charles and I had just finished rehearsing some scenes for Sweden. He left my suite for an appointment. The hotel operator rang me.

"We have a Mister Vancouver on the telephone. Shall I put it through?"

Gerry and I had spent one of our beautiful stolen weeks in Vancouver.

"Of course," I said.

"Ah. There you are finally," he said.

"What do you mean, *finally*?"

"I've been calling you all week."

"But you didn't leave a message."

"Yes. That's right," he said. "Then I had the bright idea of Vancouver."

"Oh, Gerry," I said. "And I've been expecting you and missing you. Where are you now? You sound far away."

"I'm in the country. I have a private apartment of a friend. I wanted you to meet me here."

I was flabbergasted.

"How was I supposed to know?"

"Yes, well," he said, "that's been a bit of a problem. Well, can you come here?"

"Now?" I asked.

"Yes," he answered. "It's lovely out here. I could have my aide come and collect you."

"Gerry," I said, "I'm working. And we're leaving tomorrow for Stockholm. I can't."

"Yes," said Gerry. "I understand. I can be at my office in two hours. I'll send my car and aide to collect you. I have a budget meeting in the afternoon, but I long to see you."

Two hours later I was picked up by a young man, highly discreet, who spoke only of the weather and the news of the day. I eluded the press by exiting a little known side door. He dropped me off at Gerry's private office. Since it was Saturday, nobody much was around. I looked at his door. I had never been here before. This was the place where he had taken my phone calls and sat until early morning solitarily reflecting on our relationship. I walked up to the door. It was open. I walked in. Then I saw him. His magnetism charged the entire room and he smiled with such happiness that the London fog seemed to lift. I crossed the room toward him. We shook hands and then we embraced. He felt familiarly solid in my arms. We didn't hold each other long. We both needed to look at each other, register the facial expressions. Gerry held me out from him and then, while pleasurably perusing me, he circled me and talked.

"My goodness," he said. "You certainly have become successful over the past few years. You're looking wonderful."

I scrutinized every flicker, every movement he made as I turned and took him in. The tie was askew (it was a tie I remembered). The belt was dangling as usual, his socks crept down over his shoes, and as he gestured and laughed I felt transported back in time, the same old feelings I had had for him a few years ago sweeping over me again.

"Thanks, Gerry," I said. "You haven't changed much with the hard work. You seem so full of energy and enthusiasm."

He hung forward, his gaze falling on my lips. I

remembered it was this habit of his that had arrested me
so thoroughly the first night I met him. That and the
blazingly intelligent dancing eyes. I wanted to embrace
him again, but I held back. I looked around his private
office.

"So this is it, eh?" I asked. "This is where it's all
happened for you." Marvelous how banalities help us
over uneasy moments.

Gerry took a few grand sweeping steps in front of a
long bookshelf. He moved with graceful abandon, completely unaware of how he looked or what picture he was
presenting; not even a taste of self-consciousness was
evident, whereas I stood there wondering if my mascara
had flecked on my cheek and if my flat shoes looked all
right with the long skirt.

Gerry bent over one of the bookshelves.

"I have your letters secreted away in various books
here," he said. "I couldn't bear to part with them."

He reached for a book.

"No, Gerry." I stopped him. "That's okay. I don't
need to reread my letters. I'm having enough *déjà vu*
reenacting my relationship with you on film."

Gerry straightened up and smiled. He threw back
his shoulders and thrust his hands in his pockets. It was
decidedly a gesture of pride and self-congratulation. It
was then that I understood that the role he had played in
my life was pleasant and satisfying to him. And the role
he played in my book, and now on film, was a testament
to the timelessness of our relationship—books and films
being the sincerest form of flattery and recognition.

Double vision prevailed for me as I observed him. I
had adjusted to believing that Charles Dance was Gerry
for weeks now. I had made that quantum leap in my
imagination, putting the real Gerry somewhere out to
pasture. Now as I stood before him I began to wonder
who *I* was! Or put more precisely, what *reality* was. I was
living an experience that proved I could make reality

anything I wanted it to be. I thought of Akira Kurosawa's classic movie *Rashomon*. Reality was in the eye of the beholder. Definitive truth didn't exist. Truth was relative. If I needed an actor to be Gerry for three months so that I could emote sincerely, then I would do it. Gerry had only played a part in my life anyway. But what hit me with some impact now was that *I* had played a role in my own life, and was still doing it. I stood in front of Gerry fully aware of how I looked and what I was doing. I knew the emotional buttons to push in him and what would trigger a response. It was no different from the professional exercise of acting. And each of us did it every day, every moment of our lives, except probably when we were sleeping. Even then we were probably getting direction for the next day's scene from the greatest director of all: our higher selves.

Then, as I gazed at Gerry, listening to him reminisce about us, in a kind of fugue, I found myself wondering something really bizarre. If each of us creates our own reality, then perhaps each of us creates the characters who *people* our reality. In other words, perhaps Gerry was *my* creation, existing only in my dream. Perhaps he didn't exist for anyone else at all! It was a really weird feeling, a kind of shift to some other reality. Perhaps this room, these drapes on the window, these love letters of mine stuffed between the covers of political books, were only an aspect of my dream. Maybe Gerry was the stuff dreams are made of, like the movie we were making; a player in my play, and now someone else had stepped in to play him. Perhaps Gerry had, from the beginning, spoken lines only I had wanted to hear. Were pieces of my past, my present, and my future reflected in Gerry as he moved about the room being himself? Was he wondering if *I* was real? No. Not Gerry . . .

I came to with a jolt. We sat down next to each other on his couch. The sun had broken through the hazy clouds and dusty sunbeams slanted through the window across our laps.

"What did you think of *Out on a Limb,* Gerry?" I asked, trying to ground myself into an earth plane reality.

He turned and searched for words as he gazed out the window. "I couldn't read it all at once," he said haltingly. "I read bits and pieces before I went to sleep. Some of it is beyond my understanding." He paused a moment. "Do you still believe in those spiritual things— souls and everlasting energy and things like that?"

Now I was very matter-of-fact.

"Yes, Gerry, more than ever. I think the world is in the mess it's in because we are spiritually ignorant."

Gerry shrugged defensively.

"But," he said, "these are religious wars which are causing the mess."

"I know," I replied. "That's the point. Religion doesn't necessarily have anything to do with spirituality. Each religion thinks it has a hot line to God. When the truth might well be that we are *all* attached to God. We are all part of God."

Gerry sighed.

"I don't believe in God. I believe in my work."

His words smacked the air. Charles Dance had just rehearsed those same lines with me that morning.

Gerry went on. "I don't believe spiritual ignorance is the problem in the world, even with all the religious wars."

"What is the problem then?" I asked.

Gerry straightened up.

"Nuclear proliferation," he said. "We're going to blow ourselves up if we don't stop."

I looked out the window. Birds shook themselves in the sunlight on a nearby branch. I heard a child laughing on the street below.

"Well," I said, "I don't think we are going to do that and I think the more afraid of it we are, the more we contribute to the energy of its possibility. So it won't be part of *my* reality."

Gerry looked pleadingly into my face. It was a moment of moving confusion on his part—he who was always so sure of the rightness of what he believed. He genuinely wanted to understand the outrageousness, to him, of what I was saying. Charles Dance was playing the part the same way. Charles himself was more open-minded about metaphysical truth, but still there was a legitimate confusion about the unknown that he had not dared to contemplate. The actor and the understudy were well cast in the New Age illusion of my play. I sat there wondering how I was playing myself. More importantly, why had I chosen to go back over this reality I created for myself?

Gerry and I talked about the world, Gorbachev and Reagan, Mrs. Thatcher, *Terms of Endearment,* and life itself. It was all happening again—the same interplay, same attractive chemistry, same intelligent sensuality. But he had a budget meeting and I had a rehearsal.

We stood facing each other. I finally decided to question the future.

"What would you do if you gave up politics?" I asked.

His eyes glided over every inch of my face. I could feel him want to include me in that future.

"Oh, I don't know," he said discreetly. "There will be something wonderful for me to do. I love the world and the people in it."

We stood, delicately facing each other down.

"May I have your new phone numbers?" he asked shyly.

"They're not new," I replied. "*That* hasn't changed either."

He understood. Quickly he wrote out his new numbers and handed them to me. I folded the paper and put it in my pocket. The action was identical to that of our first meeting. The feelings were, too.

"Remember me when you're in Sweden," he said unnecessarily.

"That'll be my job, Gerry," I answered. "Somewhere under every inch of that silent snow I'll feel you."

"Yes," he said. "I remember."

We parted and I knew we were still—and always—a part of each other's lives. I had no idea then how strange an impact our interweaving would have on me later.

I was late for the afternoon rehearsal with Charles Dance.

"Where were you?" he asked, enacting Gerry's tendencies to a T.

"Oh," I said, "I had a meeting with someone who reminded me that all of life is a movie and our progress is measured by how we play our parts."

Charles looked at me quizzically. Then he picked up his script to fulfill my illusion of *his* Gerry.

Our company invaded Stockholm, Sweden, the next day. We had wanted snow, but our schedule had us arriving a little early in November for such cold.

The English camera crew would now work side by side with Swedish grips and lighting technicians. Swedish actors would play the parts of the Swedes who first introduced me to trance channeling in my book. And we would actually film a trance channeling session in Swedish with the trance medium playing himself, and Ambres, the spiritual entity and teacher, playing himself. It would be the same process as with Kevin Ryerson and his entities, except it would be in Swedish.

I was deposited at the Sheraton-Stockholm Hotel, which I noticed was adjacent to a railway station. I wondered if our company manager had changed the current on my sound machine. I decided to trust that he had, even though I remembered that Sweden matched no other current or amps in the world.

After rehearsing well into the night with our Swedish actors, I retired to bed knowing I had to get up at 6:00 A.M. I closed the windows to my room as I heard a train streak by. I hated to close windows because I love fresh air. I got under the covers and turned on my sound machine. It obscured the train sounds very well.

But it wasn't long before I smelled smoke curling from my bedside table. I looked over at it. The sound machine was on fire, silently smoldering from within. And it was the only one we had. I could see the handwriting on the wall. This movie shoot was going to be about reliving illusion and the reality of a sound machine that never worked.

I sat bolt upright in bed, fully aware that I was about to make a scene. It was 2:00 A.M. I got up, put on my robe, and marched down to Stan's room and then to the room of the company manager. I woke them up and proceeded to read the riot act to them about the entire success of our film depending on the technological perfection of my sound machine. I told them that if I couldn't sleep I was a terror and I wanted them to see the first act of my terrorism. It was effective. They were properly *terror*-struck. The machine was fixed in due time.

As I lay in bed listening to the sound of Fast Surf Number II over the railway station below, I wondered in all seriousness why I had created the reality of that machine's burning up. Clearly it had something to do with testing my sensitivity to terrorizing others. I had not passed the test very well.

The word was out the next day regarding my sound machine. Several members of the crew inquired curiously about why it was so essential to me. I tried to explain "motivational suggestion," and much to my surprise, not only were they interested in how that worked but they also expressed private interest in what I had written

about. More than a few of them had had a grandmother
or relative who professed to have been into the spiritual
stuff for decades. Each crew member was interested in a
different aspect of it. Some were intrigued with the reincarnation aspect, some with the eternal energy (the more
technologically advanced related to this), some with the
philosophy of "knowing we are all connected to the
God-force," some with the laws of cause and effect. I
would have expected a California-based crew to resonate
to the material in the script, but when I heard the
English and Swedish crew members profess the same
personal interest, I was once again reminded of how
universal our individual searching was. Who are we?
Why are we here? Where did we come from? Where do
we go when we die?

As the television shooting hours unfolded I realized
that making a miniseries was a way of life, not a project.
There was time for nothing else, particularly when shooting on location. We quickly became a family attempting
to survive the tick of the clock together. Sometimes we
shot so long into the night that there was no food. I took
to stuffing my tote bag with fruit and cheese and Danish,
which the Swedes provided as a businessman's breakfast
adjacent to the morning elevator in the hotel. During the
days there were jokes about "bagging" the pigeons instead of feeding them, or at least to save bits of bird
bread for the crew. A kind of long-suffering gaiety actually developed out of the extended working hours and
the universal difficulty of obtaining edible nourishment.

The English production manager, an affable gentleman named Alex de Grunwald, whom I had worked
with before, was lovingly dubbed the new president of
Weight Watchers. They joked that he carried five weeks'
worth of food for the crew in his briefcase. Alex went to
the crew and said Bob Geldof was on the phone wanting
the crew to donate their leftover food to Ethiopia. He
told them that two "sparks" (lighting technicians) were

taken to the hospital suffering from cuts and abrasions while fighting over a peanut. He added that if Jesus appeared and offered to turn stones into loaves and fishes, he would personally put a stop to it. No one was to preempt his function. . . .

Alex came to us one night to plead with us to work another few hours with the promise of soup as a reward. He then produced spoons with holes in them. His time clock had tape plastered over the face of it. Many times he came to me to forgo my twelve-hour turnaround. (The Screen Actors Guild mandates twelve hours' rest between working hours for its members.) A crew member yelled that he could offer me another picture after this with four weeks in Moscow, five weeks in Finland—no catering. I remember that Alex had been the production manager on *Gandhi.* I asked him if he wanted us all to look like that.

Show business stories kept us going into the night as cold pizza and warm beer were scavenged from a local restaurant owned by an Italian-German couple. There were war stories about Bob Mitchum, Richard Burton, and even myself. Some of the crew remembered stories about me that I had forgotten long ago. They also remembered stories that never happened. I enjoyed them all—and had a few to tell myself. All in all, we were an excellent working group.

We were supposed to see our English location dailies the first week in Sweden, but they didn't get there until we were nearly finished. They were put on a plane bound for Tunisia. Instead, we got some interesting dailies called "Wet in Tunisia" while a bunch of Arabs were looking at my spiritual search.

So we were literally shooting in the dark, as the saying goes, not knowing what the footage, makeup, hair, wardrobe, or acting looked like, which led our cameraman, Brad May, to hold up a white Styrofoam coffee cup for a light-meter reading in front of my face.

"I may have to ask you to play your part as a coffee addict," he said, "just to make sure there's enough light on the subject."

The final shooting days in Sweden involved the scene with our Swedish trance medium. Most of the crew was looking forward to it. Others were uneasy. All knew they had a professional job to do regardless of their personal beliefs.

Sturé Johansson, the trance medium, had been my first introduction to spiritual channeling years before, when I had come to Sweden to rendezvous with Gerry. Sturé channeled an ancient spiritual master called Ambres.

The scene was set. The actors were rehearsed, the extras were present as the lights dimmed, and we all prepared for Ambres to come through, using the body of Johansson as an instrument. Three cameras were prepared to shoot simultaneously, and we had a well-stocked tape system for sound recording. Sturé said that Ambres knew his lines and the subjects he should address himself to. The hired actors would ask the rehearsed questions of Ambres and he would answer them as he had answered them ten years previously.

Butler called for quiet and then yelled, "Roll 'em." All the cameras turned over as Sturé began to go into trance. He seemed oblivious to the fact that he was being recorded visually and with audio.

We all sat mesmerized as we waited. Suddenly Sturé's right hand began to vibrate. It was Ambres' energy about to make its entrance. I looked over at the sound engineer. He was staring at the dials on his machine in front of him. He turned them in a frenzy. Then he switched on to another auxiliary machine. His hand flew to his earphones as though he was hearing more than what was happening on the set. I looked around at each camera. The operators gave me the high sign. So far so good.

Then Ambres was in. He stood up with a hunched-over posture and immediately pronounced a benediction on everyone in the room, including the crew. Sturé's right hand ceased vibrating.

The first actor asked a rehearsed question, which was about the nature of creativity in regard to creation itself. Ambres explained that we each create our world with every moment that we live. He said creation is a natural expression, that to be alive is to be creative. He expostulated on that subject for a while, sticking to the script remarkably well, until someone asked about the meaning of the Great Pyramid at Gizeh. Here he diverged from the script somewhat, explaining that the Pyramid is a Bible in stone, that it stands at the epicenter of the earth's land mass, and that we will learn to read its true message before this century is gone.

As he was explaining the Pyramid, as though on cue, every church bell in the surrounding area began to chime. The church bells continued until he was through with the subject. I could see the sound engineer was still disturbed by what he was hearing through his earphones.

The questions continued, scripted according to our first session together. Ambres was acting the part of himself, just as I was. He was precise, economical, profound, and clear.

The cameras, almost simultaneously, ran out of film. The sound man needed to reload too. Butler yelled "Cut" and then turned to me to ask Ambres to "hold his thoughts" while we prepared for more filming. Ambres had other ideas on his mind. He came straight toward me and began to speak—in Swedish, of course, which was immediately translated by an assistant of Sturé's. I wondered what his urgency was all about. The translation went something like this:

"You have greatly expanded your knowledge," said Ambres. "But now your inner wisdom must come into balance with it. You must be doubly careful now because you have seen so much of the hologram of life so quickly."

"What do you mean 'so quickly,' Ambres? And why are you concerned?"

He paused to rejuvenate the energy around Sturé's body.

"In the ancient esoteric schools we used to use the needles, too, when the student desired to see the past and future more quickly. But the swiftness exacts its price."

"The needles?" I asked.

Ambres nodded.

"Yes, the needles," he said. "You have written of the needles in your new book in English."

Then it hit me. He was referring to *Dancing in the Light,* which had just been published in America. I had not mentioned it in Sweden because it hadn't been translated into Swedish yet. The final chapters of that book dealt with a marathon ten-day psychic acupuncture experience I had undergone in Galisteo, New Mexico, with a superb spiritual acupuncturist named Chris Griscom. Acupuncture can be used to open certain channels that assist in past-life recall. With the acupuncture needles placed in strategic positions, I had "seen" many past lives of mine in conjunction with other people—which helped to clarify some of the conflicts we were experiencing today in this present lifetime. Ambres was referring to the effects of the acupuncture needles.

"The world is a schoolroom," Ambres continued. "Life is to learn. It is a teacher. But teaching is important to proceed at a balanced pace."

"Yes," I said. "I understand."

"Ah, my child." He stopped me. "But you have been plagued with sleeping problems, isn't that true?"

I was surprised that he knew that.

"Yes," I answered, "I have."

"Well, my child. You have experienced so much so soon. You see, when you proceed with such haste you alter the energy flow in your system drastically. The energy required for 'seeing' the past and the future, unless integrated steadily into the consciousness, can cause disturbance, manifesting in the inability to fall off to sleep."

"Really?" I asked. The whole crew was now attempting to understand what was going on.

"Yes," he continued. "You see, the mind is never asleep. Only the body requires rest. But the body frequency for learning during nighttime hours is quite different from daytime, because it involves the superconscious psychic powers. If those powers are overstimulated, an even frequency for the sleep state is not possible."

"Well," I asked, "how does this relate to what I did with the needles?"

"Your desire to feel cosmic union is extremely intense. You proceeded in your intensity at a rapid pace in searching out the past-life relationships with your parents, particularly the mother figure. What you did is not dangerous, but it has been disturbing for you, resulting in an upset of the sleep pattern. Do you understand?"

The past-life conflicts with my parents flashed in front of my mind just as they had done under the influence of the needles. Yes, I could see what Ambres was talking about. There had been violence involved. Violence that was difficult for me to admit had been perpetrated by my mother, who had not been my mother in that lifetime.

"You must resolve the reactions to what you saw," said Ambres, "with your feelings today. In that resolution the even-frequency sleep state will return. Whenever one rushes, one pays a price. Be careful. You have much inner wisdom to develop now in order to balance your knowledge. Wisdom and knowledge are two separate understandings."

I could feel the crew behind me prepared to film again.

"Thank you, Ambres," I said. "I will think about

what you've said. It's good to speak with you again. I've missed you. You were my first teacher."

Ambres smiled.

"*You* were your first teacher," he reminded me.

He walked back to his position in front of the roomful of extras. Now everyone knew of my sleep problems and a past-life conflict with my parents. But, as I had learned years ago, in spiritual circles hardly anyone ever abuses the privilege of knowing more about another individual than even they themselves know.

The room quieted down again. Butler yelled, "Roll 'em," and Ambres continued his spiritual teaching according to script until the scene ended. Sturé took a seat in his chair and Ambres blessed the group and left the body of Sturé. Sturé's right arm began vibrating again, signaling Ambres' exit. Sturé returned to consciousness and walked over to me and said his scripted line.

"I hope you learned something tonight," he said. "I must rest now. There is another group coming later."

I thanked him, delivered my final line of astonishment, and Butler yelled, "Cut."

Everyone began milling about. I went over to David, the soundman.

"What was going on with your instruments during the session?" I asked.

David looked shocked.

"Well, I don't understand it," he began. "All my wavelength frequencies fluctuated. And my batteries went dead in half the time. Then I couldn't believe it, but I picked up Radio Moscow in my earphones! This was weird."

I shrugged. I remembered that McPherson had predicted there would be unusual activity when we shot the scene with Ambres.

"I don't know, David," I said. "I'm just learning about the effect on electromagnetic frequencies myself. I never have been very good with technological phenomena."

David motioned to me to lean down.

"You know," he said, "I know you're going to pick up your American crew for the rest of the shoot, but I want you to know that more than anything I would like to be going on to Peru with you. I feel there is so much I have to learn from this material, but maybe I should be generous and wish the man who's taking my place a good learning experience too. There's room for all of us, isn't there?"

"Thanks, David," I said. "I'll let you know how it all goes. I think it's going to be a lesson for each of us according to what we need to learn."

The channeling session over, we gathered up our props and belongings. The crew began to break down the set. We were tired and very hungry. I stood for a moment surveying the room for one last time. I heard a banging-clanking noise outside.

"What's that?" I asked a crew member.

"It's Alex de Grunwald," he answered. "He's groveling in the garbage cans for lunch for the crew tomorrow, except that we're going to be shooting with a *skeleton* crew."

Everybody laughed. Alex appeared smiling and mischievous in the doorway.

"Thank you, everybody," he said, and then he announced, "I'm writing a new book called *How to Work on No Food, or Sweden on One Cent a Day.* I'd be happy to personally autograph it for whoever would like a memento of our time together."

The crew threw their hats at him.

That was the thing about the English. They were able to create humor out of just about anything, particularly after having been visited by an entity from another world.

Later on that night we were told that at the exact time we were shooting, the regular programming for all the radios in Northern Sweden, in homes and in cars, had been interrupted by the presentation of a strange spiritual sort of teaching session delivered by someone who was referred to as "Ambres." No one knew who or what it was exactly.

Chapter 10

*T*he last night in Sweden I walked in the newly falling snow, thinking about the drama and theatricality of life. I walked in the park where Gerry and I had fed the animals. I stood under the tree where Gerry had cried that he couldn't reconcile me with the rest of his life—while his wife waited in a hotel room. The snow fell as a silent testament to the timelessness of the human drama. We were playing our roles as though our lives depended on the performance. And indeed it was true.

I thought of my mother and father. They had had eighty-two years apiece of their drama, fifty-five of them together. On reflection that seemed overdone and outrageous to me. How could any two people stay together, inseparably, for fifty-five years? What kind of promise to oneself did that take? It had been a polarity dance of refined and colorful extremes, the likes of which I could not imagine for myself. They were hopelessly and profoundly committed to the dramatic comedy of playing opposite each other. Everyone else in their lives was simply a character on their stage.

And now it was nearing Thanksgiving. My mother

had called to tell me that Dad was ill and failing fast. She hadn't wanted to disturb my work, but her voice cracked and she wept as she suggested perhaps I should see him soon. She wanted my daughter Sachi to be there too.

Of course we would go. We finished shooting in Stockholm just before Thanksgiving. I was free until the Hawaii location the following week. It was as though the timing was guided and the impending "reality" of old age was becoming more and more interlaced in my life. It was a constant now, imposing itself with every late-night phone call.

I called Sachi. She had her own drama going. She was stunned and heartbroken over the death of her acting teacher. The teacher had apparently fallen asleep at the wheel of her car, veered into oncoming traffic, and had a head-on collision that exploded the car. She was burned beyond recognition. It was so violent an end, so abrupt, and yet, as with all events in life, so self-motivated.

Sachi and I had a long talk relating to why anyone would choose a death like that. No one else was killed— only slightly injured. We speculated on what karmic relationship she could have had with the driver of the oncoming car. Both of us believed there was no such thing as "accident," but a heartbreaking personal loss like this called for serious questioning, in order, perhaps, to help bear the burden. We talked of so many seemingly dramatic deaths occurring during these times. Was it our imagination? No, not really, and we could sense that many people we knew might elect to check out in the next few years. Almost as though, with the onslaught of New Age energy and the enormous pressures the modern world exerted, they would not be able to participate in the acceleration fast enough to be a part of the transition and would use karmic workouts to leave the body.

"Is the world going insane, Mom?" she asked, as she elaborated on the violence in the news.

We talked on for what became several hours, agreeing that something big was occurring in the world, something different from before, when international world wars, plagues, famines had hit us. It felt almost as though a giant *cleanup,* a cleansing, was in process on the planet. As though the energy of old karmic patterns was being cleared. The acceleration was on, and each event had a reason for being. It was all a learning process, too, perhaps to help our limited thinking to expand, our perceptions of ourselves to be more generous, and the conception of our future to become a certainty of peace.

Those who insisted on remaining stuck in the old ideas of judgment, blame, fear, rancor, rage, and revenge were operating not only with a limited perspective of themselves and others, but with the prospect that they would be caught in an amplification of that destructive energy that would manifest *their* negative reality to be exactly as they feared it would be.

So those who cynically assessed spiritual viewpoints as being "wishful thinking" and "desired projecting" were absolutely right. We'd all get what we believed we would. What we expected would come to pass. And with the acceleration of New Age energy, projections of *negativity* would occur and manifest faster than ever before, just as projection of positivity would.

I arrived home to see my mom and dad the day before Thanksgiving.

Dad was drawn and white as he lay fully dressed on top of his bed. I walked into his room and watched him sleep. I bent over and kissed him. He woke up, startled. Then he smiled. He hadn't known I was coming.

"Oh, Monkey," he said, barely able to speak above a whisper. "When they took me to the hospital with the drop in my blood count I shut my eyes for a minute and this tremendous sense of peace came over me like a big umbrella."

I couldn't trust myself to speak.

"Yep," he went on slowly. "I knew everything would be all right. I said to myself: 'There are some of Shirley's people taking care of me up there so I know I'll be fine.' Then I let these damn doctors make all those holes in my arms and take these stupid pictures of my insides."

I sat down beside him and lifted his white withered arm. It was hard for him to breathe. He pushed one of his hands into his chest. I looked at the long fingers and remembered how he had delicately fingered his violin strings when he was a younger man, teaching me what made the notes change and the music play.

"Remember that fluffy strapless dress you bought for the prom or the beauty show or something?" he asked.

I nodded and quietly sniffed back tears.

I remembered very well. It was a yellow organza with a white strapless ruffle around the bust.

"I was so proud of you I was about to bust when I saw you in that dress, and your mother didn't even think I'd let you have it."

As I watched and listened to him I understood that the reversal process was happening. He was becoming my child now, dependent, helpless, and longing for care and love. He had protected and provided for me when I was dependent and helpless and now the roles were reversed.

Sachi had told me of her last visit with him. He had told her that one day *I* would be dependent on her. That this was the course and cycle of life. It afforded each member of the family the experience of caring and being cared for.

"So many parents have children who don't bother with them anymore," he said to me. "But I'm the richest father in the world to have children like you who care so much."

He drifted back to sleep. I sat there and watched him breathe. How would I know if he decided to leave?

Was there a telltale sign? Was there any way to prepare? Would he choose a moment that was right for him, just as he must have chosen his moment of birth for the same reason? And more important than anything, was what I called *death* actually viewed from the other side as birth? Was the experience of living within the human body considered an entrapment of the soul, whose natural habitat was the spiritual dimension?

I watched Dad for a long time. Sachi had already seen him and was in the living room with Mother—continuity in motion.

Then Dad opened his eyes again.

"I told Sachi," he said, "not to be a sucker about men, like you were. Not to let men praise her and turn her head. We had a nice talk. Your mother says Sachi only has two things to worry about."

"What are they, Daddy?" I asked.

"Walking like a Japanese and letting her hips get too big."

I laughed out loud. Whatever the extremity, my father's sense of humor would never desert him.

"But," he continued, "I say she has to worry about men. They will con her because she's a cute little thing and she'll feel sorry for them just like you did. For God's sake tell her not to run an open charity for people the way you do."

I was holding his thin hand between mine. I patted it gently.

"Yes, Daddy, I'll tell her that. Why don't you get some rest now."

He took out his hearing aids from his ears.

"These damn things are one thousand dollars apiece or some damned thing. The price of hearing nonsense is high. But that's the most terrible part of getting old, you know."

"What is, Daddy?" I asked.

"Being a nuisance to people."

He looked at me for a long wistful time.

"Can I ask you a question?" I said finally.

"Yes," he answered.

"Have you decided to go before Mother?"

He continued to look at me intently without blinking.

"No," he said. "I haven't made my decision yet. But I can see your mother is getting stronger and I'm getting weaker. She has so much she wants to do."

"Is there more you want to do, Daddy?"

He looked around the room as though searching for an image of something.

"Well," he said finally, "I'd like to live to see your book show on the TV and to see Warren's new picture. So I might stay alive till then."

He took a deep breath.

"I remember," he continued, "I could never stand to look at the sight of blood, and now with all my transfusions I realize it's everything. I'm going to try and get stronger. But I saw you and Sachi and I'm sure I'll see Warren at Christmastime when he's back from his location."

"So," I said, "we have an agreement that you'll stick around until next spring at least?"

"Yes," he said. "I can promise you that."

"I love you, Daddy," I said.

"I love you too, darlin'," he replied. "More than I can ever tell you."

He reached up for me. I hugged him without squeezing too hard. Then he leaned back again.

"Well, I have to close my eyes now," he said. "Thank you for listening to me talk. Thank you for talking to me. Now go tell the boss I'm on top of the bed still dressed, so she'll come in and kiss me goodnight."

I nodded, kissed his forehead, and left the room.

Sachi and Mother were in animated conversation when I walked in. They had both been through their own private reflections on his condition, and life was going on.

"Mom?" said Sachi with that question mark in her voice. "Do you know what Granddaddy told me before you came?"

I sat down to a cup of tea.

"No, sweetheart. What?"

"Well, you know that old-maid woman named Helen who was by here last year?"

"Yes."

"Granddaddy says she is suffering from some terrible old-maid's Hawaiian disease."

"Oh, really? What?"

"Something called lackanookie," she said perfectly straight and with no recognizable humor.

"Isn't your father terrible?" said Mother. "How can I explain that to Sachi?"

"You don't," I said. "You don't have to."

Sachi punched Mother's knee.

"I sort of knew what he meant, Grandmother. How can he be so funny when he's feeling so bad?"

"He's never feeling too bad for that kind of 'bawdry' humor," said Mother in mock disgust. Suddenly she got up and went to her old highboy desk.

"Look, Shirl," she said in girlish delight. "This might be a good thing—I don't know." She handed me a contract coupon from Reader's Digest. "I've been paying into this thing, so much a month for years so I could get the giant payoff—look how much."

I looked. It was for $5,100,000.

"Yeah. Your father thinks I'm crazy, and I haven't told anyone else, *but I could win it, you know.*"

I looked at Sachi. She looked at Mother.

"Yes, Grandmother," she said, all full of wonder. "You could win it, especially if you believe you can."

"Then," said Mother, "I'd give half of it to you and Sachi in case you have financial troubles. Then I'd march right down to the girls at the bank, and tell them to save it for me until I got old."

I felt my eyes pop. I couldn't resist saying, "And when do you think that will be?"

Mother laughed loudly.

"Me?" she giggled. "I'm going to live to be ninety-two. I've already decided. Life is so funny, isn't it? That I'd win this money after all these years. I've enjoyed reading those little Reader's Digest books because I don't want to read a whole book. So I've gotten a whole lot of enjoyment out of the money I've been paying in."

Sachi got up to get some more tea. There were aspects to positive thinking that even we hadn't thought about.

Mother looked over at me lovingly.

"Daddy says he's still on top of the bed dressed, so I'll come in and kiss him goodnight, right?" she asked.

"Right."

She shrugged and pushed a strand of hair out of her eyes.

"How would you feel," I said, "if he went first?"

She folded her arms.

"Oh, I don't know," she said. "I don't like to think about how I'd feel." Her eyes filled with pain for a moment and then as though she could orchestrate her emotions she said, "I know one thing, though. I'd be left with trying to figure out how to work all the machines in this house, because your father never taught me a thing. He wanted to be the big shot, so he never showed me how to work anything, Shirl."

I always marveled at her disciplined practicality. Then she thought a moment.

"Evie says that when Glenn died, knowing she was in a silent house was the hardest part. But I'd miss talking about what we saw on television or what we were eating for dinner." She faltered a moment. Then she continued: "I'll miss that wonderful mind the most. That mind of his that never stops questioning and putting together connections. That brilliant, brilliant mind." Her voice trailed off.

I kept very quiet.

Then she started up again, her tone vigorous. "But I'd come to see you kids more often." She looked at me shyly. "That is, if you'd want a crotchety old woman around."

Sachi walked in from the kitchen. "Listen, Grandmother," she said. "You *have* to come and see me. I want to move away from Mother"—she gestured toward me—"so I can become more independent. So you come and we'll have a good time on our own."

Mother winked at me. She got up, gave Sachi a tweak on the cheek, and went in to say goodnight to the man she had loved and lived with for fifty-five years.

I knew both of them would be around for a while longer anyway.

During the next few days with Mom and Dad, I thought a lot about what Ambres had said regarding the trauma of my past lives with them. In a more total way I began to accept the reality that my parents—and my daughter, for that matter—were beings of extensive life experiences, just as I was.

As I sat talking with them, joking and sharing, I allowed the images of those past-life experiences to flow through my emotions while attempting to integrate my feelings for them today. Each of us had been abused by power and were abusers of power ourselves. Ambres was right. I had "seen" Mom and Dad in ways and days from the past. We had not always been parents and child. We had been involved in events that had been more than upsetting on the acupuncture table.

Now as I watched them closely over breakfast, two loving, spritely, compassionate human beings grappling with the ravages and inevitabilities of time, I was seeing them through ancient eyes in a long-forgotten time they could only barely acknowledge sharing. I was reminded once again that I had chosen these two as parental figures this time around *because* they always moved me so deeply, *because* they were the source of much of my learning and knowing of myself.

I had not only chosen them for myself *now* but in ancient times as well, and in many roles. Perhaps, indeed, I had chosen my own history. Perhaps what Ambres had really meant regarding "seeing" too soon had more to do with understanding the most profound of *all* truth: that I had been responsible for choosing to see everything I had seen, doing everything I had done. I had drawn to myself the people and events of all my lives in the long, slow, ongoing process of bringing myself, "somewhen," to a completion.

As the emotional and spiritual pieces dovetailed into place, making the tangled web of our intertwined identities and purposes more clear, I felt myself relax. An easy calm began to flow through me. My appreciation for my mother and father became so tender, so affectionate, so much more understanding, and ultimately so self-reflective. *They* were *me*. And I was them, not in a familial way dictated by genealogy, but in a philosophic and spiritually true way, orchestrated by my own desire to know more about myself.

I fell asleep on the last night of my visit and slept for eleven hours. I was finally integrating the scenes from the past with the scenes of the present. As Lazaris had said, we create the present from the future against the backdrop of the past.

Chapter 11

*A*fter the Thanksgiving holiday, our film company assembled for our next location shoot in Hawaii. That ten-year-old love affair between Gerry and Shirley had clandestinely spanned the globe.

Now, we moved as a well-trained theatrical army from the clogged streets of London to the silent snows of Sweden, from the silent snows of Sweden to the lush, swaying, balmy paradise of the northern side of Oahu. I had a hotel room overlooking a turquoise sea, with waves crashing below that put my sound machine to shame.

In Hawaii it is always easy for me to relax into a soft rhythm with the whole ambiance of the islands. I feel perfectly at peace there. The islands speak to me of a balanced texture of life which existed long ago and could again if we ceased to commercialize it.

I met the American crew at a luau that the company gave when we arrived. There were Hawaiian flowered shirts, grass skirts, ukuleles, and undulating hips.

Brad had brought his girlfriend on location and Charles Dance was accompanied by his wife, JoAnna, and their children. Stan had his wife, Lillian, and I had

Harold to hang out with (he had just bought a house on
Oahu). When locations are pleasant, families and friends
and lovers show up because there is something to do
during the actors' working hours.

Brad now had his American crew to work with. He
felt more efficient and comfortable. They had read the
script, of course, and more than a few of them were
interested in metaphysics.

Most of them were fascinated by the concept of
unseen energy. Theirs was basically a technological curiosity, but they quickly realized that when their questions
were pursued and extended, they soon touched the issue
of the Source. From what did all energy flow? And was
this Source what was known as God? The crew members
weren't religious, necessarily. That had nothing to do
with anything. They were simply aware that an intelligent
and harmonious unseen energy seemed to be governing
all activity in life whether they could identify it or not.
And as we began to shoot we exchanged books and ideas
in between setups.

Each person had a different reason for being interested. What began as small exchanges blossomed into
full-blown discussions over lunch, mainly because each
of us saw the similarity of cause and effect in technological energy to cause and effect in relationships in our own
personal lives. The way the energy worked was analogous. In sharing our experiences, we saw more clearly
that all of life, technological or emotional, was a question
of working with positive and negative energies and that
negative didn't mean wrong. It simply meant the opposite polarity—the other end of the balance—of *positive*.
Negative energy was as necessary as positive. It was the
interacted combustion that produced and created life.
The male energy (yang) was positive; the female energy
(yin) negative. Science—and life—told us that. Life could
not exist without both. Understanding the basic tenets of
that principle was helpful then in extending our under-

standing that "evil" exists only in relation to the point of view: If a child steals to live, if a man kills to protect his family, if a woman aborts a fetus rather than give birth to an unwanted child, if a terrorist murders because he has been raised all his life to believe that killing is his right and proper duty—*who* is evil? And if a person kills "simply" out of hatred or greed, *he* perceives his motives as *his need*—others make the judgment that his act is "evil."

Now this is not the kind of concept one can easily assimilate, or even accept, so our discussions were deep and colorful. At times one person would erupt with blockages and rage. Another would help him clear it out. At other times someone would have such a clear and corrective revelation that the rest of us would float on it for the balance of the day.

The shooting of the film itself became a physical manifestation of what we were learning and personally going through. The sun and sand and breeze were glorious. The hours were unrelenting. We often worked from 6:30 in the morning (to get the sunlight) to well past midnight. On one occasion Charles and I shot our love scene at 4:30 A.M. We both had to break down and cry for the scene. It wasn't difficult.

I got stung by a Portuguese man-of-war while rolling around in the surf for a scene. There was much speculation as to my past-life relationship with that creature.

Finally the "dailies" began to come in. We liked what we saw. They seemed personal, real, and well lit. The level of playing was documentarylike and whenever I heard someone refer to my character as "Shirley" I winced. It was so shockingly personal. It hit me in waves that I was actually playing myself.

Early on in preproduction we had all agreed that the color scheme of the production would remain muted; beiges, creams, earth tones, and nature colors would be our basics, and color would be used as accent. We were thinking ahead to the locations in Peru. To play down color before we got there would be good contrast. We changed our minds when we saw the dailies. I was garbed in beiges and creams. My red hair and lipstick were the only colors in the scenes. Frankly, it was boring. The burden on me as an actress was disproportionate without my even realizing it. At times like this I realized what an important part costume and production and scenic designers play in the conceptualization of screen art.

Here we were in colorful Hawaii. And I was clothed and running around in vanilla-flavored muumuus. It didn't work. It made me look lackluster and lifeless. I was supposed to be in the throes of an exciting love affair. And I was dressing like mood music in an elevator. I switched to a pink muumuu with a colorful hat. It even picked up the playing of the scenes, to say nothing of my spirits (no pun intended).

For an actress, knowing there is a bathing suit scene coming up can become an event of such anticipation that it lives with you every waking moment, particularly when the dinners at the meal break are sumptuous buffets and the piña coladas are the best in the world. There was also something about being back again on American territory that compelled me to have two eggs over easy, a rasher of crisp bacon, and lots of toast and jam for breakfast every morning. I had been so satiated with English oatmeal and Swedish herring that to be in an American hotel compelled me to eat food I never would eat had I not been away.

So, taking all my indulgences into consideration, it meant that between setups I would need to do my yoga, several hundred sit-ups, and running in place if possible. That's not fun when your makeup runs with perspiration and the clothes need to be protected. On top of that, the boredom of between-scenes leaves you with one impelling thought: *food*. Movie sets are famous for cookies, doughnuts, cakes, and muffins because they are a cheap way to feed the crew fast *and* you have the illusion you are extracting energy from the sugar. Nothing could be further from the truth. Though to turn down a coconut doughnut or a blueberry muffin in lieu of a mango is not easy. Besides, the mango could only be sensibly eaten in the shower anyway, which would jeopardize the makeup and hair. So you opt for the doughnut and coffee, cursing your hips and waistline for the rest of the day for betraying your lack of discipline. Then at dinner you feel it's legitimate to *need* to eat. So you have a piña colada, swearing that the compromise will be no dessert. And so it goes. Until the bathing suit scene comes and you may or may not hear whistles from the crew. Either way you always knew the decision about weight should have been made months before principal photography began. Yet the illusion never really dissipates that you can lose twenty pounds in one night by cutting out dinner.

Then there are all sorts of well-schooled, hard-won professional tricks an actress can employ knowing full well where her grossest physical problems are. Mine is my stomach. I can be thin, eat an olive, and look like I'm ready for the maternity ward. It's really quite incredible to me. I've tried to figure it out in therapy, past-life and otherwise, but I haven't been able to trace why I do such a thing to my body. Because of this phenomenon I cannot eat before a scene that requires a full-figure silhouette. And of course I cannot eat before I dance, all of which sometimes presents complicated logistical problems where nourishment is concerned. I carefully calculate what I put in my stomach in relation to the time I have to digest and eliminate. If my calculations go according to plan, there is usually no problem. If there is a shift in schedule, I go to plan B, which usually involves wearing a prop such as a scarf or a shoulder bag or purse of some kind in a scene. I work with the prop in front of my stomach. If I need two hands for the scene, I'm in trouble, but usually I can conceal whatever I ate with a book I pick up, or an armful of flowers, or a sweater I drape over my arm. But there are times when what I'm doing looks exactly like what it is—a cover-up. It is then that I wish I could learn some kind of meditative technique which would enable me to go straight through the working day without food or sustenance. Maybe I never fully understood the role of Alex de Grunwald's foodless days until now!

The fascination with crying scenes has always been a favorite of people who question me about acting. It is just as fascinating to me. I look at the breakdown of the scene: how many cuts there will be, how long it runs in a master shot, and of course the emotional intent and meaning of the scene itself. Since I am not an actress who either can or desires to cry in every cut, I have to make my decision when to really cry and when to break out the "Oscar bottle" (glycerine). I feel there's no point in putting myself through the associative sorrow necessary to bring on real tears in a long shot when the audience won't be able to see them anyway. So I usually play the scene out once (crying fully) so I'll know where it's going emotionally. Then, as the day and scene breakdowns occur, I make the choice. I've learned through bitter experience that if I use all the emotional associations that bring on tears too often too soon, I'll have nothing left for the close-ups—which is where it counts. Ironic that artistic human expression becomes, out of necessity in the world of film-making, a chess-playing emotional game plan. A newcomer is always overwhelmed by the intricacy of interval rhythms required to get through even one day of movie acting. I remember how Baryshnikov had come to me a few weeks into shooting *The Turning Point* with a request for help in sustaining the emotional and psychological peaks all day.

"I can dance full-out for eight hours at a time and not get tired," he said, "but I am exhausted from not knowing how to emotionally pace myself in these scenes. I am amazed that you people actually make your living at such a difficult task."

He was right. And that was where the Oscar bottle came in. Glycerine is a sweet oily substance used primarily as a solvent and food preservative—and in the manufacture of explosives. But it photographs well as tears. So an experienced makeup artist can place the tears in strategic positions on the face, leaving the actress with the task only of *looking* as if she's crying. It's never as convincing as the real thing, but the real thing is difficult to repeat take after take. Ammonia capsules are also used. Passed under the nose or close to the open eye they produce a tearing effect that soon spills effectively over the brim and down the cheeks. The problem with ammonia is that the effect occurs immediately, and unless the camera is ready to roll, your big drama is gone before it's recorded. It is difficult to describe the emotional gymnastics involved in acting deeply disturbing scenes. Obviously the highest priority is that your emoting be sincere, but the technical awareness of your marks, your key light, and consciousness of camera angle are of the utmost importance, to say nothing of the dialogue. So many times in my early days in film I believed I had been brilliant in a scene. The crew had applauded when it was over and my insides had been wrenched at the sincere emotion I touched. The problem was that I had missed my marks, hidden my face in shadow, and in one case had not even been in the camera frame. The marriage of technique and passion is the true union of an accomplished actor and there is no way to short-circuit that learning experience. You have to go through it.

In shooting *Out on a Limb,* though, the remembered passion was closer to the surface because it had been my own life. I simply let the memories overwhelm me, and my reactions were real and easily flowing. Yet it was interesting that even playing myself I found I was first and last a professional. For example, if my remembered emotion was too much for the scene, I altered it. The important thing was how it played *now,* not how it played in my memory.

One of my lasting memories of making the movie, however, is that of my big crying love scene. I had done it fifteen times. We were shooting on a romantic balcony overlooking the Pacific at 3:30 in the morning, using glycerine on my cheeks and eyes because I had dried up. The glycerine attracted the Hawaiian mosquitoes. I tried to brush them away on Charles's dialogue, thinking they would cut to him anyway, but it was no use. I finally broke down. But I wasn't crying because of the scene. I was crying because the mosquitoes were killing me.

As lovely as Hawaii can look on the scene, to shoot intricate scenes with turquoise surf sweeping over us was more like a Marx Brothers comedy than a romp in paradise. First of all, if you see two actors lying in the surf, you know there's got to be a crew in the water somewhere. If the angle is toward the land, the camera crew is definitely fighting the waves. If it's a profile shot, they are going through whatever the actors are experiencing.

If the sun is peacefully setting in the West, with a magenta hue cascading around your head, bathing your face and shoulders in illuminating light, it doesn't mean you're not being eaten alive by sand crabs as you say lines of delicate and tender affection.

If you stand profiled in the surf, drinking in the sight of a passenger steamship on the horizon, it doesn't mean you haven't cut your foot on coral and the blood is running into the water for all to see if the camera were to pan down.

And if you see an actor basking like a languid lizard in the sun, you can bet he is smeared with sunscreen and then covered with Egyptian number one body makeup. Otherwise he'd be in the bar having a beer.

So, with the Hawaiian location behind us, we returned to America and proceeded with the real nuts and bolts of making the film. Location relationships were disbanded and home and hearth took a higher priority.

Chapter 12

*S*oon, however, having arrived back on the mainland, I had an experience that enabled me to practically apply some of what I'd been learning. I was going to visit a friend and had gotten on a plane that I had not originally been booked on. I had a strange feeling that I shouldn't be on it. I wanted very much to get off. For some reason I did not want to be there.

The thought occurred to me that I now had the opportunity to experience the total fear of dying in a plane accident. I decided to go through with it. I sat back in the seat as the plane left the ground. Perhaps, I thought, it would happen on takeoff. I then decided to visualize my own fear. I didn't visualize a picture of any accident such as a crash or an explosion or anything specific like that. Instead I visualized what I would do about it. I saw the plane going down, and then very calmly I found myself rising above the airplane, knowing that *I* was perfectly safe regardless of what happened to my body.

This was not what I would call an out-of-body experience. It was more a projected imaginary experience, yet one with considerably real impact. I felt the fear course through me as though in a dream, and yet I had the election of moving away from the fear because I knew I was not going to die. It was, as far as I was concerned, a conscious enactment of a possible event—a rehearsal. And I was able to see some of my possible reactions. I saw that even if my body was destroyed in some kind of crash—*I* myself wouldn't be.

When I arrived, safely, at my destination, my friend who picked me up said, "I had the strangest feeling something had happened to your plane."

I explained that it hadn't happened to the plane; it had happened to me.

It wasn't long after settling into shooting in Los Angeles that I began to realize how many extras and crew members came to me with stories about feeling guided to work on the project. They didn't know why and neither did I. They just felt they should be a part of it. Many said they actually got calls from their agents *as* they were reading the book. Those sharings led to longer conversations about inner reality and outer reality and how they related to personal relationships. For the first time in my professional life, I looked forward to crowd scenes with lots of extras. The extras brought with them not only my books, but many other metaphysical books which they shared with me. In between shots they read and chatted about New Age systems of thought. That led to discussions, and discussions led to personal application, and personal application led to personal transformation. One person, transformed, changes many other people.

Making a movie for television carries with it a different intensity than making a feature film. I'm not sure why. The amount of time between setups may be shorter, which means the lighting crew works faster. But even that depends on the speed of the cinematographer himself. The crew takes on the pace and personal rhythm of their leader. If your cinematographer works with humor and an appreciation for the contribution of everyone around him, you have a happy and productive crew. If not, everything breaks down.

Ours was the former. And a member of a movie crew is an equal combination of artist and mechanic. I often marvel at how some burly guy knows just exactly how to create a soft shadow light to take years off my face or put sparkle in my eyes. Crews are a breed unto themselves. Their humor and honesty is largely private, because the next job may depend on what they say and do. But their sense of values is very fair, and they are mind-bogglingly professional when it comes to getting the job done. When you work the hours we were working, you easily see them at their worst and, because of that, their best.

We were shooting all over town in Los Angeles, changing locations every day or two. The "ready to shoot" call was 7:30 A.M. when we were shooting outside, because of the light. That meant that the crews had to load in at 6:00 or 6:30. Mobile homes, camera towing equipment, camera mounts, the generator trucks, the sound van, the wardrobe trucks, the prop van, the camera trucks full of lights, cables, batteries, lenses, film, etc., were the first to arrive. After that came the mobile catering—the honey wagons and doughnuts and coffee. It was an invasion of the mechanics of fantasy. Each department set up its own operating procedure, speaking show-biz dialects that only those who have worked together for years understand.

The makeup trailer was well lit inside by a generator outside. The actors sat side by side in high canvas chairs looking self-consciously or self-adoringly (depending on the person) at their *reflections* in the mirror. On a counter behind the chairs there were steaming coffee and unspeakably delicious treats that all of us took turns baking and devouring. Only those who aren't having any fun *don't* gain weight on a picture, regardless of the wearing hours.

Stories are swapped and gossip kindled as the makeup, powder, and hair curlers are applied. There are no secrets in the makeup trailer. Tabs that lift a face, toupees, wigs, and blemish coverings are soon common knowledge, and no one even thinks about them after the first day. Sometimes as we're being made up we rehearse our lines for the day, but more often than not we sit munching our sugary breakfast, sipping hot coffee in between makeup strokes, wishing we had gotten more sleep the night before. After makeup, if there was time, I'd go to my motor home and lie down. My motor home was cozy, comfortable, practical, and my home away from home.

There has always been a conflict between actors and crew in relation to the best working hours in our business. It has to do with fighting freeway traffic. The actors would like to begin later (thereby missing morning rush hour), eat lunch on the run, and shoot until 7:30 or 8:00 in the evening. This is called "French hours." The crew likes to start early, fight traffic, and quit at 6:30. They say it's because they want to be with their families at night. I think it's because they want to be with their girlfriends *before* they go home to their families.

Now, on our film, there was no way they would have time for either, because they arrived at 6:30 or 7:00 in the morning and never left before 8:00 or 9:00 or 10:00. We talked about the inhuman hours. They said they just set their minds to this professional commitment and their families would understand until it was over. But as I found out later, many of our crew went immediately on to other projects, with hours just as unrelenting. There's a reason why people in show business refer to those outside of it as "civilians." It's as though the Normandy invasion were occurring every day of the week, and if one show-biz soldier lets down the professional

collective, that person is never respected and rarely hired
again.

So we became a big transmigratory family, moving
from location to location like a functioning movable city
on wheels. There was nothing we could need that wasn't
part of our peripatetic unit, including a nurse and doctor.

The crew could build you a set of furniture from the
construction truck in half a day if necessary.

The prop truck could handle your accessories, and
the wardrobe truck had enough clothes hanging from
giant racks to outfit Macy's.

Then there was the production office bus. This was
where the head honchos hung out with their mobile
telephones to home base (the network) and their decision-
making meetings. Schedules were devised and scrutinized
there, and sometimes repressed emotions were released
over a late-night takeout Chinese meal.

And so Los Angeles became a maze of nomadic
zones for me. The restaurant scene zone, the goodbye
corner zone, the zone by the park. I completely lost my
bearings in the city and yet I had never seen so much of
it before. Sometimes we dressed our L.A. city street to
look like a New York City street by bringing in New
York yellow cabs and a few bag ladies. The director
would wince at the phony subterfuge, but the crew was
proud of their transformation. We shot downtown, all
over the streets of L.A., at the beach, in the Calabasas
Mountains, Pasadena, Malibu State Park, and sometimes
in an actual studio.

We were working from 7:00 in the morning to 10:00
at night. There was time for nothing else. Christmas was
coming up and no one had shopped. Sometimes I stayed
in hotels close to the next day's location, always accompanied by my sound machine. The crew sometimes joked
that I couldn't get a scene right because my sound machine was missing. But unless the ride to a location

would take more than an hour and a half, I usually slept at home in Malibu where the waves were natural.

As the shooting progressed, I realized I was feeling totally responsible for everything that happened on the project. If we were rained out I felt somehow that I could or should have prevented it. Because it was *my* story, *my* script, *my* life, and *my* production starring *me*, I wanted everybody on the film to be happy, collected, and comfortable.

Yet as the schedule closed in I felt serious frustration because of lack of time to myself to process what *I* was feeling. I needed time alone, time to center myself, to balance within. Because of the responsibility I was shouldering (unnecessarily) I was beginning to feel out of attunement with my own private spiritual place. I was sleeping about four hours per night. So I couldn't get up any earlier. There was no time or place to do yoga or meditation. It seemed that I was always involved with schedules, script changes, production problems, and phone calls that were about more of the same. I longed for a cool forest or a bubbling brook—or *any* private space, no matter how banal. For the first time since I had begun to work with spiritual techniques, I was feeling the consequences of not practicing them in my life. There simply was no time.

My legs began to hurt. My head ached and finally— last but not least—my back went out. I visited a chiropractor. He said I had an inflammation of the spinal column brought on by "nervous lack of attunement."

I began to think of how individual consciousness works in relation to collective consciousness. If a single person was truly centered and happy in his own being, productively and positively using his free will, how did his relationship to a project relate to the free wills of others who were negative, discordant, and hostile?

I had wanted all of us in our movie to be harmonious and happy within ourselves, mostly because the theme of my material echoed such values. On other films my expectations had not been so lofty. In fact, I don't suppose I even really cared. But this was different.

Whenever I saw any of our people on automatic self-destruct, I talked to them, sometimes feeling I was invading their privacy. They listened for a while, understanding what I was getting at, but usually continuing to allow themselves to be overwhelmed until, lo and behold, I realized I was doing the very same thing to myself.

I was feeling negative about *their* negativity until I produced an inflammation of my own spinal column, curable only by a change in attitude!

Then I did a fast objective rundown of what I was feeling during the course of a day's shooting. My assessment was anything but positive. I felt irritable with the woman who ran my motor home because she was depressed. There was no water and no toilet paper. I felt a lack of organization within the production unit stemming from the director's indecision. I didn't think anybody had much of a sense of humor during the work process. The power kept going off in my motor home when I was in it. Trash was building up everywhere I looked (most of it *mine*).

Props were getting misplaced, most of them mine.

Some of the wardrobe was missing, also mine.

But what bothered me the most was when people looked to me to make decisions that they were better off making themselves. I wished they'd use their own creativity, their own ideas, their own imagination.

One day in particular exemplified it all. I left my trailer to go to the set. There was an entourage following behind. I was going in the wrong direction, but no one said anything. I finally stopped and turned around. The entourage stopped and turned around. "Aren't I going in the wrong direction?" I asked.

"Yes," someone answered.

"Well, why didn't somebody tell me?" I asked.

"Because," someone answered, "you just seemed so self-assured."

I was struck dumb. Was this the price of leadership and taking charge? Then again, perhaps I *wasn't* taking charge. And finally, why was I creating all of this in my reality?

What should I do about it? I didn't want to expose the fact that it bothered me. Worse than that, I was feeling guilty that I was feeling negative. I was supposed to be this advanced positive-thinking person, yet with other people's insecurities I was really feeling terrible.

The Christmas holiday finally came. I had ordered some fabulous UFO books, six months previously, for Christmas presents, so lack of shopping time wasn't all that serious for me. The Christmas spirit was upon the land but not upon me.

As I felt the negative emotion building up in me, I called Colin and went to see him. He had been working on another project and had not been around much.

He said the same negative frustrations were building up in him. He had noticed it in some of his relationships, personal and professional, and he, too, was having trouble expressing his feelings about it.

The two of us stood in his kitchen outlining scenes that had occurred in our lives which were contributing to the pent-up feelings. Then we'd act out what we'd really like to do about it. It was fun—also revealing. I then made a decision to go to every Hollywood party in town during the holidays, even if it meant I would sleep only seventeen minutes every night. Colin and Sachi and I decided to pal around together, crashing parties, believing that anyone would be happy to have us.

There's nothing like a $250,000 party to make you forget your back, your responsibilities, and your anxiety over realizing the reality you create for yourself.

The first home we invited ourselves to (Colin had an

actual invitation) belonged to a very successful Hollywood agent. Never mind who his clients are—that night he had ten percent of Santa Claus and heaven.

The house was an open bank account of affluence, made not for living but for parties. Upon entering the front courtyard, we saw a black gospel choir (he handled them too), and as we glided through the open expanse of the marble-floored living room, surrounded by flower arrangements, we heard an all-white heavenly choir dressed in black tie, singing in the back courtyard around the swimming pool.

There was chamber music and an opulent bar on the other side of the pool, seen to by more black-tie attendants. In the dining room and kitchen was enough soul food to replay the Civil War: mustard greens, black-eyed peas and ham hocks, ribs, chicken, hominy grits, mashed sweet potatoes with marshmallows, plain mashed potatoes with soul food gravy, corn bread, bread, various green salads, and iced tea. The dessert counter was instant sugar shock just looking at it: pecan pies, Key lime pies, apple brown betty, bread puddings, sweet potato pie, blueberry crumb cake, chocolate fudge, homemade ice cream, and for the northerners, New York cheesecake.

Everyone was there, from Barry Manilow, who was on his own spiritual search, to Elizabeth Taylor, who had painted her square-cut Burton diamond like a candy cane to match her red-and-white striped fingernails.

As I touched on personal issues with some of my friends, it became clear that many of them were going through their own personal Armageddons. "The energy in life is moving so swiftly," became an oft-repeated refrain. Relationships and personal dramas were coming to a head, and values and principles people had never addressed before were becoming impossible to ignore. All of the insights people were having related to self-worth, self-esteem, self-love, and self-reflection. Suddenly the study of self wasn't indulgent—it was all there was. Some were using traditional psychological Freudian therapy to achieve self-knowledge; others were becoming more religious. But most had come to the conclusion that they themselves were essentially spiritual beings who had not recognized the power within themselves to bring about whatever they desired in their lives.

In discussing anger and repressed hostility, it also became clear that to feel guilty about those emotions was as self-destructive as the anger itself.

Around about this time Kevin Ryerson and Jach Pursel came into town. Colin and I discussed the question of repressed anger with Lazaris (the entity Jach channels) and I discussed it with Kevin and his entities.

"Don't hold the anger inside," they said. "Release it and forgive yourself and you'll find it's not as frightening as you think it is."

They went on to say that the honesty of the release carries with it a shift in consciousness in other people, enabling them to breathe easier when it's finally out in the open. They said that from then on, as events occurred in life, we should examine how *we* might have created the reality of things going wrong to begin with. The anger is really only the soul recognizing that it is responsible for creating the dilemma in the first place. And the most difficult aspect to admit is that we do it in order to learn.

While I enjoyed and learned from Jach and Kevin during that period, I felt the need to trace back some of the reasons inside myself for feeling so conflicted.

A year earlier, with the help of Chris Griscom, the spiritual acupuncturist, I had touched an incarnation of so long ago that it had defied identification for me. I do know that it was during a time period when advanced genetic experiments were taking place on the planet. It could have been Atlantis. I couldn't tell.

As I had lain on the table with the needles quivering

from my throat, third eye, shoulders, and behind the ears, the past-life incarnational pictures had begun to swim in.

And what I saw then was more than bizarre. I had seen myself lying on a cement slab of some sort. It seemed as though I were dead, but I wasn't. Then I realized I had agreed to some kind of experiment in which I had allowed my body to be processed into a state of suspended animation. My body wasn't moving, but it wasn't dead either. This was the simple part.

I had also agreed that I would participate in a "consciousness" experiment whereby my own soul would leave that body on the slab and enter other bodily forms in order to experience life. This process occurred over a period of centuries, and in that time I had innumerable incarnations while my original body remained on the slab. I could enter the original body any time I wanted, but I felt trapped and imprisoned because it was in a state of suspended life.

As I had lain on the table with the needles in my body, the sensations became more uncomfortable than I could bear; the dead stiffness of the joints and a kind of frozen inactivity of my inner organs were stifling. It was as though my body "today" had a cellular memory of another body eons before, when it had been involved with something I had agreed to, but thoroughly disliked.

As Chris and I had worked on the bizarre images coming up for me, I tried to pinpoint why my higher self was showing them to me. At the time it had become so physically uncomfortable that I had terminated the session.

But I knew this was an area I'd have to come back to.

Chapter 13

Now, one year later, I thought I might try again. I knew from experience that when things get rough, a breakthrough is just on the other side of the pain.

Chris had come into town from New Mexico to administer several treatments to various people. She stayed with me and we did a session. As a result of that session, several things became clear.

It wasn't long after Chris inserted the needles that the pictures began to appear again. There it was—the same familiar stonelike body lying on a slab. I knew it was me. The associated pain occurred again. I was imprisoned and entrapped inside the body. It was horrible. Chris guided me through it.

"Breathe light into the needles," she suggested gently.

I breathed evenly, visualizing light coming from the needle points. I felt myself relax a bit.

"Now," she said, "ask your higher self why you are having this pain."

I questioned my higher self. I did it in words, in English. I waited. I didn't hear anything come back. I questioned again. Nothing happened. I could feel myself resisting, as though I didn't want to hear what it had to say.

"Breathe into your third eye," said Chris. "Take light-filled breaths and tell me what you see."

I did what she said. Through my third eye I breathed light. Then I saw a picture form in the front of my mind. I was lying on a desert surrounded by lavender flowers. I was trying to beam light to another soul in the universe. I followed the light as far as I could see, but then I lost it.

On the table my right forearm began to throb with pain. I knew it had something to do with the other soul I was beaming to.

I told Chris what I was seeing.

"Okay," she said. "Ask your higher self to tell you the story of that soul and your right arm."

I asked. This time I got an answer, in English.

"The other soul wanted to depart," said Higher Self. "You wouldn't honor the desire. You attempted to hold on physically with your right arm. The soul departed anyway. You are still holding pain over the occurrence."

Suddenly the picture in my mind became very specific. I saw myself in a temple with people languishing around in white robes. The temple was made of peacock-blue marble. I asked my higher self who the people were.

The picture swam back to the desert, where I saw vases of some kind. I asked what was in the vases.

"They are cremation vases," said Higher Self.

"Who is in them?" I asked.

"Both child and grandfather," said Higher Self. "You were both."

"*I* was both?"

Higher Self nodded and said, "Yes."

I couldn't figure that out.

"Don't try," said Chris. "Just allow it to come."

Okay, I would. Then Higher Self said, "They were your brothers."

My brothers? That was even more confusing. I waited for a moment, becoming agitated and impatient.

Then I saw the slab again. There was my body on it. As I watched, a woman came over to my body with a small sculpted bottle in her hand. It was Tina Turner, looking almost identically as she looks today! She held the small bottle aloft, as though to show me I had drunk from a similar bottle. I couldn't understand. I asked Higher Self.

Immediately the picture changed to what looked like palm trees turned to stone. They were alive and standing, but stone. Then I saw the word VIOLENT spelled out. Immediately after that there was a forest of trees on fire. A terrible chest pain stabbed me. I saw little people with bald heads running around with earrings in their ears. Animals were stampeding, trying to escape from the forest fire. They were headed toward a city.

The next thing I knew I was in the city (which was more like a templed community). And an elephant was tracking me down. (I seemed to have an affinity for elephants. They were always popping up in my visualizations.) The elephant was angry with me, as though I had caused the fire. Then a previous psychic visualization occurred again. I was living with the elephants and decided to leave and head toward the city. I don't know how the fire began, but the herd leader blamed me.

The scene shifted. The pain in my chest became intolerable. I got very frightened lying on the table. Then I saw myself on the ground, unable to escape from the elephant. I looked up at him. He reared up on his hind legs and came down on my chest, crushing me. I let out a moan. It was awful. I felt I was reliving the actual event. But the most bitter memory was that I had loved the elephant and he had not understood why I left him or the herd. My chest and back were so painful now I could hardly breathe.

"Now," said Chris after I had related the story to

her, "ask your higher self if there is anything else for you to know relating to this before you release the memory for good."

I did. And Higher Self said, "The elephant lives today. He is white. He is looking for you in order to make peace and to lead you somewhere."

White elephants had been a haunting passion of mine as long as I could remember. I asked how he would find me.

Higher Self said, "He will."

I began to cry. I didn't know why. You never really do know why you're crying when working with past-life psychic energies, but you always do. I think it's because your soul finally makes contact with truths it only *sensed* before. Since we have all lived so many lifetimes over so much of the planet's experience, it is very emotional when you finally remember something that you know belongs to your experience, but which you have been unable to integrate before. I think we are all haunted by *knowing* that we are only a subtotal of much more than we realize and actually more than this life's experience. We are often touched and reminded of passions and events from some long-forgotten time and place, but we don't know how to identify them or whether we can even call them real. When you finally begin to scratch the surface of who you really are, it is overwhelming. You are never the same, nor do you want to be—and you are, whether you realize it or not, on the path of self-discovery, self-knowledge, and self-revelation.

The session didn't terminate with the elephant.

"Breathe in through the needles," reminded Chris. "Breathe into the solar plexus, so you can release the painful images and we can get on to touching more."

I breathed in and out through my solar plexus.

"Allow the past image to release, so you can draw in the future image of the white elephant bringing you peace."

I breathed. The pain in my back and chest and shoulders was worse. It went up and down my arms, throughout my whole body. I explained it to Chris.

"Ask why," she said.

I tried. The answer came back: "Suffering from love congestion."

"Why?" I asked. "What is the source of love congestion?"

"Smoke and polluted air," said Higher Self.

I began gasping for breath. My breathing was so labored I couldn't get enough oxygen.

"What's going on, Chris?" I said. "I'm a little frightened."

"Go into the pain of breathing," she said. "Let the images rise."

I tried to relax and allow the pictures to come. Instead of pictures I got an answer from Higher Self.

"Love in the human body is congested because the body is a vehicle of carbon," said Higher Self.

"Carbon?"

"Yes. Carbon is the lower frequency of silica which is crystal. It is difficult to resonate to divine love in bodies of carbon. You are on the earth plane to raise the frequency of carbon to the frequency of crystal, which will act as a consciousness amplifier. When your consciousness is raised, the love feelings are not congested because you are resonating to the Divine Source."

As soon as Higher Self ceased talking, the picture of my stonelike body lying on the slab returned. Immediately my body was more pained than before. I squirmed around on the table. I couldn't get comfortable.

"You are back with the slab?" asked Chris.

"Yes," I answered. "And it's godawful. I wish I could work out this slab thing once and for all. It's always in my mind but I can't work through it."

"Well," said Chris, "go into the body on the slab."

"I don't want to," I answered. "I'll be stuck again."

"Then go to the time when you broke free. You know you did."

"I can't."

"Yes, you can."

I squirmed around on the table, jarring several of the acupuncture needles loose.

"I don't want to be here," I said. "I want to quit. I want to get up."

"Of course you do," said Chris. "Because you are about ready to break through. You are coming to the real you who is still feeling congested about love—which is what the stone body represents. You won't accept and embrace real love until you break up the congestion."

"Okay," I said impatiently. "What the hell should I do?"

Chris's voice became softer. "Ask your higher self what you need, to be free of the bondage."

I yelled at her: "Why should I ask my higher self anything? I know it's nothing but me!"

Chris was slightly taken aback.

"Of course it is," she said. "It's the higher you, and you are out of touch with it. Ask it for help."

"All right," I yelled. Then in my head I yelled at my higher self. "What is wrong with me?!?"

It said calmly, "You are impossible."

I said to Chris: "It says I'm impossible."

"Well, we know that, don't we?" she answered gently. "Now, embrace your higher self and allow yourself to be embraced by it."

"I don't want to!" I shrieked. "Because I am impossible."

Chris laughed. "But your higher self isn't."

"Yes, it is, because it's me."

"No," said Chris. "*You*, right here on this table, are the impossible one."

"Yeah?" I asked sarcastically. "Well, what should I do now?"

"Ask your higher self what gift does the impossible one need in order to be free. Because the impossible one is imprisoned in its own impossibility."

I hesitated.

"Ask," chided Chris.

"I can't," I answered, "because I, the impossible one, and it, my higher self, are the same."

My body was virtually knotted with pain now.

"Your choice," said Chris, "is to remain impossible or be released."

I couldn't move now. I felt encased, similar to the mental picture I was seeing.

"I really am in a dangerous place now," I said, subtly blaming Chris.

"The impossible one likes dangerous places. It stays in control that way."

"Okay. Big deal," I said. "What should I do then?"

Chris hesitated, then went on: "You can focus on your higher self or you can focus on the impossible one—which of course you're already doing. When you focus on impossibility, it takes over, because that is your consciousness at the moment. Change that consciousness—that's all."

I stopped and tried to shift my focus. I couldn't find my higher self anymore.

"Remember the light," said Chris. "Fill your inner being with light. Draw the light in and expand it. You will get direction from your higher self. Your rebellious part says you can't choose light, but that is your ego talking; the immature child part of you. Draw your higher self into the light."

Slowly I forced my consciousness toward my higher self. I drew in the visualization. Light hovered in my mind. Then everything came clear. There I was on the slab, my body looking as though it were made of stone. Then I saw a group of white-robed priests lift my body from the slab and prop it up to its full height. They carried me to a place of worship and erected me upright, as though I were to be an idol of some kind. They surrounded me with the impedimenta of adoration and proceeded to teach others to chant worshipfully before the stone statue that was really me, except that I had no control over it and I was horrified that it was being used as an image for the purpose of perpetuating elitist spiritual authority.

As I watched the picture in my mind, everything became clear. No wonder I had felt so responsible for the destiny of so many people. Perhaps this was one reason for some of the problems I had today regarding adoration and fan worship. To me there was nothing more shameful than to be hyped by a studio into being adored if I hadn't earned it. It is mortifying for me and ultimately humiliating for the people being so manipulated.

I watched the past-life visualization continue. As it extended, it seemed to last for centuries. The image of me; a suspended-life statue serving as a false representative of spiritual authority. There seemed to be nothing I could do about it, *and* I knew that on some level I had willingly participated in this bizarre experiment of soul and body suspension. And somewhere on a soul level of consciousness I knew I would reap the karma of having been a part of this. Perhaps this was why I had created a role for myself this time around whereby I would be at the forefront of the New Age spiritual movement, heralding *the* giant truth that one individual is his or her own best teacher, and that no other idol or false image should be worshipped or adored because the God we are all seeking lies inside one's self, not outside.

This session with Chris was a powerful one for me. It put me in touch with why I was feeling guilty about other people's negativity, and it also enabled me to feel free to release some of my own pent-up feelings, to neutralize my frustrations. As the shooting proceeded I didn't explode in temperamental anger or anything like that. I just expressed what I felt while working. If I felt depressed I didn't bother to camouflage it. If I was pissed off I found a humorous way to let myself say so.

At first I found that people were somewhat startled at seeing that my emotional life was not always peaches and cream. But as a result they were more certain of where they stood with me. If I needed more light on my face to reveal tears in my eyes, I said so to Brad. He appreciated the interest. If Charles Dance wanted to change a line we had written, I would listen, but if it didn't sound right I wouldn't let him do it. If Anne Jackson, playing Bella, wore a dress that looked more like Anne than Bella, I changed it. I wondered sometimes if I was indulging in a power trip. I wondered if I sounded superior; if I had forsaken my democratic way of working. But no, it didn't feel like that. It felt as though I was taking charge of my own responsibility, which, as I looked back, was probably related to the lifetime that came up for me on the table—the lifetime in which I had not.

The morning after my session with Chris, a school of dolphins swam past my bedroom window. And that afternoon the pain in my back disappeared. On New Year's Eve, Sachi and Colin and I went to a small party attended by people in our business who were spiritual seekers themselves. Twenty of us sat around an oval table; a crystal was passed to each of us and we expressed in words what we would like to manifest in our lives for the following year. The open and direct honesty was heart-glowing to witness. But when the crystal came to me I found myself expressing an understanding that for me was true, but for some of the others seemed outlandish.

I began by saying that since I realized I created my own reality in every way, I must therefore admit that, in essence, *I was the only person alive in my universe.* I could feel the instant shock waves undulate around the table. I went on to express my feeling of total responsibility *and power* for all events that occur in the world because the world is happening only in my reality. *And* human beings feeling pain, terror, depression, panic, and so forth, were really only aspects of pain, terror, depression, panic, and so on, in *me!* If they were all characters in my reality, my dream, then of course they were only reflections of myself.

I was beginning to understand what the great masters had meant when they said "you are the universe." If we each create our own reality, then of course we are everything that exists within it. Our reality is a reflection of us.

Now, that truth can be very humorous. I could legitimately say that I created the Statue of Liberty, chocolate chip cookies, the Beatles, terrorism, and the Vietnam War. I couldn't really say for sure whether anyone else in the world had actually experienced those things separately from me because these people existed as individuals only in my dream. I knew *I* had created the reality of the evening news at night. It was in my reality. But whether anyone else was experiencing the news *separately* from me was unclear, because *they* existed in my reality too. And if they reacted to world events, then I was creating them to react so I would have someone to interact with, thereby enabling myself to know me better.

My purpose in mentioning this on New Year's Eve was to project a hope that if I changed *my* conception of reality for the better in the coming year, I would in effect be contributing to the advancement of the world. Therefore, my New Year's resolution was to improve myself— which would in turn improve the world I lived in.

Most of the faces around the table looked scandalized. *I* created the Declaration of Independence and Marilyn Monroe and the fifty-five miles per hour speed limit? If I changed my reality, it would change the world? I had clearly gone too far. The discussion that ensued was a microcosm of the world itself. And while the others expressed their objections, I felt *I was creating them to object,* so that I could look at some things I hadn't resolved myself. In other words I *was* them. *They* were *me.* And all because I was creating them as characters in my play.

The classic question was asked: If what I was proposing were true, would it also be true that I did nothing for others, everything for myself?

And the answer is, essentially, yes. If I fed a starving child, and was honest about my motivation, I would have to say I did it for myself, because it made me feel better. Because the child was happier and more fulfilled, *I* would be. I was beginning to see that we each did whatever we did purely for self, and that was as it should be. Even if I had not created others in my reality and was therefore not responsible for them, I would feel responsible to my own feelings which desire to be positive and loving. Thus, in uplifting my own feelings I would uplift the feelings of my fellow human beings.

How do we change the world? By changing ourselves.

That was the gist of my New Year's projection.

Chapter 14

With the holidays over and very little sleep (we worked every day but Christmas) I was looking forward to regular working days because I wouldn't feel determined to have a good time.

We finished with Charles Dance and the Gerry segment of the shoot. Our last scene together was our first meeting—typical of the illogical juxtaposition of reality in the movies. We finished late at night. Charles said goodbye to everyone and suddenly my screen Gerry was out of my life.

Enter John Heard from New York.

John had expressed some interest in losing weight for the picture. So I introduced him to Anne Marie Bennstrom, who runs The Ashram in Calabasas (the toughest spiritual health camp in the world).

John had two scenes to shoot with me and then would have a week off so he could become a tortured inmate with Anne Marie.

On his first day, there was a complete change of energy on the set. John was informal, spontaneous, and more than a little unusual. He had the kind of working

personality that challenged men and brought out mother-
hood in women. That he was an exceptional actor there
was no doubt. What made him tick as a man was soon to
provide the soap opera drama that kept the company's
gossip entertainment going for the next few months.

He lost ten or twelve pounds in one week with The
Ashram's exercise program, which consisted of twelve
miles of mountain hiking every day, three calisthenic
classes, two aerobics classes, dynamic tension class, and a
three-mile jog. All of this was accomplished on the nutri-
ents of some salad and yogurt. John looked wonderful.
During the week of his training I called him from the set
and he told me funny stories about how he was confronting his body in new ways.

John had not only been successfully on the wagon
for several months, but he had been able to stick to the
diet too. He was proud of himself and said he felt better
about who he was now than he ever had in his life. He
went over his lines and his life with Anne Marie and
joked about how he was wrong in considering California
a spaced-out dumb place. He said he had seen a way to
be "spiritually joyful" in California for the first time.

Anne Marie and I congratulated ourselves, because
his weight reduction had been relatively painless and his
feeling of well-being was very positive. That was on a
Thursday. John was scheduled to continue shooting in
earnest on Monday morning, with Anne Jackson and me.

Stan called me early Saturday morning.

"Shirley," he said in that carefully measured way of
his, "are you sitting down?"

"Yes," I said, and sat down immediately.

"Well, I've just received a call from John Heard's
manager. He quit the picture and is going back to New
York this afternoon."

I choked back a piece of toast.

"You're kidding me," I said.

"No," said Stan, "I'm not."

"But why?" I asked. "I talked to Anne Marie yesterday. She said he was doing wonderfully and was real proud of himself."

"I don't know," said Stan.

I looked out across the ocean. There were no dolphins anywhere in sight and I could feel my back pain come again like an unwanted, uninvited visitor.

"Well," I said finally, "I'm going up to The Ashram to talk to him."

"He says he doesn't want you to try to talk him into staying."

"Oh," I said. "Okay. I'll just try to be a friend and help him do the right thing for himself. How's that?"

"Hopefully that'll be the right thing by us too," said Stan with rueful shrewdness.

"What are we going to do, Stan?" I asked. "I mean, we're supposed to shoot with him in the art gallery on Monday with Anne and me."

"I know," said Stan. "I've contacted the crew, the assistants, the location manager, everybody. We'll finish up your scenes with Anne until we can hire another actor. There's just nobody available at this late date, though. But you say this project is guided, right?"

I gulped. Talk about being responsible for your own reality.

"Yeah," I said. "It is guided. So what have we got to learn from this?"

"Probably that we're going to be at least a week behind schedule and several hundred thousand dollars over budget."

"You're getting very practical all of a sudden, aren't you?" I asked.

Stan laughed. "What else would you have me do?" he asked good-naturedly.

I thought a moment.

"Listen, Stan," I said. "You want to make a bet that he won't leave today?"

"What would we bet?" he said. "We'll have nothing left to shoot with."

"I don't know. A good dinner or something. I'm going up there now. Goodbye."

I hung up and hesitated. Should I call John and say I was coming, or not call and take the chance that I would miss him if he took an early plane?

I called. He came right to the phone.

"Hi," he said. "I'm real sorry, but I can't do it."

"Yeah, John," I said. "But why?"

"Because my life has changed here. So much that I have to go back to New York and get straightened out."

I didn't expect that answer.

"So much to get straightened out?" I asked confusedly.

"Yes."

"But what about this movie you're in the middle of? I mean, I want you to do the best thing for your life."

"Please, don't try to talk me into staying," he said pleadingly. "It's because of how you've been with me, so loving and understanding and supportive, that I feel I can do what I'm doing."

I was flabbergasted.

"Oh, John," I said. "That's sweet of you."

"So, thank you," he said.

I couldn't believe it, but I said, "No. Thank *you*."

Here was a guy leaving in the middle of shooting my movie and I was thanking him for thanking me for letting him go!

"Hey, John." I collected myself. "Can I come over and talk to you?"

"Sure," he said. "My plane's not till six-thirty. And remember, I'm going to be on it."

He sounded like a tourist who had a few hours to spare before the next city on the itinerary.

I hung up and shook my head. Was this a dream or what?

I dressed and drove to The Ashram.

No one was there but John. It was a Saturday when the rest of the guests had checked out. He was sitting out on the patio with a glass of orange juice. I walked toward him. He was nervous, as though he expected me to chastise him for what he was doing. I hugged him. He had a way about him that inspired affection. He patted me on the shoulder. I patted him on the shoulder. He asked if I wanted some juice. I said no. I told him he looked great. He said thank you. He sat and looked at me.

"I've just spent the happiest week of my life," he said. "It was hard, but I was happy."

I carefully calculated how far I should proceed.

"A lot of people," I began, "don't come through the Ashram program as well as you have. Congratulations."

He smiled shyly. "Thanks," he said.

I decided to begin. "So you don't want to show your new body on the screen?"

He flashed a frightened glance in my direction.

"I don't like the mineral bath scene," he said. "I don't like the nudity."

"Oh," I said, sensing that we might be getting to practicalities. "Well, Standards and Practices dictates that we keep our clothes on in water scenes like that anyway."

He looked at me suspiciously. "Then that makes me a fraud."

This was not going to be easy.

"I quit the basketball team in high school, you know," he said.

"You did?" I asked, interested in where this was going to lead.

"Yeah. Actually the coach read me out for flirting with a girl, so I quit. My father tried to make me go back and apologize, but I wouldn't. I just wouldn't."

I sat there mesmerized by what he might or might not be leading up to. I could see the gymnasium with

John in blue satin shorts dribbling the ball for some blue-eyed cheerleader like I used to be.

"I got right up to the coach to do it so I'd get back on the team, but because my old man told me to do it—I didn't."

Hmmmm, I thought. Okay, I understand that.

"I'm no movie actor," he said. "I don't want to be recognized."

I wasn't certain whether he was serious or just testing me until I saw what happened next.

"I remember," he said. "The morning I woke up and saw my name in the paper like I was famous or something, I hated it. I still do."

With that, John broke down and cried. He was genuinely in pain at the thought of being famous. Yet he was an actor. As I quickly computed what was going on, I concluded that he imagined he didn't want to do this show because it would be seen by millions of people and he would very likely be a household name for a week or two, which would shatter his sense of anonymity. I held him and let him cry. He was a man who put you in touch with every simple maternal instinct known to womankind. Finally he straightened up in his chair. He drank some juice.

"You know," he continued, "my dentist is one of my friends. He fixed my tooth and wanted the thousand dollars right away. What kind of a friend is that?"

I took a sip of his juice.

"I guess he's a very businesslike friend," I said.

"Yeah," said John sarcastically. "Some friend."

"Yeah, I guess so," I said. "But he does make his money being a dentist, doesn't he? You know, like we make our living at acting."

I wondered if it was possible to keep the subject on track somehow.

"I wouldn't quit this project if it wasn't for you, you know," he said reassuringly.

"Why?" I asked.

"Because you are so supportive and understanding. You're not mad at me. There's no revenge or rancor in you. Why don't you run for President?"

I could feel my eyes roll.

"Well," I said, "mostly because I have this movie to make."

"New York reinforces negativity and fear," he said logically. "I have to stop doing what others want me to do. Like, I know my manager and girlfriend are back there now *discussing* my behavior. I need to blow away old habits like them. Otherwise I have to sit around listening to them not understand why I quit."

"Uh huh," I said, wondering how personal I should get.

"See," he said defiantly. "Nobody will listen to me."

I had a metaphysical flash of humor suddenly.

"I guess your name isn't John H-E-A-R-D for nothing, is it?" I asked him.

He looked at me as though he had been shot with a tack.

Just then Anne Marie came out to the patio.

"Well, John," she said cheerily, "how are you feeling now?"

He looked up at her. "I've definitely made the right decision."

"Yes," said Anne Marie, "you sound very clear about it."

I shot her a look. Whose side was she on anyway?

"Life is an adventure," she said. "We have this huge sandbox to play in. Some of us play one way. Some another."

Anne Marie put her arms around John and ran her hands through his hair.

"You feel good about what you're doing?" she asked. "I mean, are you prepared for the ABC people to sue you for the money you'll cost them?"

John's face hardened.

"Let them hang me," he said. "Let them take everything I've got. I'll go out and sell hot dogs on the street corner. Fine." Then he said the key line.

"I reserve the right to be a failure."

Okay, I thought. I'm in a little over my head.

Anne Marie reared back and laughed.

"Yes, you certainly do," she assured him.

"We all play our roles to the hilt. You're no different. From your innermost being, do you want to be a failure?"

John cocked his head. "From my innermost being?" he asked.

"Yes," said Anne Marie, undaunted. "Are you sure your choice is what you earnestly desire?"

John saw that he could avoid his innermost being by saying "Yes!" resoundingly.

"Well, then," said Anne Marie. "Then you are coming from a very pure place. Your actions flow from your thought. Your thought flows from God. Our bodies are nothing but coagulated thought anyway, so if you pick up your body and take its coagulated thought away from here, then you are acting from your God-self according to your own personal integrity."

John was speechless.

"And," she continued, "if you feel you should rearrange your life and this week has been the catalyst for doing it, so be it."

"Yes," said John. "I have to fire people."

"Okay," she said. "Fire people. I just hope you have enough ammunition left when the big lawyers train their fire on you."

John looked at me. "She's not talking lawsuits or anything. Are you?"

"Me?" I said. "What would I know about that? That's not up to me. I just want you to play the part. I *need* you to play the part and I'm real sorry that you don't love yourself enough to follow through and do it."

I was surprised to feel tears spring to my eyes. John saw it immediately. I made a conscious decision not to hold them back.

I got up. "I love you," I said. "And love is what you need in your life. You are a brilliant actor. But you have to do what you have to do. I can tell you one thing, though. The third act hasn't been played out yet. Of that I'm sure and only you know what it is."

John stood up and I hugged him.

"Thank you," he said shyly.

"You really are going back on that plane?" I asked. "You really are *not* going to show up for shooting on Monday?"

He looked at me as though he was experimenting with steadfastness.

"That's right," he said.

I turned around and walked away. I was glad I hadn't bet Stan anything substantial. I stopped by John's suitcase at the door.

I took a note paper from my purse and wrote: *Don't forget the basketball. Don't drop it now.* I put the note on his suitcase and walked out.

Colin's perspective on John's leaving was that it was a flight from responsibility. John's was that he was acting responsible to himself for the first time in his life. And mine was "He'll be back." Anne Marie, who had been with him for the entire week, said he was "coming from a very clear place, seemed to know his mind, and from his point of view was doing the right thing." Stan was on the phone to every agent in town looking for a replacement.

I called Kevin Ryerson and Jach Pursel asking each of them to consult with their entities for advice. The word came back from both that there was a good possibility that John would return in forty-eight hours.

Anne Marie called and said she felt the same thing.

"Do you want him, though?" she asked. "Will the same thing happen in Peru?"

Yes, I wanted him. I felt he was supposed to play the part—not only for the film, but for himself. I wasn't real sure what I meant by that, but I knew it would happen.

Spiritual entities seemed to be as good as anyone else when it came to professional advice in the face of crisis.

Two days later we had still not "heard" from John. The forty-eight hours were nearly up. The press had been calling. Stan fielded the questions with finesse without saying we had been advised by spiritual entities that John would be back.

On the third day I called John's manager, Bill. He said he had only found John that afternoon because John had been lifting weights in a gym ever since he got back to New York. He said John was considering marrying Melissa because he thought we had already hired another actor. He said John was sorry he had thrown off our schedule and that people were suffering, but he was just a "nothing thin actor from New York who could be replaced in a day." He said John had not liked his first day's work and didn't think he was capable of playing David.

I listened to Bill without saying much. Then he told me ABC had threatened to sue John for all he was worth if he didn't return. I could see why the entities were right.

"Is there a chance you'd take John back?" asked Bill.

I knew John would return within the forty-eight-hour period.

After a sleepless night of phone calls back and forth between John, me, Melissa, and Stan, John allowed that "I'm not running for the People's Party or anything, but

I don't like to see people being hurt, so you're killing me with kindness and ABC is killing me with lawsuits, so if you want me to, I'll come back."

"I want you to," I said at 6:00 in the morning, knowing I had to be on the set in an hour. "Bring Melissa with you. We'll have a straitjacket made for both of you."

John laughed, seemingly delighted that I now knew what I and everyone else were getting into.

What intrigued me the most was that John Heard had the guts to do what the rest of us only fantasized about—he was truly outrageous and never gave it a second thought. He was playing a part in his life, which if portrayed on the screen would have gotten all the laughs, all the sympathy, *and* probably would be the one the audience rooted for.

I looked at the way I was playing my part and asked myself if it was a role I liked enough to go on the road with it. The answer I came up with was: "She seems like a nice enough character, sincere and questing, but I wish she could be rewritten to have a little more fun with the insanity going on in the world." John Heard was clearly there to teach me that.

After work that night I went into Hollywood to see *A Chorus Line—The Movie.* It was a balmy soft night when I wandered out of the theater thinking about the film. It brought up so many memories for me, having started in the chorus myself. I stopped on a side street and stood looking into the star-studded sky trying to "remember" whether I had written the scenario of my life before I was born: the struggling, disciplined, dancing days, the night I went on for Carol Haney, the relationship with Alfred Hitchcock, the smiling-through-tears on the silver screen, the adjustment to myself as a communicator, and finally the ventures into travel, politics, writing, and spiritual questing. Did my interest in performing have its genesis in understanding that my life

always had been a role I had written long ago to be
played out on an earth plane stage today? And had John
Heard made his entrance just in time to live up to the
part I had written for him in *my* script? And if it was *my*
script, then was his character really an aspect of me?

The convolutions of intersecting realities drifted
through my mind as I left the side street and walked
farther into the balmy "Hollywood" night. Hollywood
. . . the most famous center of illusion in the world. And
the illusions created on film and stage were alternative
realities to me—not really make-believe. When entertainment was good and absorbing, nothing else existed. I
forgot my "real" life and focused on another adventure.
Was that the same principle by which we experienced
lifetimes? A matter of focus?

As I walked I began to speculate on whether my
idea of linear reincarnation was a truth or merely a
simplification. Using my present lifetime as an analogy to
multiple life experiences, I began to wonder about the
role that *time* played in my reality.

Einstein had said there was no such thing as time—as
we measure it. The spiritual masters confirmed such a
concept. They said instead that past, present, and future
were the same.

In other words, all time was happening now, and
always. Perhaps linear concepts were man's way of dealing with the dumbfounding awesomeness of totality. Our
way of measuring time, then, became a way of focusing
on aspects of the totality.

If time was happening to us all at once, then perhaps we weren't living linear incarnations one after the
other; perhaps we were only *focusing* on one at a time.

As I walked I thought of my own body. It existed in
its own totality. I was not aware of specific aspects of my
body unless I focused on something I chose. I stopped
walking. I focused on my big toe—the big toe of my
right foot. I was unaware that my big toe on my right

foot was important until I concentrated my attention on it. Then the big toe became paramount in my awareness: a kind of life in itself. Especially if someone should step on it, I thought. I stood still under the stars, focusing on the big toe of my right foot. I was creating that focus.

Perhaps that was what we were doing with each lifetime, each experience being only that which we chose to focus upon. Would that explain our feelings that dreams were real, that visions were real, that fantasies were real? Maybe I was only dipping and overlapping into parallel realities and I was correct in my assumption that *all* of them were real.

When I had premonitions of the future, perhaps I was tapping into an alternative reality which I could only define in a linear manner as the "future," but in actuality it existed simultaneously with the present. When we had *déjà vu* experiences, perhaps we were not actually seeing something in a past/future life sense, but inadvertently shifting to a different aspect of the whole—much as I had (deliberately) focused on my big toe just a moment ago.

So maybe life was essentially a matter of focus in time—analogous to film because films were also an attempt to focus on special moments of a life experience.

Those of us who made films were creating the scenario we wanted to be played out. We knew the best films were karmically balanced (the bad guys always paid). The subjects that attracted audiences were subjects they could identify with and relate to in their own lives. We knew they would suffer with the heroes and heroines because they would see themselves as heroes and heroines of their own drama. And the supporting players would be easy to identify in their own lives as well.

And even though we film-makers knew that they would know the ending of a movie was intact at the end of the roll of film, we presented it as though it would be a spontaneous experience for them. We expected them to glue themselves to our illusion, allowing the truth of it to function as a separate reality from what they knew was only a movie-making trick. We attempted to create a trick-truth for the audience and we evaluated ourselves by how completely they bought it.

I began to walk again slowly under the stars and palm trees, releasing the focus on my big toe.

So we film-makers were the purveyors of illusion, using all the tricks of the trade to convince the audience that what they saw was real. And wasn't that what we did with our lives too? We focused on a feeling or an event that created feeling, and we called it reality. We put ourselves through sorrow, exhilaration, anger, love, or whatever, and all of it was only an exercise in searching out who we were more deeply. Was life simply to experience feeling? Was that also the great contribution of films in the world? Did they reflect human emotions back to ourselves, which was just what playing our parts in life accomplished? A certain kind of film had even developed a genre term: "slice of life," meaning no beginning, no middle, no end. Not neat but, like life, just a piece of the whole. We could wander into the middle of any film in much the same way that we could wander into a daydream or a seemingly out-of-context dream at night. We woke in the morning knowing that the dream had occurred, but because of our limited concept of reality we said: "It was only a dream."

I wondered how it would feel, when I finally passed on, if I were to turn around, look at my life, and say "It was only a dream, but it seemed so real."

Maybe I would feel that the life I had created for myself had been like a movie dream. And just as I had liked certain kinds of movies because of what they had enabled me to experience for myself, I would see that I had created the dramas and events in my life from the same need to experience. Maybe I would see for sure, after I passed on, that I had created the lines I wanted, the events I wanted, the people I wanted. Perhaps I had designed them specifically to my own requirements. Maybe I would see clearly from "the other side" that I had been responsible on some level for all that happened to me. That I had created it all because it enabled me to learn and grow.

Maybe I would see that all of us had liked to experience drama in order to know who we were; that some preferred comedy; that others grew more rapidly with adventure; and still others understood themselves only by staying home. Maybe it was the same as our taste in films: each person preferring to experience a different adventure, for whatever the reason.

As I walked along the Hollywood street I thought of my job as an actress. It was to create illusion, just as my job as a human being was perhaps to realize that life itself was an illusion. An illusion of my own creation which could enable me to experience any emotion known to the human condition that I chose.

Part of me has always known that my future was already written. That part of me was what I called my higher self. My higher self was the all-knowing me, possessed of all knowledge, which put this aspect of me now called Shirley through loops of learning. It invented relationships for me, events for me, sorrow for me, and laughter for me, while compassionately looking on with encouragement and hope that I would reap knowledge and understanding from it all.

Not only was my higher self creating events in this lifetime for me, but I could sometimes feel it creating other time and place experiences as well.

As I grew and knew myself more in this dimension, I would be more maturely capable of understanding the totality of what I was.

Regardless of how I looked at the riddle of life, it always came down to one thing: personal identity, personal reality. Having complete dominion and understanding of myself was the answer to harmony, balance, and peace. There were those who would say that such a state of mind would be boring. But they were only aspects of me who couldn't admit feeling the same way.

I walked and I thought. I tried to breathe in the stars and their energy. I belonged to them and they belonged to me.

Therefore I, now, on this street on this Earth, was experiencing only an aspect of what I really was. I was more than I perceived myself to be. And therein lay the grand truth.

If I created my own reality, then—on some level and dimension I didn't understand—I had created everything I saw, heard, touched, smelled, tasted; everything I loved, hated, revered, abhorred; everything I responded to or that responded to me. Then, I created everything I knew. I was therefore responsible for all there was in my reality. If that was true, then I *was* everything, as the ancient texts had taught. I was my own universe. Did that also mean I had created God and I had created life and death? Was that why I was all there was?

A chilling wave of loneliness rippled through me. Was this what the great masters meant when they described the numbing aloneness that preceded the recognition of one's totally awesome power? Was one's inner power the point? Were all the questions and conflicts and triumphs and tragedies in our lives designed by each of us to put us in touch with our own empowerment? If we could create such negativity as war, then we could certainly create its polarity. And to take responsibility for one's power would be the ultimate expression of what we called the God-force.

Was this what was meant by the statement I AM THAT I AM?

Was the search for God pointless because God was within me? Was God within each of us? Was self-search the only journey worth taking, because what we found, we would eventually realize, was our own creation anyway?

I walked and walked under the stars. The inevitable wheel tumbled and turned in my head. Had I created everything or had it created me? How could either be proved? But if my reality was a question of what I perceived it to be, then regardless of how I looked at it, I made the choice. *I* was the one empowered with the decision-making process of how to relate to it. So in point of truth, what difference did it make? I was the one *choosing how* to experience life.

Chapter 15

Before John Heard returned to California, we shot our session with Kevin and his entities. Kevin had conducted many workshops on the nature of personal reality. But I don't think even he was prepared for the exercise of playing himself.

He stayed at my house and we rehearsed our lines late into the night. Kevin is a centered, balanced person, but when *I* went into the character of myself ten years ago, he had a bewildering time adjusting to the change in me. His eyes became confused, as though the portrayal of myself as a skeptic was a betrayal of my present-day spiritual understanding. In other words, he *believed* that I was suspicious of his role as a trance channeler. I reassured him that I was just acting, but it still threw him. The entities knew their lines, but Kevin was having trouble with his.

The day of shooting dawned clear and bright. The crew didn't know what to expect. Brad had three cameras set up so that the entities and Kevin wouldn't have to worry about matching the action. It wouldn't be a problem in the cutting room later on.

Kevin and I ran over our lines. He thought it was better not to go into trance until the cameras were rolling.

Butler decided to direct Kevin-as-himself to be detached and noncommittal about his work as a trance channeler who approached it casually and with no particular intensity of purpose. Kevin took the direction as he understood it. The crew was watching carefully because they knew that in a while Kevin would go into trance, and entities would speak through him—which, to some of the crew members, could simply be Kevin acting.

But they found him sincere, cooperative, caring, and desiring to be professional. Kevin was literally learning film acting in one day.

The cameras were ready. The script girl, Kisuna, took her position beside the cameras so she could make notes about actions and lines. Kevin was lit for each of the three cameras. The scene would be played on my back—that is, from behind me, looking at Kevin. We'd come around to shoot me later.

The soundman had a double load of tape, and the police security on the road kept the noise down to a minimum outside the beach house on Malibu Road. (Not my own place, by the way—an apartment similar to mine had been rented and "dressed" for the actual shooting.)

The crew had tarped-in the living room with black cloth to block out the sunlight, because the scene was supposed to take place at night. The resulting interior temperature was stifling.

There were times, during channeling sessions, when the energy of the entities coming through affected the electromagnetic frequencies of the electrical equipment, causing them to jam or the batteries to die—as happened in Sweden with Ambres. I wondered if that would happen to our cameras now.

Jach Pursel had come into town to watch and be with Kevin. Moral support of one trance channeler by another, you might say. So Jach was on the set. I didn't tell anybody what Jach did for a living. I thought one trance channeler was about all the crew could handle. So Jach stood discreetly behind the cameras alongside Colin, who was chuckling to himself that we had pulled this whole thing off in the first place.

The crew seemed remarkably calm about what was to transpire. They were not the same crew that had conducted the screen test.

The camera crew was interested in the science of energy surrounding the event, while makeup, hair, props, grips, and production people were simply intrigued as to why Brandon Stoddard and ABC would put up millions for this stuff.

Kevin sat in front of me. He was perspiring under the lights. Tina, the makeup artist, came in and wiped him off. I wondered how she'd feel about wiping off Tom McPherson or John. She rolled her eyes slightly as she turned from Kevin and returned to her place behind the camera. I saw she and Kisuna exchange a hostile look. I didn't understand. I had noticed that Tina made one or two remarks about Kisuna on the set, but had just put it down to between-scenes byplay. Tina was a petite blonde with a strong personality and professional workmanship who could sometimes be insensitive to other people's insecurities. I recognized that because I was the same way. She was in charge of the makeup trailer, which included other makeup artists, body makeup, and hairdressers. As far as I could tell, she ran a tight operation by never overlooking anything anybody else did, and thought everyone else should too.

As Kevin went into trance I wondered about the exchanged glances between Tina and Kisuna. On-the-set nuance in relationships always intrigues me. A movie set is a mini-society. It has its leaders and its followers. It has people who need and love power, and others who simply do their work for the sake of it. Since jobs are difficult to come by, you can sense a priority of survival permeating the ranks of the crews. Each crew member is utterly professional, yet each also watches the professionalism of fellow workers. What I find most interesting is how each member deals with the mistakes or unintended lack of professionalism of a co-worker. No one wants to be responsible for the dismissal of anyone else, yet they all know that the chain of a crew is only as strong as its weakest link. And the watchful surveying eye of management is ever present, sometimes even present in the personage of the stooge who has been singled out to report everything.

The crew *is* the movie business. As I've said, they are artists and mechanics combined. Not one person who makes the deals or handles the money can hold a candle to the artistic expertise required of a lighting technician.

Yet, as I watched them prepare for our scene I was once again reminded that the crew secures all the time it needs to insure a good take, while we actors are the least prepared and somehow are never given enough time to improve what we do. We can rehearse in our trailers all we want, but it's not the same when we find ourselves on the set with lights, props, scenery, and camera angles to deal with. Yet we are self-conscious about asking for more time to acquaint ourselves with our roles and the technical adjustments necessary to playing them well.

A cameraman can stop a take because we actors lean into a shadow. A makeup person can take twenty minutes to redo a face while everyone waits. But if an actor stops and says, "Wait a minute, I don't feel it yet," everybody thinks he's temperamental.

For those reasons, even though Kevin was cooperative, I wanted him to complain if he felt uncomfortable, ask for another rehearsal if he felt unprepared with his lines. But he, like most of us, felt that the fifty crew members waiting and prepared were more important than what the audience comes to see—the actors on the screen.

Kevin closed his eyes and began to breathe deeply. The cameras rolled. The clapper boy signified the take for each camera. I looked around at the crew. They were spellbound, and suspicious.

Within a few minutes John came through and proceeded to greet me according to script and as though it were the first time we had talked together.

A still-camera man hired by ABC publicity was shooting stills with a "blimp" on his camera so the shutter wouldn't be heard by the sound man.

Brad and the camera crew sat fascinated as Kevin's personality seemed to change completely. They strained at the biblical lingo coming out of his mouth.

The scene with John completed, Tom McPherson came through. He immediately asked for a blindfold and then stood up. The focus puller quickly adjusted for the change of move. Tom walked around the room to a closet concealed in the wall and pulled out a glass mug. Then, with the blindfold tightly tied, he poured tea into the mug from a distance of about a foot above it. He said he saw the water as luminescence rather than liquid. The crew was astonished that he didn't spill the tea. So was I. He walked to the fireplace and, still blindfolded, extracted a poker from behind a chair and began to poke the fire as he delivered his lines. The focus puller adjusted again. By now the crew was open-mouthed. Tom returned to his original position in the chair, finished his lines, and left Kevin's body so that John could return and complete the scene.

The scene ended, and before Butler said "Cut," John looked at me and said, "Will there be other requirements of channel speaking or is the scene terminated?"

I looked around at the crew. The cameras and lights seemed to be operating independently of them.

"Does anyone have anything they'd like to ask John or Tom while we're here?" I asked.

Nobody said anything. Then finally Stan said, "Ask what kind of response this show is going to get when it goes on the air."

I turned back to John. He thought a moment.

"It will sufficiently change the consciousness of those who view it," he said.

I sat forward.

"Will that be all then?" he asked.

"Yes," I said. "Except for one more thing."

"Yes?" he said, cocking his head questioningly.

"Some of the crew wonder if you and Tom would come through later after work so they can ask you questions. But only if Kevin is not too exhausted."

"Yes," said John. "However, the instrument's subconscious is jumbled at the moment. We suggest a rest period before our meeting later tonight."

The crew murmured thank-yous, John left, and Kevin rolled back to consciousness.

The crew applauded and we knew that an event in movie-making had been captured.

But it wasn't to be that easy. At least not for me. When the cameras came around on me for my side of the scene, the decision had to be made as to whether Kevin would go into trance again so that the entities could give me their stage lines.

Kevin was too tired and the entities had said it was difficult to access Kevin's subconscious (where the lines lay) anyway. Kevin couldn't sit there and play the entities himself, because he didn't know what they had done. And when he made a well-intentioned attempt at it, it was too funny for me to react to. So the only solution available to me was one that had often happened when I worked with an uncooperative actor who wouldn't stick around for offstage lines on my close-up. I said my own lines to a blank wall while Kisuna, the script girl, read the lines of the entities.

*   *   *

Later that night, after shooting, some of the crew remained for the promised session with Kevin.

I checked with the teamsters out on the road—the guys who drive the trucks carrying all the gear—inviting them also. Most of them declined with that "thank you, but we think it's weird" expression on their faces.

Then, just as the session was about to begin, Sachi and Simo came in with a bundle of white fluff curled in a basket, blinking its jet-black eyes and wagging its tail. He was an American Eskimo puppy, the likes of which I had admired in a house where we shot. Simo was giving it to me as a late Christmas present. The little puppy brought everyone comfortably down to earth and the woman whose house we were shooting in insisted on holding him because his relaxed energy was so calming.

Sachi had a date, but Simo stayed to watch the session.

The crew took comfortable places along the walls and on the floor of the living room at Kevin's feet. There was a hushed respect about them, as though they knew they were in the presence of a phenomenon that they acknowledged but couldn't quite understand. I could feel them look to me as a common leveler. They were seeing me in my element—the element that had motivated me to write the book and the script. They knew I was one of them, but I also had become part of the "other world," as they put it.

I sat next to Kevin. Kisuna sat a few people away from me to my right. Tina sat on the couch across the room next to Jach Pursel, who seemed to be enjoying the techniques of another trance channeler. I had felt Jach's energy balancing the set during the shooting that day, as some of the more astonished members of the crew were attempting to sustain their equilibrium during the time the entities were using Kevin's body.

Cynthia, the owner of the house, held Shinook on

her lap. Some crew members were drinking, some smoking, some simply there to go along with the spiritual ride.

Kevin explained the phenomenon of trance channeling in a little more detail than we had had time to outline in the screenplay. The crew asked him what was appropriate to inquire about. He said most anything. While acknowledging the presence of Shinook, Kevin thought it was as good a time as any to explain that animals reincarnate, too, but always as animals. They belong to a collective soul group and are here with us humans on earth for karmic reasons which could easily have to do with experiences we had with them in lifetimes past. I, by the way, felt such feelings for Shinook the moment I laid eyes on him.

So Brad, his camera crew, a few teamsters who had elected to come, and most of the rest of the production crew sat respectfully silent as Kevin went into trance once again for our benefit.

When Tom came through, several people asked about past lives either with their children or people they were involved with.

One man asked if he had had a lifetime as an American Indian. Another woman asked if her son was her soul mate.

Then something happened that was personally revealing for all of us.

Kisuna raised her hand, brushing her blond hair from her eyes and sitting in the lotus position as she talked.

"Excuse me," she began, "but I find myself involved with a very uncomfortable relationship on the set."

We all looked around uneasily, some no doubt wondering whom she meant. She rapidly made that clear.

"I desperately need clarification as to why Tina is acting the way she is toward me. Her attitude is very difficult for me to work with."

Tears streamed down Kisuna's face. She choked slightly before going on. "I realize in many ways," she continued, "that it is inappropriate for me to bring up publicly, but I need some help because I am making more mistakes than usual in my work and I would like to settle it with her with love." She hesitated. "Tina?"

Everyone's attention immediately shifted over to Tina, who was chatting sotto voce with her neighbor as though she took neither Kisuna nor the spiritual session very seriously. She stopped when she was directly addressed and suddenly looked acutely embarrassed—the more surprising because she was usually so well in control of herself.

"Please, Tina," Kisuna was saying, "I would really like to know why you are doing this to me."

I had never seen such an intimate movie-set problem made public like this before.

Kisuna was laying out all her feelings in front of the crew, and because of her honesty, Tina was in a position of public scrutiny. I felt deeply for both women.

But Tina said nothing.

"Could we talk?" asked Kisuna.

Tina, understandably very uncomfortable, looked over at her. "We have nothing to talk about," she then said. "I don't know what you're talking about."

Kisuna looked to Tom for direction.

Tom responded. He sat up.

"Please," he began as the room full of people watched, riveted. "Would you, Tina, please come forward?"

Tina remained in her seat. I felt slightly sorry for her. Public airing is never easy for anybody.

Tom turned to Kisuna. "Would you stand and come forward, please?"

Kisuna stood up. She walked to the center of the room in front of Tom.

"Tina," repeated Tom. "Would you please come forward?"

Tina looked at me. I gently gestured she should do it. She shrugged and slowly stood up. Then she moved toward Kisuna.

"Now, ladies," said Tom. "Would you please embrace each other?"

Neither of them moved.

"Oh," said Kisuna, "I find this extremely difficult. But I will."

She raised her arms.

"Tina?" said Tom.

"No," said Tina.

Kisuna, her arms outstretched ready to embrace Tina, found herself being stared down by a defiant look.

"It would," said Tom, "be a way of starting to resolve this conflict. Perhaps if you just looked at each other and mentioned the word *love.*"

"No, I can't," said Tina.

At that moment Kisuna embraced her—but Tina's arms remained at her sides. I was shocked. I had not realized their relationship had deteriorated so badly.

Kisuna finally dropped her arms, her attempt at reconciliation thwarted. Tina quietly turned around and returned to her seat.

Tom said nothing. It was clear that even spiritual entities could contribute only so much to solving human problems. After that it was up to the people themselves.

Kisuna returned to her place. There was nothing more to be said. After an awkward moment of acknowledged conflict, Yudi Bennet, our female assistant director, spoke up.

"I would like to know, Mr. McPherson, who is doing the stealing in this company. As we know, quite a few prop items necessary to filming are missing, and is there anything I can do to stop it?"

Tom was on the spot. It is karmically an invasion of privacy to expose someone from a perspective more knowing than our own.

"It is up to the persons involved to decide whether they will continue," he said. "Let me say, though, that nothing will seriously prevent the shooting of this film from continuing. You are all together on this venture because you have been together before. You are involved with innovative communication and you will accomplish it. More than that, the goal of the project is your own individual growth. The project will serve as a catalyst for that growth. Be aware of yourselves during the shooting and you will understand what we mean."

All other questions seemed to pale in the wake of this general reassurance and the personal promise implied. Each of us secretly knew that every job we took was another advance toward self-knowledge. This was the lesson for Tina and Kisuna and for all the rest of us observing their growth.

This was the lesson for all of us who were so goal-oriented, ignoring completely that the process was just as important, that the real goal lay not in the end result but in how we achieved it.

Brad and the camera crew questioned Tom about what we could expect in Peru. Tom cautioned them to be careful of humidity in their lenses, that it would rain a great deal, and that power could be a problem if we had no backup system. The guys took notes. There were more technical questions, which Tom answered in a way that seemed to satisfy the crew, and then he ended by saying that the show would have a tremendous effect on the consciousness of the audience, that it would be controversial but it would allow people to think more freely about spiritual ridicule. Then he concluded by saying we were all together for a reason and this project would not be the last time. We were destined, he said, to work together not only because of our desire to be innovative, but because we had much to learn from one another. A warm shiver of understanding went through us. Each of us had known somewhere in our hearts that we had drawn ourselves to one another and that we had experienced only the first act of what that meant.

Chapter 16

*L*ater that night Simo and I talked about the dynamics on the set. The conflicts presenting themselves seemed to revolve around grappling with issues that related to the growing power of female energy. The chief characteristic of New Age Aquarian energy was the emergence of the yin (female) energy. The time had come for a balance between yin and yang—and in the adjustment of that balance many conflicts arose.

I looked at our production. I, a female, had motivated the entire project—experienced the spiritual search, written about it, and was now starring in the film about the book. Our first and second assistant directors were female (in positions traditionally held by males), our co-producer was a female, and most of the men on the show were either comfortable with the female sides of themselves or were being forced to allow it. But the most graphic conflicts were occurring not among the men on the set (which is usually the case), but among the women.

The New Age was addressing itself to leadership by women, which meant not only that men would be required to make a fundamental adjustment in relation to female leadership, but that women would also. The old traditional patriarchal dynamics were going to be replaced, not by matriarchal values but by equality between the two.

As I looked at the interplay between Tina and Kisuna, one thing seemed clear to me. Tina represented the male-oriented approach to professionalism. Getting the job done well was the high priority, not really stopping to smell the flowers. Kisuna was more introspective, viewing her femaleness as a priority just as important as the task set before her. She might take longer in accomplishing the job, but she wouldn't deny herself realization along the way.

Tina expressed her female side by lovingly baking cookies, cakes, and goodies for the crew which she placed in the makeup trailer every morning. She said it was nothing, that it didn't take long. But with her hours any amount of time she spent was time she could have used for herself and her family. Yet Kisuna was more of a feminist whose highest priority was to understand self so she could be more understanding of others.

The next day Kisuna called.

"Just wanted to say I'm leaving," she said.

I was stunned at how little I had understood the dynamics of my own set.

"You're leaving the show?" I asked.

"Yes," answered Kisuna.

"Why?"

"Because," she said, "I've not been doing a good job. Production and I both think it's best that I go."

I listened. "But what's really going on?" I asked.

Kisuna paused and sighed.

"Listen," she began. "I'm ready to go on to something more creative. Being a script supervisor is too left-brained and linear for me now. That's why I'm making mistakes. I admit it. My father was a director and early on he said I should do the same kind of more creative work."

I wondered if she was listening to her heart or the heart that her father had conditioned. Then she continued with how she felt about the set.

"There's a lack of honesty among the women," she said. "They're all covering their asses, like the men have taught them to do. And they're swirling in gossip. I mean, are we seeing ugly female traits coming out because many women have positions of power on this film?"

I said I thought a film set was really a mini-society and we'd probably be seeing a lot more of this kind of thing because of the power women were destined to come into. We talked about how we had been accustomed to defining ourselves by men and that now we were in uncharted territory because we were trying to define ourselves by ourselves.

"Some of our female traits," said Kisuna, "make me wonder how much of a feminist I really am. I'm having to deal with my sexuality all the time."

I thought that a bit confused, yet I listened to Kisuna carefully. Her outpouring held heavy implications. I thought of how I did or didn't use my own sexuality in the work environment. I decided it depended on whether I found someone attractive or not; otherwise I felt like one of the boys. I thought of my own brashness and abruptness when I became impatient with someone. I saw aspects of myself in how Kisuna described others. Then it occurred to me that Tina was a great teacher for all of us.

"Yes," said Kisuna. "I can see that," she said. "And I can see aspects of me in Tina too. I know we all attract the data to ourselves which best enables us to clear up our own issues. I know I've drawn Tina and Yudi to me. They are my teachers. I know that. They are a gift for my learning. But now I'm going to move on."

There was nothing more to be said. I felt an acceleration of realized growth in Kisuna and admired her rigorous self-analysis. It was painful, yet courageous. I wondered if I would have had the courage to expose my feelings and defects publicly, as she had done in the abortive attempt at reconciliation with Tina during the channeling session. I wondered if I would have felt as Tina had felt if someone had exposed me to my fellow workers.

"When I stood up," said Kisuna, "it may not have been politically wise, but that is the old male way of repressing emotions. I needed to be honest with what was bothering me. I have to deal with confronting my emotions or I may as well give up."

Kisuna and I talked for a long time. In the conversation I realized more fully than ever how important it was to understand that the work we cut out for ourselves acts as a classroom for our self-knowledge. If we had a job we hated, that in itself said something about what we thought of ourselves. And each work environment that we experienced was a microcosm of life itself. Each day of the week could be viewed as a mini-lifetime, at the end of which we could hope to say we had accomplished a bit more recognition of who we were, and simultaneously know better the identities of our fellow humans.

I had cause to be grateful to Tina and Kisuna as teachers for me, but they were amateurs compared to John Heard, who had now arrived from New York, ready to shoot, with a brand-new excrescence on the right side of his face—indicating certain unknown pressures had been sustained in New York.

When I needled him a little, asking what happened to his conviction that he'd rather sell hot dogs on the corner than interrupt the cleanup of his life in New York, he said New York was dirty, and reinforced negativity. My brains, intricately scrambled by now, made no attempt to understand what kind of teaching this must be that I had drawn to myself.

McPherson told me that John Heard needed a transformational experience. That there were other actors in the world, but *he* was ready for a breakthrough and that was why he knew he needed to return. So maybe he had drawn me to *him*?

I wondered who would transform whom first. And whether the breakthrough would be a crash "heard" around the world.

To work with John when the cameras rolled was sheer heaven. Sometimes I wished they'd roll all day long so that I could experience that clear, direct, laser-beam talent all the time. His eyes were honest. He never made a fake, uncentered move. And each take was different, exuding its own truth and total understanding. When things don't come out exactly the same way twice in a scene, you *know* the person you are playing with is really thinking it through each time. He was a miraculous actor.

So to watch his approach to life when not on camera was a lesson for me. Colin and I were to conclude later that John was rehearsing all the time that he was not actually shooting. And there wasn't an emotional reaction or a behavior pattern that he wasn't willing to try out. It was as though he put himself through the hoops of human diversity just in case he might come across something he could use in a part. He was the quintessential example of "acting out life," but with predetermined intent. He was quite unselfconscious about experimenting, and viewed the reactions of others simply as grist for his mill.

If the crew addressed him as "Mr. Heard" and requested that he step two paces to camera right for a focus lineup, he'd step two paces to the left. The crew would be nonplussed, and John would simply study their "nonplussedness" in case he wanted to use it later. There was a childlike quality to his trying out situations and discovering limits. But as a fellow actor who wished I had the guts to be that outrageous, I was onto him. And he knew it.

Still, the truth is that probably the quality most essential to good acting is that of sustaining the child in yourself, in the sense that children can and do lose themselves utterly in the delight of role playing. And sometimes, when a role is thrust upon them, they enter the drama just as thoroughly but not necessarily with joy.

Anne Jackson and I had long talks about it as we waited for the set to be lit. She was in her sixties, but, as in all really fine actors, there was this wonderful dichotomy of child and tough adult in her. We like to please the director and, of course, the audience, but when we are honest about it we are essentially attempting to extract loving approval from our parents. When you engage an actor in retrospective conversation about our craft and why we got into it in the first place, the parents always emerge somewhere as prime movers—either positive or negative.

I guess you could say that about all human beings, really, since we are formed and conditioned by the forces floating in the family. But acting makes it all right to use and work with the child within. Maybe the reason why all of us are a little bit star-struck is because this allows us a return to childhood from time to time, the audience joining the actors in a game of "let's pretend." And perhaps this is also the reason why society never really takes actors seriously. They are to be enjoyed as amusing and entertaining, and loved as reminders that innocence still prevails in a cynical world.

So, as John went through his antics, I think most of the crew secretly felt a grudging admiration that he could get away with it.

He paced alone between shots, unconcerned that he appeared to be a caged lion. He slobbered food down his face. He burped in the middle of quiet and told obscene stories at moments when dignity was required. He was undaunted in the expression of himself.

And he was continually attempting to punch holes in our script and in my spiritual beliefs. I loved every minute of it because it honed my way of communicating to a human being who did not find social amenities tolerable. He was not the type of person who would spare my feelings and let me have my "crazy weird beliefs." He cornered me—*now*—and said EXPLAIN. And I did. But he never once said it was crazy, because his own sensitivity demanded an open mind. And somewhere in his gut he knew better anyway. Of course he was also Catholic, which meant anything was possible.

But what impressed me the most was his power— again like that of a child who takes it for granted that absolutely anything is possible. When John left his trailer and walked onto the set, brave men and ballsy women shrank in anticipation that John might perhaps force them to confront something more about themselves they had not suspected was there.

We were now into a night-shooting week in the Malibu hills. That meant turning our sleep state around completely. We went to work at dark and shot until sunrise.

Colin had "given himself" a cold because of some career decisions he needed to make. Kevin had gone home and Jach Pursel hung around for a while, until the boredom of the long waits involved in movie-making got to him too.

Glumly I sat in my trailer, waiting to be called, while outside it was alternately freezing or raining. The only conversation to have in the wee hours was small talk. "What did you eat for dinner last night?" "I think this makeup is more flattering, don't you?" "Wonder what so-and-so is going to do about the way her *friend* spends so much time with such-and-such . . ." and on and on. It drove me crazy in the makeup trailer, so I preferred to wait alone.

Also I was having a hard time resisting what Tina baked each day. Since Kisuna had left, Tina's treats for the crew had tripled. And, as everyone knows, food is also a great anodyne for boredom.

"Have the willingness to align yourself with inner beingness," I said to myself loftily.

I was trying, but maybe my inner being was a fat lady.

"Insist on being yourself, whatever it is," I continued.

"Allow people to love you. Learn to accept love," I said.

Yes, I was trying. But the pain of looking at oneself honestly was deep. I was seeing so much of my intolerance and impatience, and in that light why should I completely accept love from others when I thought *them* defective for feeling the way *I* did?

I wondered if I had been an overachiever in my earlier years *because* I was unconsciously avoiding the quest for myself. Had the drive for success simply been a way of diverting attention from the real priority of self-focus? Or had I become successful precisely so that I *could* look at myself. I was beginning to redefine the meaning of success anyway. I had seen so many people achieve stardom, fame, and material wealth, only to feel so undeserving that they became suicidal. That could have happened to me had I not understood that a spiritual dimension was as much a part of my identity as my mind and body. That understanding had saved my life, because it enabled me to feel deserving of everything I had created for myself.

Now, as I sat in my trailer, I thought of the film I was making. I hated night shooting. I hated dumb conversation. I hated to be cold. And I hated my inability to sleep during the day. Some spiritually evolved person I was. I was just uncomfortable all the way around because I was seeing so much more of me than I ever had.

I would try to meditate in my trailer to make contact with my higher self. It was always there.

"What is wrong with me?" I would ask it.

"You are impatient with time and too perfectionistic with those issues you believe are important."

"Well," I'd answer. "Perfection is part of my job."

"No," it would say. "Perfection is an addiction to the past."

An addiction to the past? Oh, yes, I could see that. How would I know something was perfect if I didn't compare it to what went before? *Okay.*

"Stay aligned with me," my higher self would suggest. "I will never fail you, because I am aligned with God."

Sometimes tears would come to my eyes with the beauty of realization, and sometimes I would decide not to listen to what my higher self was saying at all.

Colin dropped in late one night. "How's it going?" he asked, sniffling from his cold.

"Lousy," I answered.

Colin blew his nose and smiled. "Well, it's all in the playing, ya know."

I threw a combat boot at him.

The morning after our first night shoot I returned to my apartment in Malibu and fell into bed at 7:00 A.M. I turned on my sound machine and hoped to sleep until noon. At 7:30 the telephone rang. It was a friend of my housekeeper's, looking for her. I said she wasn't in, but she continued to call, saying each time it was an emergency.

The doorbell rang. There was no one but me to answer it. I let it ring, long and sustained, stubbornly resisting my desire to get up and see what it was. I should have answered it. I worried about who it might have been for the rest of the morning.

I dragged myself to work at 5:00 P.M., worked all night, and fell into bed again the next morning at 7:00.

I awoke at 8:30 to pounding right under my bedroom. The workmen had come to repair my pilings. In a fury I walked outside and peered over the balcony.

"What the hell are you doing?" I asked gracefully.

"I'm fixing the piling," said the workman cheerily.

"Well, can you come back later? I've been working all night."

He looked up smiling. "Could I just do a couple more nails?"

"What should I do?" I pleaded. "What can I say that would make you understand how much I hate it that you are here?"

"Thank you," he said nicely. "I won't be long."

I walked back to my bedroom. And then I blew. I slammed the door so hard that the rafters shook. Then I opened it and slammed it again. The doves in their hallway cage stopped cooing. I raced to the front door and opened it and slammed it so strongly that plaster fell from the ceiling. I opened it again and slammed it again. I opened and slammed about five times. I wanted to wake up my tenants in case the pounding hadn't.

Then suddenly I saw a man come into my courtyard and ascend my stairs.

"Is something wrong?" he asked.

"Of course there is," I shouted. "I can't sleep. So what can you do about it?"

"Well," he smiled sweetly, "I'm a Jehovah's Witness. I'd like to be of service in introducing God to you."

That was all I needed. I had had about as much of God as I could take and it wasn't helping me one bit.

"You know something," I said. "I'm sure Michael Jackson gets more out of your help team than I ever will."

I was angry because I thought he knew who I was and what I wrote about.

He looked at me quizzically.

"Well," he said. "I was by here yesterday and you weren't home. If you would give me your name I'd send you some of our literature in the mail and not disturb you. It looks like you could benefit from what we have to offer."

He didn't know who I was? That made me even madder. I slammed the door in his face and screamed, "Thank you!"

Wonderful, I thought. Oh my God, have I got a long way to go.

I never went back to sleep. I sat down and thought about my violence whenever I was working and couldn't sleep. I remembered the chair I threw against the wall of a hotel in Washington, D.C., because the hotel operator had ignored my "do not disturb" instructions.

I had ripped the phone out of the wall in a Houston hotel on *Terms of Endearment* when a power mower went on at 6:00 in the morning outside my window.

I remembered my plot to put sand into the Australian construction equipment because the rumbling crash of builders at work began every morning at 6:00 when I was on tour there.

I never had that reaction when I wasn't working. But if my work sleep was violated, I became violent. That was the behavior of an overachiever, all right. That was a person who didn't have the confidence to trust that all things were happening for a reason.

In fact it became a joke with people who worked with me. Whenever I was on tour we could depend on some kind of construction work to begin early in the morning, regardless of what city we were playing.

Of course my question was: Why did I draw that to myself? And of course the answer was not far behind: to develop patience and tolerance. I created the circumstances in which to accomplish this.

Stan finally asked me why I looked so tired. I gave him a quick noise-in-the-morning rundown.

He chortled, sat back, and sipped coffee from a Styrofoam cup.

"So what's new in the real world, Stan?" I asked.

"Well," he said, "ABC is going to do *War and Remembrance*. Thirty hours of Hitler and concentration camps. Hitler's become the biggest star in Hollywood. He certainly has the most work."

"Wow," I said. "We just can't figure out what that monster meant to the human race, can we?"

"He obviously means a lot of employment," said Stan, not wanting to get metaphysically serious.

"Well," I went on, "the sooner we come to grips with the fact that Hitler was a teacher for all of us, the better off we'll be."

"Nobody wants to hear that, Shirley," said Stan.

"You mean we all still need someone to blame instead of taking the responsibility that each one of us participated somehow?"

Stan looked at me with those kindly, experienced eyes.

"Who knows?" he said, with the tact that proves he always was and always will be a survivor. "Anyway," he continued, "ABC is committed to doing quality television now. So they're doing fourteen hours of *Amerika*."

"What's that?" I asked.

"You know," he answered. "It's the story of the Russian takeover of America. I said to Brandon: 'Are you *that* desperate for quality entertainment?' "

I laughed, trying to picture how doing fourteen hours of the Russians conquering America could possibly contribute to the peace process in the world.

"Well," said Stan, "if I had to choose between fighting the Russians and being forced to watch the series, I guess I'd take the series."

I stood up. "Yeah, Stan," I said. "Let's go get some

junk food." If I was going to be working, depressed, tired, and pissed off, I might as well go the whole hog and do it all with junk food.

On the way to the catering wagon, our company manager, Dean O'Brien, stopped me.

"Listen, Shirley," he said, "you know you will be the prime target for any kidnapping in Peru. So we are going to make sure there's extra police protection. Those guerrillas could make a fortune holding you for ransom from ABC."

I thought for a moment and answered him. "No, Dean. I don't think so. I'm too responsible. I wouldn't have the guts to go wandering off into the hills by myself. But John Heard—now there's your kidnappee. He's liable to stroll out into those mountains with a beer just lookin' to get kidnapped so he could tell 'em to hold out for more money from ABC. Or maybe he'd want to know how it feels to be kidnapped. Or maybe he'd want to figure out what the kidnappers felt like . . ." I started to laugh. Stan started to laugh. And pretty soon we were hysterical, swapping pictures of what John would do with the kidnappers.

"Can you see The Shining Path trying to cope with him?" Stan sputtered. "He'd drive them bananas!"

"Yeah," I said with exhausted admiration, and feeling a whole lot better. "It's people like John who could really confuse the terrorists. He's fearless, because even *he* doesn't know what he's going to do next."

The night shooting continued. The crew slogged through mud and rain while John and I sat, more or less comfortably, in a truck that was being towed along for the scene, saying our lines and trying to keep warm. A kind of trancelike perseverance prevailed. John and I didn't talk much in between shots. Melissa had arrived and he had enough on his mind. Yet I never ceased to be astonished at how he snapped into character when the cameras rolled. I wondered if he felt the same admiration for me, especially since the scene we were shooting involved my reaction to an extraterrestrial driving the truck while John's character (David) was asleep at the wheel. Once when Butler yelled, "Cut," John opened his eyes, looked at me, and said, "Good." Whether he meant because it was the end of the scene or not, I took it to mean I must have been great. Especially since his eyes had been closed . . .

John often talked about being embarrassed that he was posing as a "movie" actor. After the night-shooting period finished, we went immediately into shooting some of the heaviest metaphysical dialogue. This scene took place in daylight (thank God) on the beach.

"I don't like this mooo-vie 'acting,' " said John in his inimitable manner.

"Well, what do you like better?" I asked, setting him up completely.

"I'm an unknown, thin, *stage* actor," he stated. "I don't like movies."

At that moment the assistant director called for quiet because John's close-up was lit and ready. He had a two-page monologue scene about God and reincarnation. He had already shot the master, so I had seen him play it. He had toyed casually with sand and seashells as he intermittently looked out to sea and delivered some of the most difficult lines any actor ever had to play.

The cameras rolled. Butler yelled, "Action." John went into his casually profound attitude, and suddenly in the distance I heard an airplane. I saw John hear it too. His face began to flush crimson. The plane came closer, and of course the sound of it was more and more disruptive. No one wanted to say "cut" because John had made it clear that was never to happen unless *he* said so. So we just kept rolling. Finally the plane was so loud and John's face was so flushed with anger that he couldn't go on. He blew. He threw up his arms.

"What the fuck kind of plane is that," he shrieked, "that will go overhead on my fucking close-up! I mean, man, THIS IS MY CLOSE-UP!"

Very understandable. But my sides ached from holding in the laughter. John could not have been more upset. He bolted from the sand and went for the first thing he could kick that wasn't human. It happened to be an apple crate used to prop up chairs, lamps, and short actors. John smashed his foot into the apple box and withdrew it. Hopping around on one foot he went on a rampage around the set. The crew moved cautiously back and all I could think of was how much he didn't care about "mooo-vies."

His anger spent, the plane droning away in the distance, John came back to his mark and sat down.

"Sorry, everybody," he said calmly. "I was being ridiculous. Can we go again?"

We went again. The crew, consummate professionals that they are, began to regroup.

"All right, Mr. Heard," said Brad. "Camera is ready anytime you are, sir."

John went again and no one was the worse for wear.

In the meantime John had told me that a buddy of his had said that Christ had talked about reincarnation in the Bible. When I asked where I could find it he didn't know. So, with the weekend coming up, I decided to find it.

I hadn't a clue where to look. So I did an experiment with myself. I went into a quick silent meditation, got in touch with my higher self, and said, "Where can I find a reference by Christ to reincarnation in the Bible?"

The answer came back: "Most of the references have been discarded, but several still remain. You will find it in the book of Matthew."

I heard the answer in clear English and it was so definitive I was startled. I went to my bookshelf and pulled out a Gideon Bible.

I turned to Matthew. The page fell open to Matthew 16, verse 13. Jesus is talking to his disciples. He asks them: "Whom do people say that I, the Son of man, am?"

The disciples answer, "Some say that you are John the Baptist, some say Elias, and others say Jeremias or one of the prophets."

Evidently reincarnation was such an accepted belief at the time that it was a matter of simple discussion—not "whether," but "who?"

Jesus then asks, "But whom do you say I am?"

Simon Peter goes on to answer that Jesus is the Son of the living God. Jesus confirms that, and then charges his disciples to tell no one that he is Jesus the Christ.

In Chapter 17 there is the description of the transfiguration. Jesus takes Peter and the two brothers James and John to a high mountain. Jesus is transfigured before them; his face shines like the sun and his raiment is white as the light. Then Moses and Elias appear before them, talking with Jesus. A bright cloud overshadows them and a voice speaks from the cloud, saying, "This is my beloved Son, in whom I am well pleased; hear ye him."

When the disciples hear that, they fall on their faces, frightened. Jesus touches them, tells them to rise and not be afraid. When they lift their faces, Moses and Elias are gone.

Jesus charges them to tell no one what they have seen until he has risen again from the dead.

The disciples then ask why the scribes had said that Elias must come first and restore all things.

Jesus answers, "But Elias has come already and they did not know him, but have done unto him whatsoever they listed. Likewise shall I suffer."

The disciples understand that he is speaking of John the Baptist.

*   *   *

As I read these verses in Matthew, it was clear to me that Jesus and his disciples were talking about reincarnation. They were saying that John the Baptist had lived in a previous incarnation as Elias. And that Jesus would suffer a fate similar to that of both.

I spent most of the weekend rereading parts of the Bible, once again reminded of what a metaphysical document it really is, each teaching referring to the Kingdom of Heaven existing within each one of us, and a New Age of recognition coming that would attest to that.

I presented the Bible material I had found to John Heard and in fact worked it into one of his scenes. As a serious, but confused, Catholic, he studied it. There were moments when he seemed to put together what he was required to say as an actor with his own religious beliefs. The teachings were not that far apart, except that the Church insisted on his believing in evil and Hell. Metaphysics taught that we create our own Hell inside of us, depending upon our perceptions of reality. John saw that, but was not quite ready to take complete responsibility for his life. In fact he gave himself a prominent artistic fever blister on his chin which couldn't be covered with makeup.

"That'll serve ABC right," he said.

During his close-ups I had to chase his chin with the shadow of my hat so the three-dimensional temperamental chin volcano wouldn't be seen by the audience.

In between shots I could see John grappling with the issues we were addressing in the show. A really fine actor has to find a way to integrate foreign points of view into his belief system or it will look false on the screen. He was so good with the material that I finally told him that he really understood it whether he realized it or not In fact, I said it was material we all *know* is true. We just decide how much skepticism we will enact as we play our roles in life.

Because he was acting out his life, he understood what I said.

Chapter 17

I, in the meantime, was having my own problems with metaphysical truth. And it had to do with being a woman.

I had always been comfortable with my masculine energy, being the kind of woman who essentially knew what I wanted and how to go about achieving it. But now I had come to the point in my life where the feminine half of me needed as much attention and expression.

I didn't trust my soft, nurturing, surrendering side enough. I felt I had to make things happen actively and aggressively. The hidden inevitabilities were not going to manifest, in my masculine view, unless *I* saw to it that they did.

Perhaps that was the reason I was again having trouble sleeping. One needs to trust the night energy in order to sleep well. The night energy is feminine energy. It is the energy of relinquishing control, the energy of trusting and believing. And I was having trouble doing that.

As usual in my life, when I'm in trouble something

always happens synchronistically to help me out of it. This time it came in the form of a Russian icon.

I have always been aware of my attachment to things Russian—stemming, I believe, from several personally important Russian incarnations. Even today when I hear Russian music, or see the Russian language or hear it spoken, I am moved with some deep stirring. It happens every time. And it has been with me since I was a child.

Some time before I felt the unease with my yin energy I had encountered a young woman, a designer from San Francisco. I had met her through Natalia Makarova, the Russian ballerina who defected, and the young lady had designed a dress for me. Since that time she had called periodically to tell me how she was doing. Now she called me again, with interesting news.

"Shirley," she said, "I have something I must tell you about. I don't know why I feel it but I know it's important for you."

I listened as she explained the following:

She had been extremely depressed, physically ill and desperate. In the hospital the doctors had not held out much hope of curing her bleeding uterus. But a friend of hers had brought her a photograph of one of the oldest Russian icons in the world. It was a picture of Mary holding the baby Jesus. The icon itself was called Iverskaya and had been found in an old Turkish monastery on the mountain Alfone. She had placed the photograph of the icon on her abdomen and overnight the bleeding stopped. The doctors couldn't understand it, but sent her home.

The original icon had quite a history. It was said that a Turkish soldier, in an antireligious rage, had attempted to slash the icon with his sword. He stopped immediately because drops of blood oozed from the painting. Legend has it that the soldier was so ashamed he became a monk and lived in the monastery with the icon for the rest of his life.

Iverskaya was now in the possession of a monk

named José, who lived in Canada. Apparently, when José visited Mount Alfone the monks in the monastery recognized him as the rightful guardian of Iverskaya and put him in charge of her. José now travels with her to people who need healing. My friend had only a photograph of the icon, but even that, she said, was effective in healing.

"I just feel so compelled to tell you about it, Shirley," she said to me. "May I bring it over? I think you should see it."

I invited her over. Why I would be interested in an icon of Mary holding Jesus, I didn't know. But some small voice within me told me it related to the unfolding of my feminine energy.

The young lady arrived with the photograph of the icon an hour later. She extracted it from a brocade case and I looked at it. It was five inches square.

Mary was the predominant figure, dressed in a maroon and white robe. She held the baby Jesus in her arms. Jesus held a scroll in his left hand which contained his future teachings. There were Russian symbols above the halos of Jesus and Mary.

As I looked at the photograph I had the strangest feeling, as though I knew this icon. Then I looked more closely. Drops of oil were oozing from the photograph onto the frame that enclosed it! And there was a tuft of cotton under the frame at the bottom to catch the oil.

"For heaven's sake, what is this?" I asked.

"Oh," my friend answered, "it's been giving holy oil ever since I got this photograph."

"What do you mean?"

"Well," she went on, "whenever I am in need of help or healing I ask Mary for help and she gives holy oil."

She stopped and looked at it for a moment. Then she sighed.

"I used to take the photograph out of the frame, but

it's been stuck for four months or so. I've tried everything. It's as though she wants to stay in there."

Casually and gently I turned the frame on its back. It was a simple slip-out frame. For some reason I thought I might as well attempt to extract the photograph. Very gently I pushed the cardboard frame on the back. It came loose easily. I pushed until the photograph came out of the frame all the way.

"I can't believe this," she said. "I have *tried*. My friends have tried. We thought it was stuck by some strange power, because it wouldn't come loose."

I just held the photograph. It actually tingled in my hand. Then tiny drops of oil began to ooze from the photograph. I touched them. They slid under my finger. My hand holding the photograph was warm with a burning glow. My friend stared at me.

"You are supposed to have this," she said finally. "She is meant to be with you now."

I could feel that she was right.

"But this is yours," I said. "And I don't even know why I should have her."

"Because," she said, "you need her. You're supposed to, that's all." She left quietly and quickly, leaving the Iverskaya photograph with me.

And I did know why I should have her.

I took her into my bedroom and lay down with the icon on my chest. Instantly I felt a warm tingling glow through my heart.

Then I realized what I was supposed to learn from her. It was almost as though she were talking to me. I needed to open up my heart center. I needed to feel more compassion for myself and others. If I was going to progress with my spiritual growth, I was going to need to stop all the worrying and perfectionistic concern and just allow myself and others *to be*.

The world was so difficult to live in. There was so much harsh and volatile interaction occurring everywhere, as though millions of people, including myself, had decided to clear up their karmic debris before the New Age arrived. Or maybe the cleaning up was what would actually herald the New Age.

It was one thing to be metaphysically sophisticated; to know all the techniques and rhetoric and meditational processes. But quite another to relate to the world with simple love in your heart. That, ultimately, was the state of being that metaphysics and spiritual knowledge helped you attain. Love was the goal. Love was the process.

Study and intellectual spiritual pursuit were not where the wisdom of love resided.

Lazaris and Ambres and John and McPherson were right. I needed to own my inner love wisdom if I was to finish what I came in to do in this lifetime. When I touched that, I would be able to sleep. I wouldn't be angered and I would understand that everything I drew to me in my life was simply to learn the multiple manifestations of love that blossomed from learning to love one's self.

So I kept the Mary icon with me. She slept on my bedside table at night and watched over me. I didn't talk to her out loud, as my friend said she did, but I did have a silent inner dialogue about the nature of being a woman.

Then I remembered that I had visited a spiritual medium who contacted disembodied spiritual guides through a table that tipped and leaned and moved. The medium's name is Adele Tinning. She lives in San Diego, is about seventy-nine years old, is as kindly as anyone I've ever known, and quite simply has incredible mediumistic talent.

"It is God's talent," she will tell you, "not my talent. And maybe that's true of everyone's talent."

Anyway, Adele works with a table which is, combined with her energy, imbued somehow with the ability to spell out messages. One tip is *no*. Three tips, *yes*. A gentle rock of two is *maybe*. To spell out words it tips quickly in rhythm, stopping at the required letter in the alphabet countdown. The table hovers in the air and actually leans up on one leg. I and others have tried physically to bring the table back to the ground, but when the entity controlling it wants it in the air, it stays there.

When one gets past the physical phenomenon of the table, the implications are enormous. It tips out the spelling of messages coming from guides who need to use the table as a medium of communication.

At one of these "table-tipping" sessions Colin and I had asked who our primary spiritual guides were. The table had spelled out my guide as M-A-R-Y but I had never paid much attention to that until now. Could it be that Mary had worked her way into guiding me via a Russian icon? As far as my life was concerned, stranger things had happened.

I found myself reading all the metaphysical material on Mary that I could find. How she had chosen and been chosen to be the mother of Jesus, and the training she had gone through even prior to incarnating. And all the while I found myself learning more and more about women: what our roles really are, what monumental contributions we have been prevented from making, and how, if the world is to survive, the equality of women and of feminine leadership with men is essential. The nurturing, the resilient strength, the sensitive pragmatism, the intuitive knowledge, the respect for allowing the surrender to the God energy, the balancing of love and will, and the love for all life were all feminine traits that were in dire need of manifestation.

All of us in feminine bodies this time around were charged with living up to the choice we had made. The age of feminine energy was upon us. It was not strident or aggressive or violent or angry. It was comfortable, nurturing, balanced, and knowledgeable. It was the

Goddess-energy, the energy from which all is born. It was the energy of dominion, not domination. It was the energy of transmutation. It was the energy of service, and it stretched into uncharted territories. We would have to make our own map and lay claim to its unlimited boundaries. It would be necessary to drop away much of the past: the weary attachment to possessions, to security, to subservience. Women had been preparing for their full role for centuries, and we could now see our female identity serving that preparation. We were ready to dream and finally to live the dream. We had at last given ourselves permission to live our lives fully.

The domination of masculine energy represented the Old Age, the old way of operating. We had seen that male domination and female submission as a way of life had brought us to the brink of ruin. The dominion of yin energy was built on loving, nurturing—the New Age energy with roots deep in the very ancient worship of the mother-image, the Goddess aspect of the God-force.

Traditionally, the dialectic of divinity began with the Mother-Goddess; that being which created and gave birth. With all life there was first the attachment to mother. Then the rebellion against mother. After that came the attachment to and rebellion against father. But the initial force was feminine. Spirituality opened the feminine energy latent in all of us, male as well as female. And women were the trailblazers who would lay down a foundation for spiritual inspiration.

Slowly, as I integrated the spiritual meaning of my own feminine energy, I began to feel better.

Bella called. She asked how Anne Jackson was doing portraying the real McCoy. I said, "Better." She said, "Impossible." Then she told me that a friend of hers had been to Lazaris and had been impressed by the accuracy of his evaluation of her life.

"So listen," said Bella, "what do you know about this Lazaris?"

"I know he's good, Bellitchka," I said.

Long silence.

"He's one of the spirits, right?"

"Right."

"From the other world?"

"From the other world."

"And you go to him?"

"Yes, I go to him."

More long silence.

"Have you seen him lately?" she asked.

"Well," I said, "I see him whenever Jach Pursel is in Los Angeles, and sometimes Colin and I go up to San Francisco, where he lives."

"The spirit lives in San Francisco?"

"No, Bella. Jach, the medium, lives in San Francisco. The spirit lives in the ethers."

"The ethers?"

"Yes, the ethers are our natural habitat, not the earth."

"Oh, God," she said. "Please don't talk to me that way."

"Well, I was just trying to tell you where Lazaris lives."

Long silence.

"What was he before he was a spirit?" she asked.

Oh, brother, I thought. This is going to be good.

"Well," I began, "he's never been physical."

I heard Bella gasp.

"Never been physical? Well, he's a person, isn't he?"

"No, Bella. He's energy . . . soul energy. You and I are soul energy, too, but we are expressing through bodies at this time. Lazaris has never expressed through a body."

Long pause.

"Oh, my God," she said finally.

"Well, yes," I agreed. "We are all part of God. Or, as Lazaris would say, we are all part of God-Goddess All There Is."

"Uh huh," she answered.

"See?" I went on. "He's a feminist. He says that the feminine energy is the New Age of leadership."

"I like him," said Bella.

Another long silence.

"So?" I asked.

"So," she answered. "I'm thinking of running for Congress from Westchester."

I thought a moment. "Oh," I said, "so you want me to ask him if you'll win?"

There was a short but pregnant pause. "Yes," she said. "If you say so."

"No," I said. "*You* have to say so."

"Okay," she answered, "I say so."

"So you want me to ask him if you should run and whether you'll win?"

"Right. Okay."

"Okay."

"Goodbye."

"No, wait a minute," I said. "It's too bad you didn't do this a few years ago. It would have made a great scene in the movie."

"Yeah," she said. "You'll use it someday, in something. You always do."

"I do, don't I?"

"Yes. But that's okay."

"Yeah," I said. "You're a great character."

"So are you."

"We've both chosen great parts to play this time around, don't you think?"

She thought a minute. "All I care about is whether my part is a winner or a loser."

"That's not all you care about and you know it."

"I know it. But I'm a loser in your movie. I don't want to be one again."

"Okay, Bellitchka, I'll ask."

"But you know?" she said. "I want to help people so much that it doesn't really matter if I lose again. It's worth the risk. That's progress, isn't it?"

"You bet," I said. "With that attitude you might even win."

"Okay, ask."

"I'll ask."

"Goodbye."

"Goodbye."

And so the next time I talked with Lazaris, I asked him about Bella's race. He was very clear and very strong.

"She shouldn't do it," he said. "It would take a tremendous emotional toll and besides, she would lose."

I reported the news to Bella.

"What does he know?" she said. "He's never had a body."

Chapter 18

The last week before departure for Peru was spent shooting ten hours a day in a mineral bath.

The scene was my out-of-body experience, and the special-effects camera work was tedious and intricate. The camera began a five-minute scene high above the set and slowly swooped down, swung around, and moved into my face until it was shooting one inch away from my eyeball. I couldn't move my head or even blink. I didn't tell anyone that I had once fainted right out of the optometrist's chair when I was fitted for contact lenses. So this scene was not a piece of cake for me.

John and I were shriveled prunes at the end of each day in the mineral bath. It happened to be the week that *Peter the Great* and *Sins* were on. So I'd go home exhausted at the end of every day, eat cookies, cake, and chocolate, and watch both shows at the same time. In between Joan Collins and Peter the Russian tyrant I burned out watching the news. The Philippine elections were violent, the Haitian revolt was violent, the space shuttle *Challenger* explosion was violent, and the terrorism in the Middle East was violent. Two more of my friends died of AIDS and there was an earthquake out in the Pacific. I ate more cookies.

The tides were inordinately high along the California coast, and because I was leaving for Peru, I decided to pack some of my things and move them into town. I wondered if I was projecting disaster by being afraid. The hell with it. There were certain things I absolutely would not want to lose.

Ah! Now I found myself sifting through what was important to me and what wasn't.

I knew that the more I gave away, the more I'd draw in. I thought about divesting myself of *all* attachments, wondering what it would be like to live that way. Wouldn't it be easier to have "only" seven outfits to pick from every day? One for each day? Why did I derive such pleasure from possessions anyway? Well, for one thing, they were really great memory trips. Did that make them, as some psychiatrists suggested, just substitutes for love?

So the night before I left for Peru I sat and meditated. I felt myself get in touch with my higher self. It spoke to me in words, as it always did. Because I was in alignment the voice was clear and articulate. It told me that I was in the process of transmuting my old energy, that I was beginning to see I could take control of my destiny in every way by transmuting from passive to active. My work would not only be person to person now, but person to humanity. It was now important for me to take complete responsibility and to be aware of what was going on around me, but not afraid. It said I was evaluating and sifting through my "pasts," and that that was what the evacuation of my possessions was all about.

I recognized and acknowledged that I had prepared for our trip to Peru for a very long time; that the first time I went I had decided to use that trip as a vision quest and knew then that I would write the book that would become a film that would take me back again.

My higher self told me it was necessary to shoot in Peru because of the energy there, that the crew was going along on my quest, invited and motivated by me, and moreover that they would go through subtle but profound changes; and that the real trip would be between takes, and inside of each person.

Each of us, it said, would use Peru to grow internally. It would be difficult but awe-inspiring, and we would learn that the process is more important than the goal. I asked H.S. whether we'd see UFOs. It said that was unimportant but would depend on the collective consciousness of the crew, that their individual growth was more significant than seeing UFOs. But I asked again: What would it serve if UFOs were recorded and the crew freaked out? H.S. replied that some were ready to see them, but many were not, and that the collective consciousness could progress only as fast as its slower members.

It said we would feel strange and yet familiar sensations on some of the locations; that some would have an Atlantean vibration, which carries with it a beautiful, sad longing. Others would have Lemurian vibrations, which were more tranquil and peaceful.

It confirmed what McPherson and John had said: that we should be careful of humidity in the camera equipment and make certain that security was tight.

And finally I asked H.S. about what was going on in the world. It said the reason the time seemed so negative was because tragedy had taken on a more personal quality. The crime we were experiencing was more perverted than ever before. It would continue in that vein. Tragedy wasn't a mass event now. It was a personal event because it was necessary for us to see that each human life has value. It said even the pain I was feeling in my body was a reminder that someone somewhere was suffering all the time, and what good was spiritual knowledge unless it helped to ease the pain of being in the body?

Finally my higher self reassured me with this statement: "The human beings alive in the world today will learn that they can preserve the beautiful world they have created for themselves—or that they believe 'God' has created for them. It makes no difference. There are many paths to completion. And the point of being alive in the body is to emulate 'God.' That is achievable. That is the New Age."

With that assessment of the future I fell off to sleep, and the next morning we were off to Peru.

But first, several members of the crew had expressed concern about the martial law declared in Peru. In fact some of the guys didn't want to go. So Stan called a meeting and announced that he had spoken to the U.S. State Department and to our ambassador. They said that martial law, The Shining Path, and terrorism were all nothing compared to the problem of pickpockets.

So, as Colin and I sat together on the Aeroperu flight, we chatted about how we had created a dream fiction for ourselves. We dozed, we read, we talked, ate, slept, read some more, ate again. John, sitting behind us, leaned over at 35,000 feet and handed me a note that said: *From the desk of God. Happiness is landing.*

We arrived at 3:00 A.M. Peruvian time. Stepping off the plane I remembered my first arrival years before and how alone yet expectant I had felt.

Now, we were met by representatives of the Alan Garcia government who told us that we had permits to be escorted through the city of martial law without interference.

The government representatives were zealously attentive to me and to Stan, but they ignored John Heard, who was relegated to waiting for his luggage with the peons. We had been traveling for twelve hours and were going to be in Lima for only four hours until we got on yet another flight for Cuzco, which would serve as our base of operation.

I realized John was missing. In a South American environment his particular personal power went unnoticed. When I sent people to collect him they thought he was John Hurt and congratulated him on his brilliant performance in *Elephant Man*. John wished we had left him alone.

Walking out into the dank and silent night of a city under martial law was chilling. There was no activity in Lima. At this hour it was against the law. The only vehicles visible were armored tanks flanked by soldiers with machine guns at the ready.

Our company was divided up into cars and vans as we made our silent and nervous trek into the Lima-Sheraton Hotel, where we would hopefully obtain a shower, rest for the few hours we had, and begin again.

No one knew what to expect. All the way there were tanks and soldiers at every main thoroughfare crossing. The soldiers were young and swaggering, a trait easily amplified by the loaded machine guns swinging from their shoulders.

Only a stray dog or two reminded us of normal life.

Otherwise, Lima was as I remembered it, gray and depressing, with a thin veil of pollution hanging in the air even in the deserted night.

Colin and Simo and I were sitting together in the back of the designated car. Simo had come to Peru to take care of me, although clearly, dealing with macho and possibly trigger-happy soldiers was not part of his job.

The three of us didn't say much, being both tired and watchful. Our car was stopped at the first tank checkpoint, and the pass that our driver presented didn't seem to have much of an effect. I tried to understand the rapid flow of Spanish. The soldiers pointed their guns at us. Simo and Colin flashed looks at me. I wasn't sure if it

was because I was a famous movie star that they thought
the soldiers wouldn't dare to knock off, or whether they
knew I had been in several life-threatening circumstances
before and survived. Whatever, I patted their hands in
nervous reassurance, not really knowing what the hell
was going to happen.

The security pass seemed to make no difference
whatever—the soldiers were not about to let us through.
I thought of all the banana republic movies I had seen
about "the disappeared ones" in South American countries. If they didn't know who we were, what did they
care?

Then I heard our driver mention my name and *Irma
la Douce*. The soldiers peered into the back seat at me. I
tried to smile, but in fact I have difficulty being civil even
at the security check in an airport. So I probably just
looked blank. They asked our driver more questions and
I could make out bits and pieces of the conversation. He
was telling them we had come to Peru to make a movie.
Much exclamatory light began to dawn.

I think my role as the Happy Hooker finally did it.
They waved us on just as our driver mentioned that the
other seventy people were with me too. This they seemed
to understand, probably because all South American ce-
lebrity dignitaries travel with an entourage. No doubt I
was no different. And besides, we were the only vehicles
on the road. . . .

Nevertheless we were stopped at least five more
times with somewhat the same charade to play out. I
wondered what the checkpoint personnel thought we
had said to the previous checkpoints. I was pissed off for
sure, but I kept very quiet, finding it easy to allow fear to
prowl around in the gut, stabbing every now and then
with a real jab.

But we made it safely to our hotel.

The authorities wanted our passports for security
reasons. I refused, saying my passport was more secure

with me. They flashed me a "don't mess with her" look, and didn't bother me. I knew that having a passport in a foreign country was as important as having a right hand.

We dispersed to our rooms and dealt privately with whatever would make us comfortable until 7:00 in the morning. The security forces searched my room, looked under the bed, and left.

My idea of comfort then was a hot shower, some yoga postures, honey-roasted peanuts, and some fruit. I read a Lima travel magazine until I fell into a strange sleep for about two hours with my passport in my hand.

The wake-up call came accompanied by a waiter bringing fresh fruit, mud coffee, and a basket of toast and rolls. It was the first day of decisions about what to eat in Peru.

In the lobby the crew congregated, our gallant band of illusion makers, having the personal courage to be uncivil, mumble-mouthed, sleepy, and somewhat pissed off. John, of course, headed the list of pissed-off ones, but that was only because he was better at experiencing *any* situation. I reminded him that he was an unknown, thin, New York stage actor who loved struggle. He said, "No, that's what John Hurt is." John was the kind of guy who made you want to hug him, pinch his cheeks, and kick him in the rump at the same time.

We hung around in the lobby until security said we could go. Then we piled into a bus, each of us lugging our own hand luggage and valuables.

The airport was another world in the bright light of day. Long lines of people waited for news about flight departures. The airline personnel themselves had no idea what was happening.

I went to the newsstand. I spotted an *International Herald Tribune,* a lifesaver, the best newspaper in the world in my opinion, and one that has always enabled me to feel that the human race and its events are available for me to know about, wherever I am in the world.

I can go into a peaceful reverie even when I'm in the middle of chaos if I have a news magazine or paper to enthrall me. That's what I did with the papers I found. Colin and Simo chatted with people.

Three hours later the plane for Cuzco decided to take off. It was as though it had a mind of its own, the people being too bureaucratically disorganized to make any lasting and trustworthy decisions.

And so, looking down at the magnificent terrain of Peru, we were finally on the last leg to our destination: Cuzco. The snowcapped splendor of the Andes below us seemed so gracefully feminine to me. And of course it made sense. The Andes were the gateway of the feminine energy on the planet; the Himalayas, the gateway for the masculine. My old stomping grounds had been the Himalayas in Bhutan, Sikkim, Kalimpong, and Nepal. As I looked back on it now, that was a time when I was more comfortable with activating, manifesting masculine attributes. I challenged authority, went to the barricades with my political beliefs, was angry and outraged at injustice, and aggressively calculated how I could effect change in the society where I lived in a forceful fashion. I was operating with yang energy, emulating the very power structure that I found fault with. I was exemplifying the establishment techniques that I abhorred. But that was the old days.   •

The new days would be smarter, more centered, more effective, and frankly, more personally rewarding, because I was beginning to see that I had been responsible for creating all the unrest in my old reality as a mirror through which to see myself. Now I felt ready and willing to see myself as a more peaceful candidate for harmony. Hopefully I would no longer *need* to feel deep, hidden anger, or flaming outrage, because I would have already lived through that part of my scenario. I would have tried on those feelings, acted them out, and would have resolved most of them. Flash-flame would occur every so often but it would be largely superficial. And eventually I would learn; I would not need even that anymore.

That was the wisdom I was beginning to feel.

So the Andes moving slowly below me represented the gateway to the profoundly feminine aspects of myself I hadn't yet been willing to trust and touch.

I put my hand around Mary the icon in my purse.

Just before I left America, my friend had presented me with a small reproduction of the icon, which was closer to the original than her photograph. The monk from Canada had sent it to her to give to me.

I knew it was, indeed, a talisman of sorts. But talismans work in human understanding because we ascribe magic to them. And magic works wonders. The loss of magic is the denial of unlimited possibility. I had kept it by my bed as a reminder of the feminine vibration I was trying to transmute in myself—I would *need* reminders.

As we landed, Cuzco was sunny, crisp, clear, and inviting. It was also 11,380 feet high.

The company was ensconced in two hotels. The "above the line" talent (actors, writers, producers, etc.) were at the Libertador. The "below the line" talent (camera crew and grips) were at the Savoy. Neither was the Ritz, but both were comfortable.

My room at the old Libertador adjoined Simo's, so he could field the calls and whoever might walk in looking for small talk. It was originally a suite with a step up between the rooms. My room had a window onto the cobblestone street below. Simo's was a closed-in box. But he set up a hot plate and soup kitchen to make it seem like home. There was a small sitting room off my room which, stripped of furniture, I saw immediately would work, for my yoga and a massage therapy table.

We had brought a massage therapist with us. I figured massage would be beneficial for everyone at the end of the day.

Since the hotel would be our home for at least a
month, people were doubly concerned about their rooms.
Mine seemed to be fine. The carpet and bedspread were
clean. I was just a little concerned about the picture of
Jesus bleeding and in pain hanging from the cross over my
bed. The maid removed it and put up two men under a
sombrero instead. I went with Colin to look at his room.

We opened the door. It was stuffed with piles of
dirty laundry and twenty-four used mattresses.

"What are they trying to tell me?" he said. They had
given him the wrong room number.

Colin settled, we sought out John Heard. It didn't
take long. His door was open and he was expressing
articulately how he missed the Statue of Liberty and
Manhattan streets. Nevertheless in no uncertain terms he
announced that the traffic outside was more than he
could "fucking" stand. So they moved him to a room
next to mine. It was either divine justice or John manag-
ing, as always, to experience everything to its utmost.
The two forces could be the same, of course, so as
matters developed, I felt justified in thinking it all probably served him right. . . .

That night was one that will go down in my book
antisleep-wise. Part of the construction crew that had
preceded us by weeks decided to have a party. And they
had it in a private dining room located right under my
bed. The floors and walls were not exactly reinforced, so
I heard every toast, every joke, and every rowdy, raucous
dance number—backed by drums that could have soloed
at any first-class Independence Day parade.

It was the one night we had to catch up on sleep,
and the production company had warned us to go to bed
immediately in the high altitude so that we'd be ready to
work early the next day.

I turned my sound machine on full blast. Thank
goodness the current was correct. But it made no difference. The sinking of Atlantis couldn't have been louder.

At about midnight Simo went to the production office and complained. The American secretary who had sent out the memos warning us to get to sleep immediately said, "Oh, she should tell us when she's sleeping." Simo marked her name in his little black book and finally called the hotel manager.

An American film company listens to no one but the director and sometimes a temperamental star. Neither was present in our case, so I did the best I could. What I also didn't know was that Cuzco power sometimes suffers an upsurge in energy which often blows out electrical equipment. So, of course, my sound machine blew. What was interesting was that I didn't. I sat up in bed and said to myself: It's all happening for a reason and everything will be fine. At 5:00 A.M. I fell asleep.

At 6:00 A.M. a trumpeter attached to an army barracks near us began to sound reveille, followed by a military band joyously rendering a rousing march, fortissimo, to accompany the soldiers as they went out on maneuvers. First they had to practice marching in the vicinity though, until around 7:00 A.M. So I slept from 7:00 to 11:00.

I got up saying to myself: All of this has already happened. It's an adventure I'm simply reliving: It all took place in another time.

Simo, however, put in a distress call to Los Angeles for two more sound machines. I couldn't depend on alternative realities to get me through the movie. And I didn't want to look like Marjorie Main playing myself.

After all that we went out to look at the Inca city which would be our home for four weeks.

No one really knows how old Cuzco is. As with all pre-Hispanic cultures, the facts are diffused because of the tradition of oral history. But modern archeologists now claim that Cuzco had been inhabited by unrecorded pre-Inca cultures. The word *Inca* is a Quechua term used to describe just one person—the ruling emperor himself. Quechua is still the language of the Inca. The creation myth of Cuzco goes like this:

In the beginning there were wretched barbarian creatures who lived in a land of darkness. The great Sun lord sent his son to earth to bring enlightenment and culture. His name was Manco Capac. The great Moon goddess sent her daughter to be his bride. Her name was Mama Occlo. They emerged from the waters of Lake Titicaca and began a long odyssey together which culminated in the fertile valley of Cuzco. Applying the test of the Sun lord, Manco Capac plunged his golden staff into the ground. When it sank and disappeared, he knew this was "the navel of the earth," and founded an empire upon the spot. So Cuzco was more than just the capital city of the Inca Empire. It was a holy city, a place of pilgrimage with as much significance to the Quechuas as Mecca has to the Moslems.

The Incas built their city in the shape of a puma. Within that animal form I marveled at the Sun Temple, the Plaza de Armas, the Wailing Square, the cathedrals, and the palace of Pachacutec.

The cobblestone streets of Cuzco wound and beckoned to us with new colors, sights, and sounds. Each junction was ancient history. After many earthquakes, it was the Inca structures that remained. There were craft shops selling rugs, baskets, bags, jewelry, sweaters, gold, and paintings.

Later on, Colin and I met and went to look at some of the locations the production crew had selected. Although my actual experience in Peru had taken place in Huancayo, which had entirely different terrain, it wasn't possible to base our production company there because of the requirements of accommodations and surrounding locations. I could feel the art department strain for my approval because they knew it was quite different. But they did a superb job in the main in scouting out places which were reminiscent of what I wrote in the book; except for the "hotel" where I actually lived.

The original experience was more primitive than the movie version. I had lived in a mud hut called a "hotel," with a dirt floor and no windows. That was it. No running water, no heat, no nothing.

Maybe it was difficult for them to believe. I don't know, but instead of going with what I wrote, they found an actual hotel, rather quaint, almost European, trimmed with red paint and sporting a courtyard abounding with flowers. Zsa Zsa Gabor would have been happy honeymooning there. They had, however, confirmed to the man who ran the hotel that they would muddy up one whole wall and the courtyard. He looked on in disbelief at what was happening to his treasured hotel—which he believed the company had chosen for its charm. Mud was loaded into the courtyard, splattered on the walls, and even dumped in the room interiors. He had suspected Hollywood was insane, but this was proof.

In the end we just couldn't make it look primitive enough. So the company paid the man, restored his place to normal, and went searching on the other side of the tracks for a better way to purvey our celluloid dreams. I hoped the hotel owner's feelings were not too badly hurt. No doubt he took the whole Hollywood madness in good stride.

Since we had shot the interior mineral bath sequences on a Hollywood sound stage, we needed to get the exterior shots in Peru. That meant digging a huge hole and duplicating a natural phenomenon that did not occur in Cuzco. The water also needed to bubble and emit steam.

The hole was no problem. There happened to be a giant one deep beside the Urubamba River. But where to get the water to fill it with?

Someone said the mayor of Coija had a heated swimming pool with freshly chlorinated water in it. Chlorination was essential, they felt, because John and I would be in it for days.

The art director went to the mayor and asked him if I could use the water in his swimming pool for my movie. When he said yes, they moved the shooting date up on the schedule because things were going so smoothly.

However, when the company backed up the fire truck to drain the mayor's pool, they found that he had already drained it to make room for cool, fresh, un-chlorinated water for me. The art director tried to explain I hadn't wanted to use his *pool*—I wanted to use his *water*. The local fire department, which consisted of one truck, was brought in. The guys lost count of the trips that truck made to fill our hole with 80,000 gallons of water which then needed to be heated and fitted with artistically primitive surrounding rocks so that the whole thing didn't look like a manicured rock-garden special from the San Fernando Valley.

But once the local fire department's water was in the pool, the pool sprang a leak. Fifty thousand gallons of water leaked into the Urubamba before it was stopped.

They then put a liquid rubber sealer on the bottom, filled the pool again, and brought in the heaters. The heaters melted the sealer, which appeared on the top of the water as floating rubber scum.

Someone suggested throwing dry ice into the water so the steam would camouflage the rubber.

It worked. John and I would just have to say our dialogue fast so our mouths wouldn't stay open long. Obviously the mineral-bath shoot was scheduled for later.

The art department did a superhuman job in the wilds of Peru. So superhuman that the art director had to be sent home with altitude sickness precipitated by movie pressure.

A word about what 11,000 feet feels like. First your head aches, constantly and relentlessly. The food you eat is difficult to digest. The oxygen in the blood is obviously thin, causing dizziness and heart pounding which can be extremely disconcerting. Those are some of the physical effects. The mental, psychological, and psychic effects are even more profound.

I had been there only a day and a half when my dreams and mental associations began to be unlike any I had ever experienced.

I think it was a combination of the altitude and the Andean energy. Later on I was to hear stories from nearly every member of the crew relating to what was going on in their heads.

Our dreams were more vivid, more definitive, more real than usual. They made me more aware than ever of the possibility that we might very well be living two or three levels of reality at the same time.

Colin and Simo and I shopped in the marketplaces the day before we started shooting. The Peruvian handicrafts were exquisite: hand-woven shoulder bags of multicolors, and soft baby-alpaca sweaters woven in fairy-tale colorful designs. The alpaca fur rugs were perfect thrown across a bed. I did all my Christmas shopping in Cuzco and never looked back.

Our stomachs were beginning to rumble with the food, even though we had had only soup and bread. Later we would find that we should have stuck to that.

I had brought a quart of chunky peanut butter with me along with a case of crackers. If things got really rough I could live on those.

The company was settled in and ready to work. Then we found out that already someone had stolen my combat boots (boots that I needed to match those in scenes we had already shot). And maybe worse than that, all the booze stored in the production office was stolen.

Joie, our costume supervisor, had thought to bring doubles of my combat boots, but our company manager had no solution for the missing liquor.

We began shooting in the Plaza of Cuzco. Crowds gathered and gawked. The crew was organized, professional, and fast, and even though the rarefied high-altitude light stung my blue eyes (Andean eyes all seem to be brown), Brad was able to rig an overhead tarp to reduce the glare.

Stan had wanted to shoot one of the most dramatic scenes in the script on the first day of shooting because it was much better for the production schedule. I felt that John and I had not had enough time to adjust to the altitude and that we would have a hard time with the screaming dramatic dialogue. John was in a good mood. He had been learning Spanish and was interacting with the local people. When I asked him how he felt about tackling the big Plaza scene he wanted to take the chance. He seemed to relish overcoming the adversity. After that we were scheduled to move out to the airport to do the arrival scene, because that was the only day they would give us permission to shoot out there. And in the afternoon we were to head for Machu Picchu.

We got through the morning, although the airport scene took far too long, headed back and had lunch, and then rounded up the crew, baggage, John, assorted paraphernalia, and technical equipment, and somehow got it all to the station and onto the train going up to Machu Picchu.

We were on a train that was supposed to take three hours to get there. As it turned out we arrived seven hours later.

The terrain we traversed made it worthwhile. The Urubamba River tumbled from its Andean paradise above, running alongside the train, actually spraying our hands as we stretched them out the windows. Jungle undergrowth, ever-changing trees of storybook varieties, and huge boulders raced past with the speed of the river—which was traveling much faster than our train. Handcrafted bridges of hemp and mountain vines were the only indication that humans lived in the wild countryside we were passing through.

There was no food other than picnic boxes packed from the hotel restaurant. And at each mountain stop the crew gave away more boxes. Peasant women in bright-colored serapes, their hair dressed in twisted thick black braids, accepted the boxes with dignity for their children. They lined the railroad tracks when the train rolled in. Many tried to sell us handcrafted necklaces and bags.

Tina and Julie, our body makeup girl, cried for the poverty in which they saw people living. John went to a window. He saw the outstretched hands and turned away, unable to cope with it. Then he reached in his pocket and threw all the money he had out of the window without looking at where it landed.

No one else saw him do it. It is one of the strongest memories I have of the trip to Peru.

The bright day turned to darkness as our milk-run trek proceeded. The crew had brought along cases of beer and by now they and John were feeling no pain. He enjoyed drinking with the crew. We swapped movie stories about people we had worked with. Nothing is sacred when a crew gets going.

We hung out of the windows together, with the rain and the Urubamba spray dashing against our faces.

Finally at 2:00 the next morning we pulled into the train station of Machu Picchu. And as we suspected, it was raining.

We loaded ourselves into a bus which would take us up the winding road to the ruins. If the weather broke we would have to shoot in three hours at daybreak.

"Listen," said Brad. "It's war. We all know that. We'll just pull together and make it work."

And so I returned to the haunting ruin of Machu Picchu which had so captured my heart ten years before.

Machu Picchu was known as the Lost City of the

Incas and was not discovered until 1911 by an American named Hiram Bingham, who was to become governor of and senator from Connecticut and a professor of South American studies at Harvard. The Indians themselves had not known it was there. The ruin is situated at the top of the mountain with no access for vehicles or construction. How it was built, even why, still remains a mystery.

I stepped from the bus into the rain and mist. The old hotel was still there. I looked up and saw the shrouded outline of the ancient stones, and at that moment, out of the wispy clouds stepped a giant alpaca. He stood outlined in the rain—almost as though he were guarding the place until we could be there in the morning.

I climbed the stairs of the hotel veranda. A million tourists had been there since I had first been so moved by the place. So much had happened to me. So much I had learned, so much to understand.

We had to bunk in together because there was a shortage of rooms. So Colin and I stayed together. Even though the rain was soothing, I pulled out my sound machine and turned it on.

"So this is what you sleep by," said Colin.

"Yep," I answered. "And you'll be off to sleep before you have time to wonder what Peru is going to come up with tomorrow."

Chapter 19

When we woke it was Colin who came up with something I didn't expect. Because it was still raining and our shooting call was on hold, Colin felt it was the right time and place to tell me about something about which I knew nothing. It had to do with the dialogue at Machu Picchu.

"I had a meeting with a cultural man dealing with Machu Picchu," he began.

"Oh?" I said. "What's he like?"

Colin made a face. "Right out of a bad Costa Gavras movie."

This was not a good sign. "Well, what happened?" I asked anxiously.

"He says if we don't take out the references to extraterrestrials in our script, he won't let us shoot here."

I looked at Colin, trying to understand. I had been used to ridicule where my views on extraterrestrial life were concerned, but this sounded serious.

"Why?" I asked. "What does he object to?"

"Well," answered Colin, "he feels there is a neo-Nazi conspiracy in the world spreading rumors that Third

World cultures such as Peru are too backward and unintelligent to have built monuments as splendid as Machu Picchu without extraterrestrial help."

I had never heard of such a concept.

"You're telling me that this guy thinks that to speculate that extraterrestrials might have helped build Machu Picchu is a neo-Nazi idea?"

Colin nodded his head.

"According to this character, yes. So we can't have David speculating that it might be true."

I thought a moment.

"Okay," I said. "Let's have Shirley ask him if ETs could have helped, and John could do one of his seductive 'could-be' shrugs and not answer. We'd get the same point across but on paper it'll just say *David didn't answer*."

Colin smiled that Harold smile. The smile that crossed Harold's face in the movie just before he strung himself up on a rope to bug his mother.

"Good," he said. "It's settled. Shirley will ask and David will shrug."

"Right," I agreed. "Then I'll give a press conference and say that the ETs probably helped because the Incas were the only culture smart enough to understand them."

"You should go into politics," said Colin.

"Thanks," I said. "But the politics of the spirit is enough for me."

It seemed so simple sitting in a wet hotel room in Machu Picchu. We would change one line, period. But as it turned out, the man called a press conference that day for Peruvian and international reporters. He accused me of being a neo-Nazi and gave them his conspiracy thesis. The reporters were aghast and amused. The Peruvians knew he was a media groper, and the international foreign press knew it was a good story. Because I had refused to give any interviews until after the shooting was complete, I couldn't, nor did I want to, say anything.

So once again in the papers around the world it looked as if I had gotten myself into yet another controversial, colorful situation. At least they were becoming more and more cosmically oriented.

When Colin and I left our hotel room for the lobby, we found the crew reloading equipment onto the buses and milling around. I found Stan.

"We're leaving," he said. "This has been the most expensive day of my entire career. We're on double time. The trip here cost, I don't know. The crew is bone tired. I don't want them slipping on the rocks. We've lost a day anyway, we only have a permit for one day, and the hotel can't accommodate us tonight, so we've made the decision to go all the way back and come again another time."

Well, that was what I called a creatively risky decision.

"How do we know it won't be raining the next time we come back, Stan?" I asked—rather legitimately I thought.

"Because *you* are going to project otherwise, Shirley," said Stan simply. "You are going to show us that positive thinking works."

Oh, brother. Practice what I preach and all that. If this stuff works, show us. I see. He was absolutely right.

Quickly I said I was going to take a fast hike to the top of the ruins. Stan said fine.

In my boots and rain gear I began to climb the stone steps of the ruins. Misty clouds floated below the mountains. The rocks were slippery as I climbed. I saw what Stan meant. I remembered the story of the Inca ghost at the clock tower who appears often and says he wants no one to be there. I wondered if that was why we had rain as I followed the stone paths. I remembered how some archeologists believe that the Lost City was built solely for Inca princesses. As I gazed over the sides of the mountaintop ruins, I imagined hovering spacecraft levitating the huge stones from quarries that were visible across the valley. Other than that it was difficult to imagine how the Incas got the twenty-ton blocks up there.

I stopped for a moment as I climbed, still and alone. I tried to evoke the feelings I had had when I was first there, long before I really understood what I was looking at.

I had never felt I had lived there or even really been there in a past life. What I had felt, though, was that I was familiar with an energy that was part of that time, a high technology that spoke to an understanding of forces above and beyond what we were familiar with today. It was almost as though I felt we had regressed in many ways, fixating on priorities that were not serving us properly or wisely, priorities that in the end might just mean the end of us.

Sadly I turned around and headed back to the hotel. The alpaca I had seen the night before stood gracefully in the mist, blinking at me. I wondered if the next time I saw him would be in sunshine.

When I returned to the lobby, John Heard was sitting with Michael and Cowboy drinking beer. As with Simo and myself, they were there to watch out for John and take care of his needs. They hadn't informed him yet that he was off the train, hence, no doubt, the beer.

Stan drew me aside and offered me a cup of coffee. He sat for a moment and then he told me something I could scarcely believe.

"Listen," he said. "I think you should know. Three people have come to say that our bad luck began after you and John had the scene where you shouted 'I am God.' They think it's God punishing us."

I stared at Stan.

"Are you serious?" I asked.

"Very," he said with real sincerity in his eyes.

"But, Stan," I began. "I'm not sure we've really had

bad luck. I mean everyone has been so helpful. And as far as this weather is concerned, well, one of the first things you learn is that nature follows consciousness. Nature cleanses however it has to."

"Well," said Stan, "they don't all know that. Those three think God is having his revenge."

"Wow," I said, really shocked. I suddenly felt out of touch with the crew again, even if only three felt that way. I wanted to know who the three were, but I didn't want to ask. I didn't want to get into a religious conflict, but I wanted to help them understand my point of view. It seemed so much more peaceful and nurturing than to believe that God was a wrathful, vengeful entity prepared to wreak havoc when not subserviently obeyed. Was God punishing me for blasphemy? No, I think he would want each one of us to recognize the God within ourselves and take the responsibility for that immediately; to recognize that each person was divine. Each person was God. I thought God would have loved that scene. To say "I am God" was to fulfill and respect his love for us, because we were all part of that same divinity.

"Well," I said to Stan, "maybe those three people are afraid of themselves."

Stan put down his coffee cup.

"Well, I just wanted you to know," he said.

I nodded and sighed.

"Thanks for taking what they said seriously, Stan. And don't worry," I went on. "We won't have bad luck. We might have a hard time, but we won't have bad luck."

Stan looked deeply into my eyes. He was a remarkably open and kind man. I was glad he was the producer of my show.

I got up from the table and walked to the balcony. It was funny. Whenever I came to what Butler would call a "glitch" in my feelings I reminded myself about the totality of time—that our show was already on the air.

What was important now was the personal growth and transformation of everyone involved. In my view the objections to the "I am God" scene were not so much objections to the material as an expression of fear of the personal and individual responsibility that the scene suggested we take as humans who recognize our own divine energy. To blame God for anything was so easy. I remembered something I had read once and it made such sense. *"God needs us because we are a way He can express Himself."*

Meanwhile, the world was waiting for us to get on with living. . . . We piled ourselves back onto the bus. For some reason John was colorfully muttering to himself about Judas's effect on Jesus Christ. I couldn't decipher whether he saw himself as the betray*er* or the betray*ee*. Probably the latter, and probably it had something to do with the rain. John had the gift of turning any situation into a personal matter—one of the devices that made him such a good actor.

He hunched down next to me.

"Do you know I have this big mother-fuckin' crush on you?" he said.

While I tried to sort this out he stuffed his stereo earphones in his ears. He was out of hearing distance. He swayed and tapped to the music he was hearing.

"Do you know the greatest love song ever written?" he asked.

"No. What?" I asked. He looked blank. I shook my head.

"Well," he said, "it's about wanting one more loving spoonful from my baby, and the guy who wrote it shot his mother."

I tried to speak, but my mouth opened and nothing came out. John leaned back and howled.

I wanted to contribute something to his free-flowing insanity, but all I could think of was that he smelled like vanilla.

*   *   *

On the bus trip down the mountain an engaging tourist entertainment occurred. Young boys left the top of the mountain at the same time as the bus. They slid down waterfalls, gullies, and wild mountain footpaths. Then they lay in wait as the bus made its curve in the road, indicating that on foot they had gone faster than the vehicle. For people like Cowboy who had an affinity for belief in magic, it was a mystifying mountain trick. At the bottom he gave them a huge tip. That was how they supported themselves.

At the train station we all pitched in and loaded equipment back on the train, wondering what drama would be in store for us the next time we came.

On the train ride back I talked with some of the crew. The discussion revolved around the troubles some of them were having with family members who were only comfortable with what they could see and measure and were spooked by dimensions that they sensed were true, but couldn't be controlled. Not many actually ridiculed the search, but instead some found it dangerous and foreboding, as though the dead could come back and refute their "safe" accepted reality. What I found interesting was that the crew members who openly discussed the personal effect their questioning had on others in their lives understood that they themselves had created the opposition as an aspect of themselves which was also still not sure.

The train ride was becoming more revealing with each mile. Tina and Julie were now buoyant as they flung American money to the children of the poor.

"Oh, look at that sweet little one," Tina would say and fling the child a piece of food or a coin. They were relieved that they were helping someone less fortunate than they. I looked the other way. I'm still not really sure why.

John's pain for the poor was infinitely more profound to me. He was literally sick about it and couldn't eat. I wondered how he was when he really loved someone.

At the end of the train ride Colin and Simo and I got into our car to go back to the hotel in Cuzco, which was still another two hours away.

Presently we found ourselves in the Sacred Valley of the Incas and from that moment on I spent the rest of the day in an altered state of consciousness. I was to remind myself many times on this Peruvian location that making the movie was not the highest priority reason for my being in Peru.

There have been a few times in my life when I was absolutely certain that I had been somewhere before. It doesn't matter whether I'm in a city or out in the wilds; the feeling usually comes initially as though borne on a soft wind. Then an uncanny cloak of memory settles over me. As I look around, it nudges and jabs my mind until either I gently concede that memory will have to wait until another future, or I haltingly feel I can place the time and circumstance.

Such was the feeling I had in an Inca ruin called Ollantaitambo. Ollantaitambo overlooked the magical sacred Valley of the Incas where the Urubamba River tumbles freely and the surrounding landscape is emerald-green. Terraced hillsides slope under skies that look like a turquoise backdrop spattered with fluffy, wispy paint. It is sacred all right, just by virtue of what it does to your heart when you stand in the midst of it.

But Ollantaitambo was what got me. I saw the other company cars veer to the right toward Cuzco, but as though pushed forward by an invisible arm, I asked our driver to stop. He casually related some of the history of the ruins: They stood at a strategic point where the Sacred Valley narrows and the Urubamba plunges steeply toward the Amazon. Ollantaitambo defended Cuzco against incursions by jungle tribes from the North. The ruin was

named for a local chieftain who had a forbidden love
affair with the daughter of his sovereign, the Inca
Pachacutec. He rebelled and was crushed. Great battles
took place during Manco Inca's rebellion. When the
Spaniards finally besieged the place, it was abandoned.

That was the history as related by our driver, who
was also a tourist guide. But I felt something different.

The invisible arm pushed me from the car. Colin
and Simo got out too. But I wanted to walk alone
through the ancient stone blocks of ruined history which
somehow spoke to me. The twenty-ton stones seemed
constructed with a kind of flexible perfection.

I walked toward the hillside ruin. A misty wind
came up behind me and there was that feeling again. I
began to climb the stone stairs leading up the mountain.
The arm supported me as I went. I saw Colin and Simo
talking to our driver and then going off on their own as
well. I climbed the two hundred steps, looking down on
them occasionally from above.

Then somehow I knew I had to climb all the way to
the top of the mountain ruin. I was compelled to do it. I
didn't know why. There was no rail—only stone foot
ledges jutting out from under the earth, and intermittently obscured altogether. But I somehow knew where
they were. I felt that I had used them before. Then I had
had sandals on my feet and some sort of plumage around
my neck. It was the most bewitchingly haunting feeling I
had had in a long time, quite different from the past-life
regression memories I had experienced in a clinical environment with the acupuncture needles. These memories
were coming back to me with no stimulation but the
environment. I continued to climb. The mountain was
very, very steep. I knew I was climbing to the lookout
tower where I used to spend a great deal of time. I was
breathing hard now because of the altitude. Then I made
the decision to relate to the altitude as though I were
living in my past experience. I did a kind of focused

mental gymnastic with my concentration. I felt my body straighten up and a powerful strength surge through my thighs, as though on such a climb the pressure should be held in the legs, not the solar plexus.

What happened next was a lesson in mind over matter. Suddenly I found I had no trouble breathing. I was free of concern because I *knew* there was no reason for it. I climbed higher. Then I looked down again for Colin and Simo. I saw only Colin. Simo had disappeared. I continued to climb. The sun was falling and I wanted to be able to descend in daylight. I began to see narrow animal trails winding through the mountainside under-brush. The nature of the undergrowth changed; the wind hugged my body in forceful gusts. The clouds forming over the Sacred Valley began to gather in charged moun-tainous shapes. It began to rain at the top of the moun-tain. I looked up. Then I looked around me, breathed deeply, and smiled. I felt totally happy all the way through to my heart. I was in sheer and absolute heaven. No, I thought, my memories of this place are not of battles and war and disease and killing. My memories are of rever-ence to nature. I knew that I had waited on the side of this mountain for sunrises and I had chanted and held my palms to the sun in a collective exercise with thou-sands of other people around me. I knew we worshipped the rising sun on one side of the mountain and the setting sun on the other side. I looked up ahead. I had to get to the top and see what associations came up for me. Just then I saw someone below me rounding a corner of the mountain ruin with his head down. He was climbing quickly to catch up with me. I looked closely. It was Simo. His brown curls swirled in the wind.

"Wait for me," he shouted. "This is so incredible."

I stopped and wiped my face. I did a plié to feel the strength in my knees.

Simo was not breathing very hard when he reached me.

"Isn't this weather like our house in the mountains?" he asked. "It all feels so familiar."

Then a thought occurred to me as I gazed at him silhouetted against the misty drizzle.

"What do you mean, familiar?" I asked.

"Well," he said, "I just needed to climb this mountain here and I needed to because I saw you doing it. I mean, I think the two of us have climbed above this ruin before. I can feel it."

I looked at him.

"Do you really?" I said.

"Yes," he answered straightforwardly.

"So do I," I answered. "I know we've been here before and if you say you feel that way, then I think we were here together, and maybe one of the reasons we're associated with working together now, especially in Peru, is because we know each other from this place."

"Maybe it goes back further than Inca," said Simo. "It feels secret, almost as though no one is supposed to know."

Yes, I thought. Maybe so. Maybe my associations of collective meditation spoke to a time long before the Incas. Many anthropologists believed that the Incas borrowed much of their administrative and agricultural knowledge from a culture much older than theirs.

"Shall we go all the way up?" I asked. "I have to."

Simo began to climb again.

"Yes," he said over his shoulder. "That's why we're here."

Now there was no path at all. Tourists and guides clearly never came this far. As I looked across the mountains I could see the remnants of ancient Inca footpaths. Again I felt myself fly along them, barely skimming the ground.

The sun was beginning to set now. The trunks of the mountain trees looked golden. The clouds played roller coaster among the trees as if they were alive. Simo and I climbed higher as though driven by an omnipresent force.

We looked up to the last ledge. Above it was a temple tower of some kind.

We carefully picked our way through cactus and prickly underbrush. A mountain goat darted in front of us, stopping and challenging us with a stare that seemed to request our credentials. We smiled.

"It's just like home," said Simo.

The goat set about eating a prickly bush. We passed. Carefully we climbed the last ledge. A full-blown wind enveloped us on the top of the mountain. There was the temple tower, stark and resilient, a monument to a time of splendor, I thought. Just adjacent was a compact windswept courtyard surrounded by stone structures which enclosed it. The stone structures formed niches waist-high from the ground. I had seen niches like that in Egypt, but now as I saw them again I thought I knew what they were for. Immediately I walked to a niche and leaned the top part of my torso into it. Then I began to hum. The vibrational amplification from the walls resonated through my head and body. For me the niches had been used as a form of sound therapy.

I chanted the scale using OM. With each ascending note I felt a different vibration in my body. I felt the amplified vibration touch internal organs as well.

Simo chose a niche and began to chant and hum. Then we chanted the same notes together. Despite the wind, the sound echoed and reechoed, bouncing off the walls and reverberating around us. It was a healing exercise.

I stepped back from the niche and contemplated the surroundings. From another level of consciousness I saw pictures form around me, materializing as though out of the air. There were women dressed in garments made of some kind of crystal fabric and decorated with bright plumage. The skin tone of the women was golden-brown-orange. Gracefully they fitted themselves into the niches, leaning forward and chanting. The exercise seemed to put them into some kind of alignment and reverie. They were smiling and peaceful, not communicating so much by language as by mental pictures. I felt that I had known how to communicate like that too.

I walked away from the courtyard of niches and out to the temple tower. It was a simple structure with lookout points on all sides. I climbed into the tower and looked down. From my altered mind state I saw how the twenty-ton stones of the ruin were being transported from the quarries miles away in the valley below.

On the valley floor were long lines of priests of some kind, sitting about twelve feet apart. Clad in white crystal-fabric robes, they sat peacefully in the lotus position, collectively meditating. And hovering in the air above the long line of priests were great monolithic stones floating toward the mountain, guided by the meditative power of the priests' minds. The pictures I saw in the valley were astonishing, but I knew they came from an alternative, yet parallel, consciousness which I knew I possessed even today if I could just get out of my own way and allow it to flourish. What I saw didn't frighten me. It was as though I was observing another truth within a bubble of time, and within the bubble I saw myself seeing it all.

Simo came away from the courtyard and joined me in the temple tower. I didn't tell him my vision.

"I don't feel this was a fort," he said, "or anything like that. I don't feel war. I feel it was a very advanced society and although I can't remember what it was like for me, I know that even today it is sacred."

The wind whipped around us.

"I see," he went on, "priests and ritual ceremonies praising the sun and moon and God. I see all the people in total harmony with nature."

I never mentioned the images I had seen that matched his.

"I'm glad," I said instead, "that we are here together. I'm so glad you decided to climb."

Simo looked over and touched my arm.

"Nothing is an accident," he said gently. "We're together for a reason, but then we've always known that, haven't we?"

I squeezed Simo's hand and left the temple tower. I climbed to the edge of the mountain and raised my arms. I felt I should make a pledge of some kind to myself, some kind of a promise. I could feel the invisible presence behind me relax. I could also feel the presence of other beings with me.

I lifted my face to the misty wind.

"For all you invisible guides and teachers and Gods around me," I said out loud. "I know you're there and I know I'm not letting you help and love me enough. I am going to change that by allowing myself to receive your love and help. That is what it means to be a woman."

I lowered my arms. That was all I had to say.

There were those who would say that I was "allowing" them to help me too much already. But I had learned one thing a long time ago. The safest place for me was out on a limb, because that was where the fruit was.

Chapter 20

The scene for the next day was to take place in a broken-down bus. It called for chickens, pigs, and goats to ride along with John and me. To convey the sense of culture shock, we had written into the scene that a pig would be handed across the laps of Shirley and David while they were eating a sandwich. It took eighteen takes of pig-handling and uncounted numbers of curves in the road till we had the right sunlight for the "background." Why background was so important in a pig-handling scene was analogous to the classical conflict in film-making between front-of-the-camera people and behind-the-camera people. In all my years of movie-making I could never get it clear which was the higher priority. It would seem obvious that the actors' reactions to the pig would take a higher priority (front of the camera). But then if there was darkness in the background, the long shot wouldn't match the close-ups which would come later.

In any case, irrespective of John's good morning health and my sunny attitude, it wasn't long before the whole thing descended to the pits of movie-making madness. The pig got sick and threw up on me. The goat grabbed my sandwich and ate it, and the chickens thought nothing of backing up, leaning out of their cages, and relieving themselves on my Peruvian poncho, which had no double because it was the original I had worn when this whole experience unfolded in the first place. Life imitating art? Art imitating life? I don't know. I was too sick to analyze. I'm not good in moving vehicles anyway. Curves always make me nauseous. And clean smell is a favorite for me. Well—I had neither. Clearly this reality was a learning experience. I tried to make myself believe it.

John went into one of his smiling trances—out of it, away somewhere—and I used every visualization known to metaphysical circles to keep from throwing up even further on my wardrobe. To exacerbate the difficulties, a toothless woman holding her baby in full view of the camera decided it was time to nurse her child. She pulled out a beautiful bulbous tit, stuffed it into her baby's mouth, and began to sing over our dialogue. Butler yelled, "Cut."

She of course spoke only Quechua and continued to suckle her child and sing. The cameras stopped, the sound tape stopped, the bus stopped, and the script girl exited the bus and vomited. The pig threw up again on the floor, the goat went for my hat, and the chickens leaned farther out of their cage. The baby nursed silently, with unperturbed concentration. One of the crew asked for the door to be opened. He fled down the steps and leaned over just in time. John smiled his secret trance smile and Butler winced. He couldn't deal with the nursing baby. He decided to take control of the situation anyway. In his best Beverly Hills television dialect he shouted to a woman in the back of the bus: "Now listen, babe, let's have you wing that basket full of vegetables up here a taste more rapid. Ya dig?"

The woman stared at him. I stared at him. The crew

stared at him. Not only did she not speak one word of English, she didn't even speak Spanish. She spoke only Quechua. That didn't seem to deter Butler at all. He repeated his direction with a kind of blind faith while the rest of us prayed to be rained out.

Two hours later we got the shot *and* the rain, which meant that we were relegated to walking, sloshing up to our ankles in Peruvian mud mixed with all sorts of organic waste assembled by Mother Nature. This was to be the standard operating procedure for the rest of the shoot. McPherson had warned us about the rain, but I guess he figured mud (and whatever else) was too earth plane to mention. Either that, or from his perspective, everything looked like light.

Since a movie company could be termed a mini-society, it wasn't startling that a mini-revolution broke out among the ranks of the Peruvian and American crew. The Peruvians insisted they weren't being fed properly and were angry. The Americans *were* being fed and were angry because they didn't want to eat in front of their brethren who had worked just as hard in the rain and mud as they did. So everyone was hungry and angry.

Yudi, the assistant director, inherited the problem. She came to me pleading for something to be done with "these penny-pinching ABC money people." I agreed and told her to send the driver back to the hotel to get one of them who was having lunch in a dry dining room.

The driver elected to tell the ABC production brass that they'd better get out to the location quick because I was quitting the show. (He was probably one who got no food.) They showed up as though borne on lightning. (When the star quits or refuses to work, that's real bucks to be worried about.)

Brass Number One spoke first.

"It's all fixed," he said.

Yudi didn't wait for more B.S.

"Listen," she accused. "I've brought up this problem to you guys five times in the course of this shoot and you've done nothing about feeding the Peruvian crew. *You* stay at the hotel all day. *We* have to work with them."

"Well," said Brass Number Two, "you know Americans aren't welcome anywhere anyway."

His logic slid by me.

Brass Number One spoke up.

"They don't like our food anyway. They have their own ways, you know."

I guessed that one of their "ways" was to handle hunger silently.

They both continued in unison, overlapping each other. "They're supposed to bring their own food. Besides, our crew probably hired more Peruvian help on the sly and that's why there's not enough food. They make more in one day from us than they do in one month from anyone else. They know what they want. They don't want our ways."

Everyone turned to look at me.

"Well," I said, "our American crew is really pissed off at your human insensitivity while they and the Peruvians are slogging away in pig shit and mud. They are buying the food for their co-workers out of their own pockets. Make some kind of new arrangement. Okay? I hate seeming like ugly Americans when we're supposed to be doing a spiritual picture here."

The guys blushed. I knew they were only trying to save money—as, indeed, they were supposed to. Like so many location problems, this one probably arose from a breakdown in communication. The Peruvian firm delegated to hire the Peruvian crew probably neglected to tell them to bring their own food as part of the deal. Sooo . . . there we were: in the crap, literally.

"Look," I finished. "I don't blame them for not wanting our ways. But they would like some food. So order some Peruvian food from the caterer. Okay?"

There was a condescending collective nod as they got up to leave.

I was to learn later that Yudi had a private meeting with them where she really let them have it:

"There we were with a director who speaks television English no one understands, a vomiting crew, a vomiting pig, chickens with diarrhea, goats that eat props, an oblivious-to-time nursing mother, a bus stuck in the mud, a Peruvian revolt, and a schedule to keep. You apologize to every member of our crew and don't let me hear one of you say I'm stirring up trouble."

The Brass complied. The mixture of art and business was not easy on human sensibilities, particularly when each individual had his own set of priorities. I, however, was really proud of Yudi.

In the meantime, the bureaucratic cultural representative telephoned Stan and said, "No flying, no UFOs, and no people perpetrating a neo-Nazi plot to discredit the intelligence of the Third World."

Colin said, "Think of it as someone who says the Brooklyn Bridge was built by a New Yorker, and someone else says, 'No, it was built by an extraterrestrial.' Let the someone-else guy say it. That's freedom of speech. That's democracy."

"No, Colin," said Stan. "Let's let John do one of his famous 'it could be anything' takes. The guy won't know what that means."

I walked into John's trailer. He was smiling and mischievous. I was to learn that adversity made him happier because it helped him define his identity. Cowboy, John's assistant, was frying Spam over a Bunsen burner.

"So you're going to eat that fried stuff?" I asked.

John smiled. "Sure I am. The heartburn feels good. I have to hurt myself, since everybody else is being so nice to me."

Wow, I thought. "You know you're no Catholic, John. You're a terminal Protestant, because you always need something to overcome."

John bit into the fried Spam.

"That's why I like Cowboy. Like I tell him, he has the good grace to allow me to fail."

The drama of the crew revolt carried with it enough gossip to occupy us for days. I had learned early on that on a shoot, somehow it seemed necessary to have someone to hate, someone whom everyone considers the heavy. It's unfortunate that having a common enemy draws people together but at least then they don't attack each other. In that respect, a "son-of-a-bitch" makes it possible for the rest of the group to operate harmoniously. Such was the role that the ABC Brass selflessly played. Stan knew he had to be the good guy, the one everybody loved and respected. And I had to be the "creator" who was crazy enough to attempt to initiate all of it in the first place. And John? He was the teacher and the entertainment, since we didn't have television, and our Gauchos cookies, See's chocolates, and Nutter-Butter cookies were held up in Customs.

The shooting progressed regardless of the weather. Making a movie must be comparable to a military invasion, I think. Human individuality takes a back seat to the overall project, yet without the idiosyncratic contributions that only individuals can make, there is no successful theater of "war." There is a mathematics to the precision required, compounded of human selflessness, a desire to please, and a fear of displeasing the person in charge—who in feature films is the director, and in television, the producer.

The terrain we were shooting around was breathtaking. The rarefied altitude of the Andes caused us to feel the vividness of our waking hours as intensely as our sleeping hours, each of us experiencing strong dreams, having powerful impact, sometimes nightmares, sometimes exquisitely lovely images, sometimes idealized romance. It was as though we were centered in an energy power point that amplified what ordinarily would have been a more low-key experience.

None of us slept more than a few hours a night. And when we did, it was in fits and spurts. Sometimes we weren't even sure whether we were sleeping or not.

Rain came several times every day. We shot through it if possible, chilling our feet and legs to the bone. It didn't matter that we were ankle-deep in mud because we were being shot from the waist up. I thought of McPherson's warnings. Such simple pleasures as hot coffee and the warmly welcomed Nutter-Butter cookies, which finally arrived, made us feel we were being given a treat. We were reduced to almost childlike pleasures and interreactions. Sprightly jokes were prevalent when the sun was shining. Bathroom humor was the rule of the day when the mud squished in around us.

The Peruvian crew and extras did the best they could with attempting to understand why we had invaded their land, why we were requesting them to do such strange things as "hit marks," "do it again with more animation," and the like. It was doubly difficult for Yudi and Butler because there were *no* words in Quechua for *movie, camera, once again,* or even *thank you.* I remember asking one of the Peruvian crew if it was difficult to speak Quechua. He said to speak it well you had to be born to it. Later on I asked him about the fermented native drink *chi-chi*; I wondered how potent it was. "One sip of *chi-chi*," he said, "and you speak fluent Quechuan."

Brad May tried to balance artistic perfection with efficiency and speed, and his desire to win an Emmy for cinematography was not lost on the rest of us. Stan, as a good producer, said we were all pulling for him (particularly with such glorious scenery to work with), but we needed to pull faster. Brad knew I squinted in the sun, so he took time to erect a silk tarp over my head. "The movie is about the lady's adventure, not squintage," he would say. "And I don't want to be responsible for launching Shirley into character parts." Another few hours would go down on the production chart by Brad's name.

Butler promised he'd shoot more master shots and not fall prey to his television conditioning, which dictated that every scene end with a close-up.

"Awfulness," Butler would say. "The awfulness of conditioning."

Yudi, who was in charge of organizing the production to make the shooting run quickly and smoothly, was faced with extras who wondered why we were pushing them around, difficulty in communicating, and because of the unpredictable weather, rarely knowing which scenes were next.

However, all problems paled when John Heard dunked me in the so-called mineral bath. I swallowed water the grips wouldn't put their feet in, and of course my hair and makeup were ruined. I was stunned. The crew shrank back into a mudbank, wondering how I'd handle it. I wasn't sure myself. When I surfaced, John was just standing there smiling at me. I truly do not know what the hell he had in mind but the effect was somehow to put everything else in perspective. It was such a spontaneous act that in many ways I thought it was funny. Outrageous, but funny. And so I shook the dirty water from my hair and face and couldn't think of anything to say but "I don't believe you did that."

The crew knew a long coffee break when they saw one. I retired to my trailer. There was no hot water, so someone got me rainwater in a bucket to wash my hair. All my makeup was streaked with mascara and mud, so I washed it off and Tina applied it again.

Stan walked in.

"We always say we'll never make another movie

again, don't we? But somehow when it's all over we forget the pain and difficulties."

I nodded, almost chuckling to myself.

"It's like childbirth, isn't it?" I asked.

"Yep," answered Stan.

I stared into the makeshift mirror, wondering if John would survive a push into the Urubamba River.

Just as Tom McPherson had predicted, several of the crew members were experiencing serious cardiovascular difficulties with the hard work in such high altitude. Most everyone had intestinal and stomach problems, and was losing weight. Tempers were short over such mistakes as the hotel operators calling the wrong rooms in the middle of the night.

The most serious sickness was that of the leading man on our sound crew. An old soldier from many wars, he refused to put his own health ahead of the production. He was close to cardiac arrest every day. So Stan took charge and told him he *had* to go home. No film was worth dying for.

On the day he left, we stopped the cameras and waved to his plane as it circled overhead. I heard someone say "The lucky cuss." But another guy shot a look at him and said, "What's the matter? Is what you're learning about yourself too much for ya?"

As each of us dealt with the difficulties in our own way, it soon became clear that we each had different lessons to learn and problems of self-esteem to solve. I heard the word *karma* everywhere as relationships were buffeted about in storms of emotional conflict. "What goes around comes around" was on everyone's lips. A kind of clear karmic harmony began to become evident. If someone was cruel and short-tempered at ten in the morning, it took no longer than till eleven o'clock for that person to experience the same treatment from another.

"It used to take three months for my karma to come

around," I heard someone say. "Now I'm experiencing it in twenty minutes."

And so it went. Sometimes the rain would come in flashing torrents, drenching us with such swiftness that there was no time to run for cover. There were many "towing" shots, where John and I had to do scenes in an open jeep with the cameras chained securely to the windshield and on "door platforms" while the camera crew huddled in a truck, hunkered down under yellow rain slickers. Sometimes they sang between gusting flurries of rain; sometimes they shivered in silence. I think John, as a New York actor, must have reassessed his respect for making movies. There was no way to know what the cameras were recording. There was no room in the jeep for Brad, and Butler sat in the back seat unable to see us. The dailies never did arrive, so we were, in effect, shooting blind, with only the crackling long-distance telephone assurance of someone back home in the editing room telling us that what we were getting was okay. They couldn't possibly understand what it felt like to pull trucks out of the mud every morning while living on peanut butter and crackers. Our feet were wet and frozen inside our combat boots, and our stomachs rumbled with Peruvian dysentery. The Peruvians themselves stood in open sandals in the cold driving rain with such patience, peering at us from under drenched ponchos and wondering if these invaders from North America's Hollywood were really from another planet.

Every now and then someone would bring lollipops to the location. The huge macho grips would pounce on them, licking away on a grape sucker while pulling a camera out of the mud.

The llamas and alpacas would periodically look up from grazing the rain-soaked knolls, blink those incredibly long eyelashes, observe our madness with judicially pursed lips, and go back to the sanity of being one with nature.

Whenever I could, I returned to the peace of my trailer, a gutted-out bus, wide and very comfortable. I wanted to invite every crew member in with me, but where would I start?

I carefully hoarded and slowly consumed each bowl of custard I had found in a bakeshop in the Cuzco Plaza. Sometimes the electric power in the trailer worked, sometimes not. The Peruvians said the gods at Machu Picchu were responsible for whether the power worked anywhere in the country.

Returning to my hotel at the end of every day, I looked forward to a hot bath to remove the mud. There was no stopper in the bathtub, so I used the heel of my foot to prevent the water from leaking out. Instead of a sheet, I slept with a blanket next to my skin for warmth, and when I wondered how I could ever communicate what we were going through, I huddled over my notebooks and jotted down my feelings. Day passed day, yet time seemed to be standing still.

Chapter 21

The second assault on Machu Picchu was rapidly approaching. And the ire of the cultural representative was rapidly reaching a boiling point. He had taken to calling me a neo-Nazi in public again. He had telephoned not only members of the local press but the foreign press as well, in order to call attention to the problem. He claimed he was going to shut down shooting of our picture unless I rewrote the scene in Machu Picchu.

I, in the meantime, had met a good friend of his. She was a woman who knew him and his family quite well. She told me that his son was a mystic, deeply involved in researching esoteric subjects. She said the man himself had seen spacecraft on a number of occasions. ("It would be difficult to avoid them, living in Cuzco," she added.) He had even speculated that the Inca ruins could not simply have been built by people from "here."

In any case, there had been an archeological and anthropological seminar held in Cuzco the previous year. Several factions were represented, attempting to explain the splendor of the Inca civilization, not only in Machu

Picchu but throughout Peru. One faction strongly contended there must have been extraterrestrial help of some kind, since so many craft had been sighted over the centuries and the technology required to build such monuments was beyond present-day explanation. Another faction objected vehemently to that. This was the political faction that claimed that recognition of extraterrestrial help was a neo-Nazi plot engineered to undermine belief in the intelligence of the Third World. This faction garnered a great deal of publicity. For whatever reasons of his own, the cultural representative had decided to embrace that position and was continuing to make it as public as possible. Several wire services had picked up this story, saying that shooting on our show had actually been shut down. All of it was engineered to pressure me into cutting the extraterrestrial speculation from the script. Frankly, I was more interested in whether we'd have sunshine, because the scene the man appeared to be worried about had already been shot in Los Angeles. But he didn't know that.

Esther Ventura was an Argentinian woman working for the production outfit that hired our crew in Peru. She was a cultured and sensitive woman with dark eyes and naturally curl-tossed hair who understood my script because she was on the path of her own spiritual quest. She knew of my concern about the one-shot chance we had to shoot Machu Picchu in good weather.

"I suggest you let me bring a broujo to you," she said in her husky voice. "They can be very effective in helping you control the weather."

I had never met a broujo. I had heard about them in my metaphysical readings and I was attracted to the notion of asking one for help with the weather, particularly in view of the fact that there seemed to be so much negative energy building up over the Machu Picchu shoot.

"Benito" was accepted as the Inca high priest of the

Andean area including Cuzco and Machu Picchu. His blessing would be needed in any case, according to Inca law. So the ceremony that was arranged was not a mere occult adventure; it would have taken place on some level, whether one had been aware of its implications or not.

Esther brought Benito to my trailer during a night shoot. It was particularly dark and cold. I expected an elderly man garbed in a traditional poncho and cap, but to my surprise Benito, dressed in a tweed suit with a vest, stepped out of a Toyota. He wore a brown felt slouch hat and was accompanied by his wife, who was dressed in a long skirt and a shawl.

Simo ushered them into my trailer and offered them cookies, liquor, coffee, and See's chocolates. Though Benito had very few front teeth, he polished off most of the chocolates in the first half hour while we chatted by the light of a candle. From the moment I looked into his sweet, wise face I liked him, which made it very difficult for me when I realized he was suffering badly from emphysema and could hardly manipulate his arthritic fingers as he pulled out his bag of coca leaves.

The bag of leaves seemed to be his prized possession. Through the leaves and the way they fell when he tossed them, he could see the past, future, and present. The coca leaves were somehow empowered to hold the secrets of the universe.

Immediately I thought of a drug arrest I had read about in New York City. Some man had gotten a long sentence for bringing through Customs a souvenir from Peru of a bag of coca leaves. I wondered what they'd do with old Benito.

With slow and attentive tenderness (and labored breathing) Benito placed a small felt packet, held together with string, on one of the orange crates I had set before him. For a moment he almost seemed to gaze through the fabric of the packet, his eyes a soft watery brown. Then with arthritic difficulty he untied the packet and extracted about a dozen tiny silver objects. As I looked closely, I saw they were representations of a star, a llama, numbers, a goat, zodiac symbols, and so on. He held the tiny silver cutouts securely in his hand. Suddenly one of them fell through his fingers. He looked at me and gasped. I didn't understand what had happened.

"Very unusual," he said to Esther in Quechua. "Never happen to me—don't understand."

I looked at the silver object that had fallen. It was a tiny silver star.

"What does it mean then?" I asked.

Esther translated and asked Benito.

"We will know in the days to come," he answered in his labored breathless way. Then he looked deeply into my eyes. It was almost as though the falling star represented a disaster of some kind (*dis-astrado* meaning torn, or separated, from the stars). But I couldn't imagine what it was. Could it be that the weather in Machu Picchu would be really bad and we wouldn't get the shot?

Then for some reason I felt that someone had died. I didn't know why.

Benito held the little star for a few minutes in the palm of his hand as though tuning in to its message. Then he looked up at me again with a sad smile on his face and waved the thought away.

Apparently having ascertained what he wanted from the rest of the silver objects, he bagged them again and put them away in the pocket of his suit jacket. He then gestured toward his wife, who was swaying on her feet where she stood above him, beside Simo. She handed him a package wrapped in newspaper. Placing the package on his lap, he opened it and slowly began to extract what was contained inside.

With crippled determination he placed the following objects on the daybed beside us: an ear of corn, a wad of animal fat, some seeds, a crystal, a coin of silver and gold, a small book made of silver and gold paper, some seashells, a sponge, several marzipan candies, a piece of a llama fetus (as I later learned), and a condor feather. He then sprinkled sugar over everything, on top of which he splashed some anisette liqueur.

I thought the daybed was going to enjoy some interesting aftereffects, but this was clearly the beginning of some kind of ceremony.

Just then there was a knock on the door of my trailer.

"They're ready for you," said one of the second assistants.

I got up and explained that I would return after we got the shot. Esther translated and Benito nodded.

When I stepped out into the cold wet night, the second assistant said, "What kind of voodoo ceremony is going on in there?" I laughed and said I'd do anything for good weather in Machu Picchu tomorrow.

I trekked to the set, which was the interior of the jeep lit for a small scene between John and me. John was sitting behind the wheel in a somber mood and didn't say much. I was glad—I could get the shot and return to my trailer.

Benito was waiting for me. As I sat down he made the sign of the cross and held his head in silent meditation for a long time. When he finished he said, "I talk to the high priests of Inca at Machu Picchu. They govern the weather. You have seven titular spiritual guides who guide you. They talk together. You are sincere in your search, but you must make ceremony to high priest of Inca."

"All right," I said. "What should I do?"

Benito waved my words away as, one by one, he lifted each of his displayed objects and meditated on them separately.

Esther whispered to me: "He told me they each

represent an element of life at Machu Picchu which must be respected and recognized."

His meditation ceremony was well into the hour mark when another rap came at the door.

"They're ready for me again," I said. "I'm sorry, but that is why we're here."

I left Benito and company and walked to the set again. By now there were whispers and sidelong glances cast toward me.

"She's doing one of her out-of-body astrals or something, you know," I overheard someone say.

We got the shot and I returned.

I was called to the set about five times during the course of the rest of the evening, and each time left my trailer as promptly as I could. I made a point of that because I was afraid that what happened later would happen.

Anyway, during a time period when they didn't need me, Benito earnestly conducted his ceremony and talked to me of my life. By now he had spread a gigantic bag of coca leaves across the daybed and proceeded to caress and meditate on each one in turn, as though each told a story. I had been to enough psychics to know that tarot cards or tea leaves or palm reading or *I-ching* were only tools that enabled the psychic to attune to a higher level of awareness. That awareness is available to all of us because it is only contact with the higher self, which is all-knowing and directly connected to the Divine Universal Energy Source. But psychics have had more training in attuning to that energy level, so they are able to trust it more readily than the rest of us are.

As Benito studied the shape of the coca leaves, I could see him go into a space with his spiritual mind which enabled him to see and sense more clearly.

"You have encountered many obstacles in your life," he said.

I nodded.

"But you have overcome. You will use your seven guides into the future to help shepherd your project through."

He stopped a moment.

"Why are you so interested in the lives you have led in the past?"

I shrugged.

"You must give that up. Your present is more interesting."

He stopped breathing for a moment. Then began again.

"You have separation from someone because you opened big trough in life he could not understand."

I said nothing but I thought of Gerry. Benito looked at me sadly again but didn't continue. He then got to the business at hand.

"You must do ceremony for good weather at Machu Picchu. The high priest of Inca agrees to help if you will do your part. Everything stems from feeling within. You will manifest what you sincerely believe. Do not doubt. Do not be afraid. Do not be mistrustful. What you believe is what will occur."

Benito then poured more anisette into a glass which he passed around the trailer to his wife, Esther, Simo, and me.

"It is not the liquor that is important," he said. "It is the sharing."

We each took a sip of the sweet liqueur and passed it on.

Two and one half hours had passed. The energy output Benito had exuded just psychically was demanding for a person in such ill health, but the ceremony was winding down. After blessing each coca leaf he gathered them up into his large bag and put them aside. Then he piled all the natural objects together and made a separate package out of them. He tied the package tightly, blessed it, and handed it to me.

"You must take this," he said, "to the highest point of Machu Picchu, face the East, and burn this packet. While burning you will think only of your vision of good weather, and your wish of good weather will come to pass. Do not doubt what you wish to happen."

I took the packet and handed it to Simo, wondering if the animal fat and llama fetus would keep until the next day. Benito took a small packet from his jacket.

"This is infusion tea," he said. "You may become ill when doing the ceremony. If so, drink this."

I took the tea packet from him. Benito stood up. The candles were burned nearly to stumps and the company crew had gone home. There was a cold drizzling rain gently drumming on the roof of the trailer. Benito gave one last hacking cough.

"You must see a doctor," I said. "You have done this for me. Let me do something for you."

Esther translated. He nodded and said something to her.

"He says he hears you are famous. All he wants is a picture of you."

"Certainly," I said, making a mental note that I would have the company doctor see him as soon as possible.

"Thank you, Benito," I said. "By the way, what is your last name?"

Esther told him what I asked. He looked at me triumphantly.

"My name means the condor of gold."

With that he bowed to me, and with his wife in tow, he left my trailer and stepped into his Toyota—which, I was to learn later, had been rented so that he could come to me. Through the misty rain I waved goodbye to him. Then I looked up into the night drizzle. I said a silent prayer that the package he had given me would work. I also noticed that I was too self-centered to say a prayer for him.

*   *   *

Simo woke me at 4:00 the next morning. This was the big day. Crew members all over Cuzco were rising and wondering if the arduous train trip would be worth it this time.

I did a quick yoga in my cold room, ate a piece of toast popped into a toaster by my bed, and determined to myself that everything would go perfectly for the day.

I wasn't in the car for five minutes before it was clear that "swimmingly" was not how the day would go.

The drive to the train for Machu Picchu would take several hours, particularly at zero ceiling outside. The fog was so thick that a snail would have beaten us. I wondered how the camera truck with all our equipment was going to make it in time to load onto the train. Never mind, I thought. I patted Simo's arm, which was holding Benito's weather packet for safekeeping.

"Oh," said Peter, our driver. "You should probably know—the security guard who has the key to the camera truck was out drunk all night and no one can find him. He never came back to the truck and he is the only one with the key, so unless they get the camera equipment to the train, how are you going to shoot?"

I clutched my stomach. I could literally feel it turn over. I couldn't talk. I stared out the window as though I could see through the fog. Simo cleared his throat.

"How do you know this?" he asked Peter.

"Well," he said, "they were going crazy in the production office when I left, but none of the bigwigs know about it yet."

"I do," I said, finding my voice.

"Yes, ma'am," he answered.

Well, well, well. Talk about trying to find the purposeful good in everything. This was my big chance. The security guard got drunk and shacked up all night with a hooker who probably rolled him afterward (keys included) because his destiny was to learn something? But what about me and the rest of us? What the hell was going on? I tried to stay calm. If the camera truck missed the train, what would be the point of the rest of us going? Sometimes the finer points of higher consciousness eluded me.

As we crawled along in the fog we passed the camera crew van. The guys inside had no idea that there would be no equipment to shoot with. What were they supposed to learn from this?

As we plowed through the rain and fog I realized that my lesson was probably "Stop projecting the worst. Somehow it will all work out." That kind of attitude had been guaranteed to make me irritatingly perturbed whenever someone quoted it to me. I thought it was irresponsibly idealistic, unprofessional, and all-in-all hopelessly undisciplined and capricious. In sum: "spaced out."

Yet there I was having no recourse but to accept it. Now, as I felt myself helpless to change anything, why not believe that it was all happening for a *good* reason? This attitude of mine being one of them.

In a slightly more positive—which is to say, resigned—frame of mind, I sat back. Well, at least I didn't jump out the window as we drove.

We pulled into the train station to find Dean and Stan having coffee in one of the train compartments.

"Well," I said accusingly, "what are we going to do? Will the train wait?"

"Wait for what?" asked Stan.

"The camera truck," I answered.

"The camera truck will be here any minute," he said reassuringly.

"Oh, really?" I asked. "What did you do, fly it in?"

"What do you mean?" he asked.

"The security guy went AWOL with the keys. It hasn't left yet because no one had another set."

Stan and Dean went white and jumped up. I didn't see where they went or whom they checked with. I only knew the fumes inside the train compartment were so toxic that I had to leave. Simo handed me an umbrella, so I took myself out in the rain, marched down to the Urubamba River, and stared into it wondering where it would take me if I jumped.

Three hours later the camera truck arrived. Someone had uncovered another set of keys. The security guy never did show up and the train for Machu Picchu waited. The lesson? The realization that we wasted three hours *worrying*.

The train ride seemed shorter (in fact, it was) and certainly less lugubrious than the first one. John Heard seemed struck with wonder to learn that he had actually taken it before.

The crew was in fairly good spirits because if we got this scene we were coming into home plate of location completion. Colin had departed for L.A. several days before, so Stan and I were left holding down the creative part.

With prayers in our hearts we scanned the skies as the train pulled into the station just below the Machu Picchu monument. Perhaps it wasn't necessary to take the drizzling rain at the train station seriously. I closed my eyes and tried to project. Simo lifted his face to the clouds and did the same. I couldn't find Stan. Perhaps the three-hour wait at the station had prevented our seeing even worse weather. Esther patted my arm.

We piled into the buses and with uncertain emotions made our way up the winding road to the mountaintop.

Fifteen minutes later our fears were confirmed. A solid thicket of fog accompanied by a cold drizzle enveloped the Lost City. Machu Picchu wasn't even visible.

I took Benito's "element packet" from a bag. Simo had tied together dried twigs to make a fire which he carefully held protected from the wet. I wondered how long a fire would burn in this drizzle anyway.

I couldn't find Stan. Esther offered to locate him in

the melee of disembarking crew members. I watched each of them as they looked up, looked around, and laughed.

"Are you kidding or what?" I heard one of them remark as he bundled up inside his raincoat. "Who can shoot anything in this and still see it?"

"Okay," I said to Simo. "Let's start climbing. If ever it was necessary to trust in creating my own reality, it's now."

Esther returned with Stan in tow.

"What's up?" he asked.

I explained everything that Benito had said. He didn't scoff or smirk at all. Quite the contrary.

"Let's go," he said. "We have a lot of projecting to do so we can get in a good day's work. In fact the *only* day's work at this place."

The crew looked askance as the four of us—Stan, Esther, Simo, and I—trudged into the fog and rain and disappeared from their view.

The climbing entailed in getting to the top of Machu Picchu is no joke. Even if the sun did come out, I wondered how the guys would lift the equipment to the top. No matter. That's show business. We climbed in the drizzle with the twigs and the package for about fifteen minutes—straight up the very narrow steps of the monument. We stopped, took a collective breath, turned around, and looked below us. Nothing was visible. It was as though we had ascended into a sprinkly fog-heaven and left the earth below us forever. We could hear voices in the lower realms, but they were only haunting reminders of those who doubted and had no faith in the potential of expectation. Miracles being opportunities that work out better than expected.

We smiled at one another and continued to climb. Near the very top we spotted a flat-surfaced rock that looked as though it might have been used for ceremonies of some kind. We made our way to it. Climbing above the fog still higher, we found ourselves standing on the rock with a 360-degree view of mist and floating clouds around us. At the same moment a giant alpaca—no doubt the one that is said to guard the monument—materialized above the veiled rocks and—I swear—floated toward us. We didn't move. He stopped, looked at us, chewed his cud, and as though giving us his blessing, he regally turned and disappeared back into his shrouded kingdom. A chill of wonder went up my spine. I had learned to trust those chills. They almost always meant that whatever I was thinking or saying was the truth.

We had already determined which direction was east, so we placed the packet facing the obscured, yet rising, sun. We each took a moment to acknowledge that the sun was actually above us, however invisible it was.

Then Simo placed the twigs under the packet. The packet was so wet each of us dragged Kleenex from our pockets and leaned down to light it. Slowly the twigs began to smoke. Then a thin flame appeared.

We stood up and faced the east and began our visualizations.

"Picture the weather you would like to have," Benito had said. "Your mind's picture will manifest if you trust it."

Rain birds chirped in the drizzle. Stan spoke. "As a producer who has prayed for weather in many different countries," he said, "I don't have the chutzpah to ask for more sunlight than we need!"

"Okay," I said. "I'm going to visualize a third-dimensional misty quality with sunlight shining through. I'd like clouds to hang suspended in the air." The four of us exchanged looks as we each prepared to do what we could to enhance Machu Picchu.

Silently the "element package" began to burn. Then it crackled and snapped. Holding hands, each of us projected our collective weather desire. As I did mine, I found myself wondering what projections felt like to other people. Did their minds respond more readily to what they wanted to see than mine did? I thought of all the stories about Lourdes and the miracles. "They occur because people want them to" was the oft-repeated repudiation. Yes, I thought, isn't that the way it should be? Shouldn't the patient always participate equally with the doctor? If you believe you are well, you are, and vice versa. Body following conscious belief. It was best never to acknowledge that doubt is real.

I closed my eyes as I pictured the sun shining on third-dimensional clouds. I could feel the fear of failure creep in momentarily. I pushed it away. I opened my eyes and observed Stan, Simo, and Esther. Each was meditating with eyes closed.

About five minutes went by. A spiraling curl of smoke rose above the twigs. Then suddenly, coming toward us up the stone steps, was a man. He was dressed in an official raincoat with a rain hat and had a badge on his shoulder that indicated he was the fire warden for the ancient ruin.

He began to gesture and yell at us in Spanish. It startled us out of our reverie, but nobody said anything. And then, as though we were conducted by a puppet master, the four of us turned and looked at the fire warden at the same time. He stopped talking. He stopped gesturing. No words were exchanged, and as though guided by an invisible force he looked away from us and, completely changing the direction of his attention, walked up the hill until he was out of sight. It was an out-of-focus, dreamlike encounter. He actually stopped objecting to our fire in midsentence and never looked back. None of *us* had uttered one word.

Esther glanced at me and winked. We then returned to our misty meditation. Then rain birds began to sing again. A rush of energy went through my body. Then I became profoundly peaceful. I could almost hear the clouds drift through the mist. The seven guides Benito had talked about swam into my mind. I meditated on them. They didn't have form really. I just acknowledged their presence. I asked them for help. I visualized the way I wanted Machu Picchu to look. I could feel the others meditating with the same intensity.

About half an hour went by. Then, as though on cue, the four of us broke our meditation. The "element package" was ashes now. There was only a thin waft of smoke left from the mystical ceremony. We stretched, as if to signify its conclusion, and then we embraced each other. There was nothing left to do or say—except for something I felt very strongly. So I said it out loud.

"It will be sunny in about an hour," I announced, absolutely sure of my words. The others nodded and shrugged. "So I'm going down to the hotel to get made up and dressed so I'll be ready."

As I began to descend through the mist down the steps of the ruins, a queasy dizziness came over me. I was suddenly very sick at my stomach and could hardly keep my balance. I thought it was the altitude, or maybe the jam cookie I had eaten on the train. I kept walking. The nausea became worse. What was going on? Then I remembered the small packet of herbs Benito had given me. "You will become ill because of the energy swirling through you. Make a tea with this." But I hadn't remembered where I'd put it. I kept walking. When I came to some of the crew at the bottom I could hardly speak, but I heard them talking to me.

"What were you doing up there? Making more rain?"

"When do we leave? We'll never get this today either. . . ."

I couldn't answer. Just smiled. I needed to walk until I could lie down in my room. I could feel a strange pressure on my body, a sense of literal decompression. I'd never felt anything like it in my life. I made my way to my room and lay down for a minute. Then something made me get up immediately and go to the makeup room, where Tina was set up. I sat down in the makeup chair. She commented on how white I looked and wondered why I was bothering to get made up at all, considering the weather. I could hardly breathe. I needed to hyperventilate to keep going. I sat there nauseous and dizzy until she was finished. Then I put on my wardrobe, which felt as though it belonged to somebody else. My body felt detached from me. I heard some of the crew talking excitedly outside. With painful difficulty I walked to the window and looked up. The clouds were lifting. The drizzle had stopped. The crew was carrying the equipment to the top of the mountain.

"Hey," said Tina, "look at that. What did you guys do up there?"

I couldn't answer. I walked outside. Simo could see how sick I was. He walked beside me.

"Let's climb now," I said. "I want to be ready when the sun breaks through."

Someone had already alerted John, so he would be ready too.

As I climbed I found my legs wouldn't work properly. There was no strength in my knees. I needed to climb stiff-legged which meant bearing down on Simo's arm for support to raise my body step after step. Thank God he was powerfully built. The sickness was worse now. It was overwhelming. I didn't understand what was happening. It felt as though some energy pattern was grounding itself through me, and the intensity of the vibration was more than I could take. I looked up. The sun was breaking through. A few crew members applauded. I climbed higher, wanting to vomit with each step, yet unable to. Simo helped me walk. It felt almost as though he were a battery of some kind—that I needed the physical contact of his arm.

The cameras were set up above me. As I walked toward them a few crew members rushed forward to help me. I explained it was the altitude and a drop in my blood sugar which was creating the nausea and lack of strength. That seemed to satisfy them, but some of them were enough in tune with me to understand there was more to it.

John was ready to shoot. The script girl held the script in front of me. I took a quick glance at my lines, took a deep breath, and was ready.

"Are you okay?" asked John.

"Sure," I answered.

"I guess when you witch out the weather, it makes you sick, eh?"

He was remarkable, really.

"Yeah," I answered, hanging on, not eager to spend energy on anything but the shot.

I looked around me. The sun had broken through the clouds completely and was shining over them so as to cast an outlined aura around the ruins as well as the trees. The third-dimensional mystical quality was even more pronounced than I had visualized. It was a poetic painting . . . perfect.

"It's beautiful," said John. "Worth it."

That was all that was said and the cameras rolled. The scene called for me to walk to the edge of a cliff, look down, and say some dialogue. John saw that I could hardly walk, so he helped me. I found myself lifting my legs much higher than I needed to because I was so unsure of my footing. We got the scene.

The camera guys set up quickly in another location. We got that scene too. All the while I was stabilizing myself so I wouldn't throw up. My face was white, my skin clammy, and I couldn't wait for it all to be over with. I desperately wanted a bottle of Coca-Cola. Someone ran down the mountain to the hotel dining room and found a Coke. I needed sugar to ground me. I drank it all at once.

For two and a half hours we shot. I was suspended

in a bubble of sickness. The crew wanted to stop and take a lunch break.

"Please," I said to Yudi. "Ask them if we can shoot straight through. I can't hold this energy much longer and if I let go of it, I'm sure it will pour with rain."

Yudi asked the crew. They complied.

Esther came over to me.

"You know," she said, sounding impossibly assured, "you are going through a cleansing process along with everything else."

I began to cry immediately. What kind of cleansing? I didn't know. I only knew it was true. I hadn't eaten since the early morning, and the thought of rich food repulsed me. I hadn't had a cigarette all morning, either, which was unusual for me. Suddenly it was difficult for me to be around those members of the crew who were smoking.

We continued to shoot. We shot every conceivable angle of the Machu Picchu ruins so we'd have plenty to choose from in the editing room. I stood and sat with tense rigidity so I could hold the energy, whatever it was.

Finally we got the last shot. The crew applauded. I relaxed. We looked up. As God is my judge, a cloud drifted in front of the sun. In fact, clouds seemed to materialize from out of thin, clear air.

"Quickly. Quickly," yelled Yudi. "Let's get a crew picture of all of us here. Everybody line up."

The still photographer set up his tripod, checked his focus, and shielded his camera with a plastic coat while the rest of us lined up dutifully, feeling the drizzly mist moving in around us. There were hurried shouts of direction. And then something happened which I will never forget as long as I live. The photographer took about five shots of the entire crew. We all smiled and shouted as though the camera could record it. Then, as though by direct cue from an unseen director, the still photographer said, "That's it—I'm out of film." And immediately the skies literally *dumped* sheets of rain on us. Our small band of movie-makers was drenched within one minute. It actually made us laugh, it was so "coincidental." Everyone turned to me and at that moment my nausea and weakness went away. If it hadn't happened to me personally I wouldn't have believed it. But somehow the pressure of holding the energy was released, and with it I was back to normal.

I raced down the narrow steps of the ruins until I reached the hotel, whereupon I collapsed on my hotel bed and slept for three hours while the crew got some second-unit footage and finally packed the equipment onto the train.

In my sleep I had several visions (dreams, images, apparitions—whatever word applies). First I saw Gerry. It was so strange, because I hadn't really thought much about him since our meeting in London. But there he was—sort of hovering over me, curious and somehow needing to make contact.

Then I saw a funny vision which had such impact that its message continues to hold me in its meaning even today.

I have never been a really heavy smoker, lighting about a pack a day. I *never* inhaled. It was a social habit, not an addiction, something to do with my hands, or to induce a sense of relaxation by being companionable. Nevertheless, I stuck to one brand. I smoked Vantage 100's.

My vision was a huge package of Vantage 100 cigarettes. The package was the size of a human being. I climbed up the side of the package and looked over the top of the interior. It was empty. There were no cigarettes in the package. As I peered down into the empty package a voice rang in my ears: "See to it that it stays empty."

I laughed at the vision. It woke me. It was as though

my higher self had painted a picture so graphic I couldn't ignore its message.

I am now one of the legions of people who have given up the filthy habit. I haven't had even a puff since that bizarre vision. I'm not sure I can recommend my method of quitting to anyone else, though.

All the way back on the train I gazed out at the wild Urubamba swirling and crashing against the rocks of the Andes. I thought about my original trip to the Andes, how the whole adventure had inspired me to write *Out on a Limb*, how the conflict with Gerry had propelled me to understand more of what life meant. And Gerry was still a part of me, still a character who seemed to impose himself on the drama of my life, even if it was only in a dream.

But then what was the dream? Was life the dream or was life the theater? Where did one stop and the other begin? Or was there a difference?

When we returned to Cuzco it wasn't long before the word got around that I had controlled the weather and made sunshine happen in Machu Picchu on a day that was intrinsically gloomy. After that came the Peruvian newspaper articles that claimed I believed I was the reincarnation of an Inca princess. Between that and the extraterrestrials the papers said I claimed built Machu Picchu, I could have started my own *Peruvian National Enquirer*.

Chapter 22

*T*he next day's shooting in the Chinchero market began pleasantly enough. The mayor of the town honored me with a ceremony and a presentation of an antique textile representing the color combinations of the village. Bob Butler was honored with an antique plow which was the symbol of work.

I heard some of the crew saying they might stay on after the shooting because they found the people so simple and pure.

During one take I fell down in the mud.

I read some Spanish movie magazines at a vendor's stand.

I was having a sense of disjointedness. All day I felt a sort of longing loneliness, as though something I couldn't touch was missing. I tried to brush it aside, but it was like a gentle, gnawing pain, the kind you keep worrying at even while you are trying to ignore it.

I kept thinking of Gerry, as though I should call him or something.

At the end of the day I looked forward to a hot bath with my heel stuffed in the drain.

Just as I had undressed, the telephone rang. When I picked it up I realized it was long distance, and then I heard Bella's voice.

"I've been trying to call for two days," she said. "You're in a place that doesn't exist."

"Well, I never got your message."

"I know," she said in a tentative way.

"What do you mean?" I asked.

"I didn't want to tell you what I have to tell you. I didn't want to be the one."

I couldn't imagine what she was talking about.

If it was something to do with my daughter, or Mom and Dad, Bella wouldn't have been the one to call.

"Tell me what?" I asked.

"It's Gerry," she said.

"Gerry?"

"Yes," she said. Then she hesitated. "He was in an auto accident on vacation in the South of France."

My thoughts of him swirled back to me; the longing, the feeling something was missing. I stopped thinking for a minute. Then I knew.

"He's dead, isn't he?" I asked.

There was a slight strangled gasp.

"Yes, my darling. I'm so sorry."

I didn't say anything. She went on.

"It's so strange," she said, "that you're shooting a film about him and I'm yet again the character in your real-life play that tells you he's gone."

I didn't know what to say.

"I didn't want to tell you. That's why I didn't leave any messages."

"Oh," I said, the full implication of her reluctance hitting me.

I thought of the tiny silver star that had fallen through Benito's fingers, and how distressed he had been.

"When did it actually happen, Bella?" I asked.

She told me. I figured out the time difference, but I already knew. It was at exactly the hour of Benito's visit.

"How did you find out?" I asked.

"The English papers carried it first. I saw a squib here. Then I made some calls."

"How's his wife?"

"Devastated."

"Is there going to be a funeral?" I asked, wondering if we'd be through shooting in time for me to go.

"I don't know," said Bella. "But if there is, you shouldn't even show up in the city of London. That wouldn't be wise for anybody."

I couldn't concentrate. I was thinking of our last meeting.

I put a hand over my eyes and tried to block out my surroundings. I tried to put the karmic pieces together. Had I, on some level, known it was going to happen and during our meeting made contact with him one more time? Had he known he was going to check out? Didn't everybody know on a soul level when and why they were leaving? Was that our one monumental act of free will? But why did he do it?

"Are you all right?" asked Bella.

"Why did he do it, Bellitchka?" I asked.

She hesitated, knowing that she was suddenly into a metaphysical spiritual conversation, on a level beyond not only her comprehension but mine too. Maybe that was why she hadn't wanted to be the one to tell me.

"You mean, why did he die?" she asked.

"I mean why did he *decide* to die now, when he had so much to look forward to, so much to accomplish? We had so many things to discuss together. So what changed his mind?" I asked, never expecting her to answer me really.

"Well," she said, "he didn't decide to die. I told you. It was an accident. Nobody decides to die. It just happens. It's one of those mysteries."

"No," I said. "No. It's not as simple as that. It's *connected* somehow, Bella."

I could feel my voice trailing off with my thoughts. I didn't feel like crying, but I desperately wanted to go away somewhere, someplace I could just be quiet, by myself. I thought, I'm not emotionally involved with Gerry enough anymore to be stunned on a personal-loss level. But *some*thing had been bugging me the past couple of days. Was this why I had been thinking about him in Machu Picchu and today? Was he actually *around*? Was he trying to contact me as a soul energy now, because he no longer had a body? *Then* it hit me that I wouldn't ever see him again. Instantly a picture filled my mind of the last time we had met, when he had prowled back and forth in front of his bookcase. Then an odd thought struck me—as such apparent irrelevancies do at times of stress. . . .

Bella's voice on the phone was saying, "Are you there, my darling? Are you all right?"

"I'm okay, Bella," I said. "Bella? Listen. What if they find my love letters stashed in those books in his bookshelves? Who goes through those things?"

"God. I don't know," she said. "But I'm sure they'll respect his privacy for many reasons."

Yes, of course they will, I thought. They always did.

"Is Mr. Dance playing me well?" he had said that day in London. I wanted to say, "Excruciatingly so; with all the spiritually closed-minded familiarity he can muster up." But I hadn't. I could see Gerry was still operating in the dark ages of his own spiritual self, while functioning with all cylinders ignited, intellectually. At least I had learned to let him be. Let him have his own reality, his own pace in life.

And now he was not in that intellectually empirically provable body anymore. He was suddenly operating in territory the very existence of which he had always denied. He was now only a soul. Had he gone home and not recognized it? Was I feeling his presence because he needed guidance and had no one else to consult?

"I've been feeling him around, Bella," I finally said.

"What are you talking about?"

"Well, it's like he's been in my thoughts for a few days for no reason. Now I see why. God knows how he'll contact me now that I know where he is."

"Oh," said Bella. "Well, my darling, like I said, this whole thing is too Pirandello-ish for me. I feel like I'm in somebody else's play bringing you this news."

"You know, Bella," I said, "when I saw him last time I sensed so much that he was abusing people with his intellectual superiority and not asking enough spiritual questions. I almost wanted to warn him to develop that spiritual side of himself or he'd be in trouble."

"Yeah," she said. "You told me. But did you tell him?"

"No," I said. "I couldn't. He was so intimidatingly sure of himself, sort of ordering people around and stuff. But, God, I still found him attractive. I really felt we had another few rounds to go with each other."

"Yeah," said Bella. "I remember you said."

"Soooo," I said, not knowing what else to say, "I guess he had his reasons for going now."

"You really believe that, don't you?" she asked, very seriously.

"Yes," I said. "I really do. And I'd say this if it were Sachi or you or anyone else I really, really would hate to lose."

"So you think everyone decides *when* they want to go?" she asked, trying to clarify what I was saying.

"Oh, sure," I answered. "Not only *when,* but *how.*"

"I see," said Bella simply.

"He knows from my book that he was a catalyst for my own spiritual search. That was the role he played in my life and now on the screen. He knows that he was one of the most important people in my life because he made me realize that intellectual pragmatism is not enough."

"How do you know he understands this?"

"Because he's now on the other side, where brains and pragmatics don't matter all that much."

"You really think he's over there, or rather over *you*, hovering around or something?"

"Yes," I said. "I know it. I can feel it. And now he wants to understand."

"So how are you going to help him?" she asked.

I thought a moment.

"I don't know."

"Yeah, well," said Bella. "Like I said. I'm really sorry, my darling. Let me know if there is anything I can do to help."

"Okay," I answered. "But I really think it's *him* that needs help now, not me. I think he's really shocked to find that death is not oblivion. I need to help him over the problem of realizing, perhaps even of recognizing, that he is now disembodied."

"Whatever you say," said Bella. "I just can't think like that. Sometimes I wish I could, but I can't. So I'll speak with you in a few days."

"Thanks, Bella," I said. "How's Martin?"

"He's fine. He sends his condolences. But he says you had closed that chapter of your life with Gerry, but here it is, an ongoing play, and I'm still playing the same part."

We hung up.

I paced around the hotel room. I had to move around, walk. So then I got dressed and went out. I walked around Cuzco by myself, into the bazaars. I bought some baby-alpaca sweaters, some earrings, anything that felt like a familiar activity to divert my attention from what had happened. I stopped and listened to the church bells, to an old Elvis Presley record spinning on a jukebox somewhere. Then I heard a refrain of a song that Gerry and I had loved together. I seemed to be moving through my own drama, watching myself react.

The gorilla-chasing dream came back to me. The dream where he chases me to the edge of the cliff and I turn around and say to him, "What should I do now?" and he says, "I don't know, kid—it's your dream." I felt as if my life was a dream. An illusion, as the Buddhists and Hindus claim. If we created our dreams at night out of the stuff of the subconscious, superconscious, or whatever level of consciousness we utilize, then perhaps we were doing the same thing during our working-day hours. Perhaps we could make our daydream anything we wanted it to be, depending on what we wanted and needed to get out of it, "to rise out of the muck and the mire of the delusion of life," the Hindus said in the old Vedic scriptures. Life was a dream, an illusion, a play, a delusion, an entertainment. Some of us enjoyed being entertained by violence, some by tragedy, some by comedy and adventure. And some didn't like being entertained by the illusion at all anymore. When that happened to people, they decided to end the dream, draw the curtains on the magic they had created for themselves in the first place.

The question was this: Did I draw the curtain on Gerry? Or did he draw the curtain on me?

From the time I knew that Gerry had left the body, everything changed for me. I felt that he was constantly around. It was an unusual and yet reconfirming experience. It wasn't disconcerting, but more reassuring, because my spiritual principles were based on a belief in the eternity of the soul. Often I asked myself whether I was creating the feeling of his presence because I wanted confirmation of my beliefs. But it really didn't feel like that.

Nothing bumped in the night, or materialized in a blaze of light at the foot of my bed in the darkness. No form of ectoplasm came to visit me when I least expected it, tapping out messages on tabletops. Nothing resembling anything I had read of other people's experiences happened to me. It was more a constant, continually pressing, yet gentle presence, as though Gerry were asking for clarification and guidance. I literally *felt* the questions, almost signifying that he might be stuck in some dimension between his earth experience and the higher truth of his next adventure. I felt that he found the result of his departure extremely disorienting, rendering him nearly incapable of adjusting to what he had done with any balance or acceptance. That was where I felt I came in. The conflict in our relationship had centered around my developing understanding that man was essentially a spiritual being, and his conviction that man was essentially a mental and physical being. He had been a confirmed atheist, actively denouncing the role of God and the Church in the culture of an advanced civilization, and as a good and intellectual socialist, he based his compassion and humanitarian impulses on the sociological shrewdness of the necessity for peace in an otherwise violent world.

He believed that mankind's problems were essentially economic, where I believed that spiritual ignorance was the basic problem, therefore setting up the conflicts in a have and have-not world. Whenever I pointed out that most of the wars on the planet today were being fought over the interpretation of God (Arab versus Jew, Hindu versus Moslem, Protestant versus Catholic, communist atheists versus capitalist Christians), he said no, they were based on economic disparity. When I argued that belief in God gave people hope and literally kept them going, he said it was necessary to perpetuate such a myth in order to bear the tragedy of poverty.

When I said that I believed that the God-force was within each of us, not outside or above in a pink cloud surrounded by harps and milk and honey, he said that to believe God was within gave man a license to self-righteousness and cruel abuse of power. I said that those who professed not to believe in God (communists, for example) abused their power more than anybody.

He kept saying we were in an age of economic disparity, and I that we were in an age of spiritual ignorance that caused a particularly destructive form of fundamentalism, each faction intolerantly believing *their* God was the only one because they couldn't accept anyone else's God, much less that God was within each of us.

And so it went, around and around. Neither of us got to the point of agreeing that our thinking was not necessarily mutually exclusive.

Since Gerry was such a brilliant economic and sociopolitical pragmatist, I was fascinated with the demonstration of his mental gymnastics. I was even more intrigued by the cold truth that spiritually he was so adamantly of a closed mind. This was an irresistible challenge to me, giving me something intriguing to try to overcome. How a man that compassionately brilliant and intellectually advanced could be so closed and threatened by the subject of God and soul became an adventure for me.

Of course he found it upsetting to contemplate such dimensions, because he couldn't see them or prove that they existed, but I always had the feeling that it was upsetting to him because, if he had recognized the potential truth of the alternative realities, he would have felt swamped by the accompanying sense of lack of control. And one thing Gerry needed to feel was autonomy.

The other reason for his closed-minded intellectualism was more complicated. It had to do with his own self-esteem and his need to believe he was taking complete responsibility for the life he was leading. Because he was an insistent pragmatist, this had to relate to the things he did, rather than to who he was. It would seem that the natural base of his intellectual arrogance would be a high opinion of himself. But that was not the case.

When he had told me he liked to be admired, but not by people who meant anything to him, I understood that he meant he would have had to live up to those qualities that elicited such admiration on a daily basis and under scrutiny. He didn't like the personal pressure which on closer examination *always* accompanied the question of the spiritual self on some level. He understood that man could not function without the unseen dimension of hope, but looking at the world through his admirably reasonable eyes, he couldn't see where the hell it came from. Better to deny the basis for that hope, do the best he could in pragmatic terms for the large, unseen, impersonal masses. Yet somewhere deep in his gut, Gerry did know that he was failing both them and himself. Somewhere on some level he understood that his intellectualism was arrogant and that he really was afraid to admit that he, as well as everyone else, was aligned and attuned to the Divine, whether one went to church or recognized that one had a soul or not.

Now that he had crossed over, was he being forced to acknowledge that his earthly insistence on actively ignoring the dimension of the Divine had been a profound oversight? Was that why I felt him around me asking for help? Would I be able to give it to him if I could just figure out a way to do it?

In the meantime I finished up the movie. Some members of the crew were suffering so badly from various forms of dysentery, insomnia, and just simple human maladjustment disorders that they were on automatic pilot, longing for the day when they'd be able to pop down to McDonald's or Love's Barbecue Ribs, sit in front of the TV with a beer, and enjoy the simple American pleasures that included the family and loved ones they often took for granted. Others had transcended the primitive trials of the Andes and could be anywhere from now on and feel happy. Neither was more advanced than the other. As a matter of fact, several who were having the best time seemed not to have progressed one iota in their personal growth. Some of those who slept well and functioned in a perfectly ordinary manner were simply treading water and had opted not to look into themselves and stir up what was unresolved residue. Of course it could be that they didn't have any. . . . Some of the most uncomfortable had taken quantum leaps in their personal self-knowledge because they had dared to confront their personal conflicts by giving themselves uncomfortable reactions to the primitive conditions.

One thing was certain. Everyone was beginning to view life and its working conditions through the eyes of perception rather than evaluating it all as objective fact and reality. As a result, they were coming to the understanding that they were responsible for how they experienced the location. We were not victims of the location we saw; we were victims of the way we saw the location.

I was in for a learning process of my own on that score. It had to do with the abuse of power. As the production department brought our business to a close, the question of bonuses came up. I heard that ABC would not give Esther a bonus, because "she had not been a good influence on me." Irately I demanded to see the Brass and Brass Number One showed up. We happened to meet in the bar, with surrounding crew members well within earshot, when I asked, in no uncertain terms, what the hell this was all about. *Why* wasn't Esther getting a bonus?

"Because she brought that voodoo expert to your trailer and you got so interested you held up production because you wouldn't come out."

This was news to me. I remembered being so careful to report as soon as they called me for each setup.

"Listen," I said, "I don't know where you got that. I was out of that trailer so fast just *because* I didn't want to be accused of this."

"That's not what the production sheet says, and my job is to go by *it*," he answered.

"Then fuck the production sheet—it's *wrong*!" I shouted. "And besides, even if I *had* held up production—which I didn't—I was having a ceremony that I believe ultimately helped us alter the weather in Machu Picchu."

"Yeah," he said. "And that ceremony made you sick."

"So *what*?" I said. "What the hell difference does it make to *you*? We got the sun and we got the shot, didn't we? What do you care how we made it happen or how I was feeling?"

He looked at me with a baffled expression. Maybe he really did care. I realized then that we weren't talking about production problems. We were talking about spiritualism, and he was using my sickness and supposed tardiness to attack something that looked as though it might have been a metaphysical "miracle" that he found difficult to accept.

I hated the subterfuge. Why couldn't he come right out and say that it was voodoo black magic bullshit to him? Angry all over again I rushed on to attack further, berating his intelligence, his honesty with himself, dragging up the mess about not feeding the Peruvian crew, accusing him of abusing his power—and finally stopping dead in my tracks, appalled that I was acting out what I felt he was doing. Shaken both by my anger and by the unpleasant discovery about myself, but still unwilling to admit to it, I stood up, said something like, "I can't deal with this," and stalked out. I didn't have the guts to apologize.

Once again I had failed myself, had reacted with strongly expressed negativism to a situation which might have been remedied if handled with reason and understanding. If I had had the sense to step back and gain some perspective on the role I was playing in the conflict of interests I might have been able to take the sting out of my own anger.

When I realized what was really going on, I found myself attracting people to me during the last days of filming who hadn't connected to me before because I wasn't ready for them. I was so busy playing out the drama of emotional conflict that I hadn't taken the time

Gerry never left me. He seemed to be hovering over me, watching and curiously listening to what was transpiring in my life. On an earth plane level he would have pooh-poohed what was happening. "Aberrations of imagination," he would have said. But now—who knew? —perhaps he could not only afford to be open-minded, but found it necessary if he was to go on to complete his own higher understanding.

Meantime, there were aspects of higher understanding that *I* intended to explore.

Chapter 23

Mr. Anton Ponce de Leon is a cultural anthropologist in charge of investigating UFO sightings in Cuzco. He is a gentle, unassuming man of kind patience yet rigorous curiosity. Since so many sightings had been reported, he was a busy man.

"I never really understood any of the reports I received," he said, "until I had an experience myself."

Anton then described a sighting he'd had near a lagoon in the mountains outside of Cuzco.

He said he was driving home late one night, through the mountain pass, when he noticed a string of lights hovering above the usually quiet lagoon. He got out of the car to observe more closely. All he could hear were the frogs in the water. Otherwise, silence. Then suddenly the string of lights began to move, without sound, until the two ends linked up with each other, forming a circle. He said he couldn't see whether the lights were from craft or not. Then from the opposite direction he saw another light hanging over the city of Cuzco. It began to move toward the circle of lights above the lagoon, becoming larger and larger until it hovered above them.

Now, lit from underneath, he could see it was a giant craft. He watched as it linked up with the lights over the lagoon.

"It looked as though the lights were supplying energy to the craft," said Anton. "I watched for three and a half hours, until I was too cold."

"What was it?" I asked.

He looked at me, not certain whether to go on.

"I don't know," he said. "That was my experience. After that, I no longer called anyone else crazy for what they reported. And those who call me crazy now will stop after they have their own experience."

Anton had not read *Out on a Limb* and was not aware of the story we were filming. He had simply been told that I was interested in extraterrestrial activity. We took a long walk together after shooting one day and I attempted to make him feel comfortable in sharing more of his experiences.

He told me he had met a woman who had changed his life with her philosophy and spiritual knowledge. I didn't think much of it at first, but then I realized he might be describing someone I had very likely heard of before.

"What did she talk about?" I asked.

Anton was reluctant to be very specific except to say that she discussed the state of the world with him, how negative thinking was ruining human relationships, and how a deep internal spiritual belief in the God within each of us was what would be the salvation of mankind, particularly in the face of nuclear disaster. She discussed something he described as "spiritual technology," outlining energy patterns and electromagnetic vibrational frequencies emanating from a person who is peaceful as opposed to the kind of energy coming from a conflicted and tortured individual. She said inner peace was the most valued state of being in the cosmos.

"Well, who was she?" I asked.

He shrugged. "She only had one name."

He said nothing more.

"What did she look like?" I asked.

"She was small, with dark hair and dark almond-shaped eyes, not really Oriental. I've never seen eyes like hers. She was so beautiful. She seemed to look through to my soul, and when she moved she was floating almost."

"Where was she from?" I asked.

Anton brushed lint from his coat and shrugged again.

"Let me tell you something," I said.

I then proceeded to describe Mayan, the extraterrestrial character in *Out on a Limb*, with whom David claimed to have had contact.

"She was just as you described and her name was Mayan," I finished.

Anton's eyes lit up like diamonds.

"That was the name of the woman I met. And she had a 'commander' who worked with her. I met him, too."

I remembered David describing the commander of the craft he had claimed to go on. He said the individual looked human except that he was small, with ears very close to his head, and had no eyelashes or eyelids.

"What did her 'commander' look like?" I asked Anton.

"He was very small, maybe five feet tall. He looked very human as we do, except that his eyes had no lids on the top. His ears were round and flush to his head and his eyes had no lashes either."

It was rich material for a cosmic comic strip, no doubt about that. But it wasn't a cartoon. It was really happening. I had not included David's space ride in my book because my editors had said no one would believe it. Therefore I hadn't included any of the descriptions that Anton had just duplicated. So he couldn't have gotten any of it from my book.

"So, Anton," I said. "Are we saying that both you

and David have had contact with an extraterrestrial female who imparted knowledge to you that is not part of our education here on Earth?"

Anton nodded. "I believe that is what we are saying, yes. There is a gentleman in Lima, a Yugoslav—he has also had contact and has written several books on the subject. He has been aboard the crafts. I will give you his address and number and when you finish here you can contact him in Lima."

Anton Ponce de Leon and I walked for many hours together, discussing the implications of potential extraterrestrial presence on our Earth.

He told me of the legend in Cuzco handed down through generations. An extraterrestrial was supposed to have landed outside the ancient city thousands of years ago. He stayed to teach the people of Cuzco art, science, government, and self-expression. An ageless stone monument to his being still stands.

When Anton and I said goodbye I knew it was only the beginning of our separate investigations.

That night Esther took me to Benito's house. I wanted to tell him about our manifested weather in Peru. I found him in a corrugated tin hut with dirt floors, one electric light bulb, and dogs, cats, chickens, and fleas everywhere. It was nighttime and he was so congested with phlegm and pleurisy he couldn't sleep. As I walked to his bed with my autographed picture and a new wool sweater for him wrapped around a bunch of money, I saw that he was interested only in the bouquet of wildflowers I was holding. With painful difficulty he sat up in bed, hardly able to draw a breath, and one by one he touched and said a prayer over each flower.

He lay back down in his bed, covered with dirty blankets, wearing a shirt and a maroon vest-sweater with a pattern of white llamas knitted into it.

I had brought the company doctor with me. He sat beside Benito on the bed, no doubt wondering if he, like the rest of us, would pick up the fleas that abounded freely in the hut. The doctor listened to Benito's heart and lungs, felt his abdomen, and so on.

"Emphysema, possible TB, enlarged heart, possible pneumonia, edema," said the doctor. "He's over eighty and is in need of help. I'll arrange for a vehicle to pick him up and take him to the hospital for X-rays and treatment."

I looked around the hut. Old cooking pots hung from nails embedded in the mud walls, and there on an orange crate was Benito's suit and vest with the brown slouch hat. I looked back at Benito.

What did this mean? The man who gave me the secrets to changing the weather was not able to nourish his own body because of his poverty? Or was it poverty? Could it not also have been lack of education? Benito didn't understand about the body's need for protein, the issue of cleanliness was not part of his education, and as he lay sick he still continued to devote himself to prayers.

Oh, Gerry, I thought. Couldn't it have been his spiritual faith that sustained him through the comfortless pain of his life? Couldn't it have lessened the burden? Wouldn't he have been dead long ago had he not been such a master of unseen powers? I could feel Gerry there with me. Contradictions tumbled in my head.

I leaned down and touched Benito's shoulder. "Thank you for all you've done for us," I said. "You made it possible for us to get the shots at Machu Picchu."

He looked up at me, regarding my thanks as irrelevant and unnecessary. He handed me the bouquet of wildflowers.

"Give these to my wife," he said. "And tell her to make an offering to God."

I left his bedside, feeling Gerry accompany me. I wanted to touch him over my shoulder and allude to the fact that the polarity dance between spirituality and materialism was continuing.

*   *   *

Feeling Gerry with me every moment, I headed into the scene where John (David) tells me (Shirley) about Mayan. We had gotten the master shot of the scene a week earlier. The weather had prevented us from going further. To come in for coverage now, after establishing the emotional mood seven days before, would not be easy.

So once more the two of us stood by the jeep, memorized our marks, and rehearsed so that we would match both the moves and the emotion we had established a week earlier. Even the weather was identical to the master shot: windy, misty, ethereal—a joyous painting.

The cameras rolled—three of them to save time. John began his long monologue—not easy under any circumstances. Everything went fine, for a while. Then the script girl fell down and wrenched her knee, two camera batteries went dead, and a squall sprang up. It seemed as though some direct authority was letting us know we were not to shoot the scene the way it was going. John kicked the mud. I patted him on the shoulder, muttering something like "Everything happens for the purposeful good," and went to my trailer so I wouldn't get the wardrobe wet. I sat down in front of my mirror, the rain beating on the roof, to check my makeup. Something didn't look right. I leaned forward. As I looked at myself closely, I realized I had forgotten to put my earrings back in my ears after lunch and we would have had a colossal mismatch when we came in for the close-ups. Only we wouldn't have noticed until we were back in America!

I went to my purse, extracted the earrings, and put them on. Immediately the squall stopped. The rain lifted, and as I peered out the window the ethereal mist returned. Within moments one of the assistants knocked on my door and said they were ready for me.

I wanted to say: "Are you ready for 'why'?"

As I walked back to the set, I looked up and said to an invisible Gerry: "Are you watching all of this?"

I told the camera crew about my earrings. They looked at my ears. They looked up at the sky. They looked at one another, shrugged, and we got the shot. When it was over, John Heard said, "What is it with you and your 'guides' anyway?" The script girl's knee returned to normal and the camera batteries were recharged.

The return to Lima was different from our original arrival from the United States. We had not known that the American Embassy had been bombed until someone in Los Angeles told us, and the lilting tropical climate that met us now seemed to belie the fact that a curfew was still on. Of course we were staying in the Miraflores district at the El Condado Hotel, which diverted one's attention from any kind of trouble.

They had a nice suite for me with a Jacuzzi and a television set, which pointed up clearly how out of communication we had been for so long in Cuzco.

One of my primary pleasures became breathing with ease once again. My rapid heartbeat and blinding-swift altitude headaches were gone. Instead, at sea level my sore throat developed into a full-fledged flu. Still, I could drink two pisco sours and not be drunk, and the sun shone all day.

The mood of the crew changed. They were more comfortable on some levels, yet on others they were alarmed at how swiftly and easily they returned to old habits that city life naturally promulgated: too much booze and rich food, excessive shopping, and a demanding rhythm that tended to dissipate the inner peace they had partially achieved in the mountains. There was only a day-and-a-half layover before departing for the States, so some elected to stay longer. We shopped, went to the Gold Museum, sat on the terrace watching ourselves and Peruvian life go by, and thought, each immersed in what we had learned or what we somehow couldn't bring ourselves to learn. Every individual on the picture had experienced a drama, a novel in itself, the lessons not quite clear yet. And so we avoided discussion as we encountered each other drifting in and out of the restaurants and shops in the Latin quarter.

We gave John a big fortieth-birthday party in a dinner club with dancing and elaborate interior decorations. He was sweet, embarrassed, and very sober. We exchanged gifts and I thanked him deeply for being so superb at interpreting David. He thanked me for insisting that he play the part.

I did my press conference relating to the UFO controversy. Straight-faced I said I was sorry that anyone in this beautiful country should feel I was a Nazi. I had been called many things, but never that. Then I said something about the extraterrestrials.

"If they had come," I said, "they never would have cast their pearls before swine. They would only have imparted higher knowledge to a civilization which could have comprehended it, such as the Inca."

The press thought that made sense somehow. Actually, they were far more interested in whether I thought I had been a reincarnated Inca princess. I said, why not? I've played all kinds of parts.

I went to the beach, to a nightclub, and to as many restaurants as I could fit into two days. Sometimes I went with people from the company and caught up on show business gossip. But most of the time I was still preoccupied with the passing of Gerry. I tried to call Bella to see what was going on, but I couldn't reach her.

And before I knew it, all the people who had made up the professional group interpreting my life story were on their way back to the home base of a profession that would send them out to another far-flung dot on the planet to do it all again with somebody else who believed he or she had something to say.

Simo and I stayed behind. I had people to talk to about Unidentified Flying Objects. It wasn't long though before I believed they should be called IFOs: Identified Flying Objects.

Chapter 24

One of the most interesting people I spoke with who claimed to have extraterrestrial contact was Vitko Novi, a Yugoslavian gentleman of about seventy-five years of age. He was a retired businessman who said he not only enjoyed going to his office every day to dabble, but also was devoting his life now to writing about the UFO contacts he had had.

He came to my hotel room with slides and Spanish translations of his books. We sat together with Jenny Gago, an actress who played Maria (the psychic) in my film. Jenny translated and did not seem at all surprised at what Vitko was saying. I recorded what he told me.

"My first encounter was on March 10, 1960," he said. "Late one night, while I was working at a power plant high in the Cordillera Blanca, the power went out. I went to a window and looked out. The night was bright even though there were no lights. I went outside. There, hovering over the power plant, was an oblong craft emitting light so bright that I couldn't look up into it for long. I didn't feel afraid, because there was a worker with me who said he had seen craft like it many times.

Together we watched the craft descend silently until it landed. I stood transfixed as two very tall human-looking men, with shoulders that sloped more than usual, exited from the craft. They were dressed in tight bodysuits made of fabric that was shiny, almost like the wet skin of a seal. It was all one piece with very fine threads. And they wore no shoes because the bodysuits covered their feet.

"Their faces looked as though they were combinations of many races, a mixture of coloring and features I had never seen before.

"The two beings peacefully walked toward me, sat down, and materialized a fire to warm us up in the cold night!"

As Vitko talked he was calm and matter-of-fact. No matter how many stories of this kind I heard I was always astonished, slightly suspicious, and yet somewhat envious because nothing like that had happened to me. Vitko said that at this point he looked into the fire, with the two space beings beside him, trying to give himself time to get sorted out. He said he wasn't frightened and didn't want to leave but was hardly able to credit what was happening. Then one of the beings spoke to Vitko in his own language. Vitko quoted the gist of what they said for Jenny, who translated to me.

"We sense in your cellular structure that you are rejecting us," said the spokesman. "That is your right. But our greeting to you is 'all for others.'"

Vitko didn't know what he meant.

"We mean," said the being, "that we want nothing for ourselves. That is our creed where we come from. We do everything for others."

Suddenly the two beings touched something on their bodysuits, and Vitko saw them hanging in the air. Then they moved themselves around in various directions. He said it was like looking at James Bond. But they explained that when they reversed the positive ions in the atmosphere around their suits, they could control their movements by degravitating themselves.

Vitko said the two beings gave him a pyrotechnical display of degravitation and then came back to earth and sat beside the fire. Vitko said he was ready to believe he was going crazy, but his friend was comfortable and laughing because he was used to them.

As Vitko told me his story, I remembered the David character in my own book and screenplay—a composite of several people who had had their own space being contacts. How prevalent was this stuff? Was it true or did they simply want it to be true? Vitko flashed his color slides from a projector onto the white wall of my hotel room. I was fascinated by the pictures. I had seen so many like them. The craft (saucer-shaped) hung over the mountains above a power plant below. Were they real or somehow faked? And were there actually beings inside? So many people around the world were relating stories similar to this. What did it mean? Were they all making them up?

Vitko told me that the beings said they were from a star called Apu and had been visiting the Andes for centuries. They were legendarily known as "angels" because they could make rain (by manipulating the negative ions in the atmosphere) and they were very sought-after as healers.

"The Apunian angels," said Vitko, "often landed their craft and called for the sick and maimed to come aboard. Each of their patients always returned to their homes cured."

"How did they do it?" I asked. "Explain it to me."

"Well," said Vitko, "they said they disintegrated the diseased cells and then reintegrated them again with Divine energy. When they first learned to reduce the atom they learned how body atomic structure works too. They said we are all capable of doing this if we could understand and utilize the component parts of the atom, but that requires a knowledge of the Divine energy, the understanding of the physics of the soul, and a willingness to accept that each being in the cosmos is made up of that energy. He said if we feel hate or fear for ourselves or others, we will not be able to do it."

This was the spiritual technology that I was hearing more and more about. It was as though we were on the threshold of understanding that the success of outer technology depended entirely on the success of understanding our inner technology. It felt as though we humans were spinning close to the center of our own energy transformation if we'd just allow ourselves to embrace the potential. We were in a metamorphosis because we had exhausted our old mode of consciousness. The winds of change were upon us; everybody could feel that. So why wouldn't those winds bring higher and more aware beings to help us raise our own awareness of the infinite potential we possessed.

Some of the beings were in physical bodies, and came in craft of various kinds; and some were without physical bodies, such as those using mediums as instruments. In either case the message to us always seemed to be the same. We defined ourselves by our limitations and fears. We experienced poverty because we had not yet understood that we deserved abundance as a matter of right. And the creation of abundance was within our conscious and *aware* control, and could, if we really wanted it for everybody, be created. We created wars and killing and greed for ourselves because we were deeply afraid that otherwise we would be deprived: of sustenance, of freedom—of many things. The result of fearful consciousness was that most of our energies were channeled into destructive enterprises. The most amazing human truth of all was that killing and the destruction of life actually still existed as part of our human experience.

By this time in my life Vitko's story of space teachers was not something I felt inclined to scoff at. In fact, more than ever I wished that his encounter had happened to me.

"The beings asked me if I would like to go aboard their craft," Vitko went on. "So I did. To tell you the truth, I thought they were spies or something, so I was curious even though I was afraid."

Vitko and his co-worker followed the two beings into the craft.

"I noticed," he said, "that when they walked ahead of us, the grass didn't bend under their weight. When I asked them why not, they said they would harm nothing on this gentle earth and took great pains to control their weightlessness."

Vitko said the room he entered was round, with no angles. There were soft fat sofas to sit on.

"Immediately," he went on, "I had a strange sensation of degravitation. My body had weight, but something inside of me felt lighter. Suddenly I saw that I was surrounded by screens. The two beings asked me if I wanted to see my life enacted in front of me. I didn't know what they meant. Immediately, before my eyes on the screens surrounding me, I saw the story of my life. I saw everything. My birth, my childhood, scenes that I remembered that affected me deeply. It was incredible. I saw myself acting out events that had actually occurred in my life. In fact, everything I *thought* showed on the screen as well. I was watching my life in emotional Three-D."

Vitko stopped talking and turned to me.

"I found it very disturbing," he said. "I didn't understand anything. So I was sure they were sophisticated communist spies. I went to the police. I told the sergeant what had happened: everything, along with my deduction that the craft carried enemy spies. The sergeant said I was crazy and should seek psychiatric help. I knew I would have to pursue it alone after that."

Vitko then outlined how his life became a series of encounters.

In the next year he had several more visitations. On June 4, 1960, he was hiking alone in the Sierras when the craft landed again. He was afraid because he knew he had reported them to the police. But they were not upset at all.

"You must pursue your truth however you wish," they said.

And the same two beings invited him in. There were books, magazines, flower petals, herbs, and various other paraphernalia of human life, along with a cap made of rabbit fur. One of the beings held the cap up and, while shaking his head sadly, said, "You still take the life of another being." Vitko said he felt so embarrassed and sat back on one of the fat sofas. The screens went on again. This time he saw a retrospective of the natural earth changes that had occurred in that part of the world. He said he saw the formation of the Andes Mountains plus the construction of the original city of Cuzco. The city was built by the people of Apu and the construction was accomplished with degravitational techniques to lift the monstrous stones. The original design of the city was patterned after a flying butterfly. There were no angles.

Then he saw Cuzco destroyed by a cataclysm—a cataclysm that also destroyed and re-formed part of the Andes. It disturbed and affected the atmosphere in space so much that extraterrestrial craft had difficulty landing.

By now Vitko was afraid that what he had seen was real. He left the craft.

Two months later, on August 21, 1960, he encountered the craft again. They invited him in, and the beings discussed their past incarnations. One of them had had 504. They discussed the family unit on Apu and revealed that there really was no such thing. A child was born into the family of the ALL; all loved and nurtured equally. There was no feeling of proprietorship. The discussion of the family led to a problem that Vitko was having with his daughter.

"You are possessive of your daughter," the beings gently chided him. "You have the right to those thoughts and feelings, but it would be better for you to share the love of all beings—that is your noble mission of birth."

Vitko left the craft resolved to improve his relationship with his family.

The next encounter stunned him. On the screens he was shown the beautiful mountain city of Yungay. It was his favorite place. Immediately afterward he was shown the destruction of Yungay which would occur ten years later. The beings revealed the future destruction to Vitko so that he could exercise his free will by going to the authorities to plead for evacuating the city of 20,000 to another location. The mayor-judge in charge accused Vitko of being an extreme alarmist and again he was recommended to a psychiatrist. Vitko said he left the mayor's office and walked alone until he encountered one of his being friends who reassured him: "You have done your part. But ridicule is difficult to bear, is it not?"

On another occasion he entered the craft with three mountain women. Each was shown some of their past-life incarnations on the screens.

"We show you what you need to understand," said the beings. "What you already understand is not necessary."

On still another contact he met a woman who had been born here on earth and taken to Apu to learn her own internal power. She said that within one year's education on Apu she was using mental powers she had never been aware of possessing. She elected to remain with the Apunians.

During a visit to a town that was suffering from drought, he was told that the inhabitants said prayers for the craft to come. It did. It hovered in the sky manipulating the positive ions in the atmosphere. When vibrating at different speeds, the positive ions caused clouds to form which then created rain. The town was drenched in a much-needed storm.

Vitko told me story after story of his encounters with the space beings. And basically they were trying to teach him that all of mankind and each individual within it was a masterpiece of spiritual potential; that the Earth was a learning center where spirit could interact with matter; that our physical world was only a result of consciousness intention and by changing our consciousness we could change the world. They said that beyond the physical spectrum of our Earth, there were companion intelligence systems of nonphysical guides, as well as physical guides, who continually interact with us and with every life form on Earth whether we are aware of them or not. They all hold the spiritual intention of our Earth in their consciousness, because we are all brothers and sisters of the cosmos. Many of our forefathers were their forefathers, so they are karmically intertwined with the human race.

Vitko said they told him that whenever we treat any form of life carelessly it is because we don't recognize it as a part of ourselves. They said the flow of conscious energy among all levels of life on our planet was instantaneous; that there was no life form, however small or large, that did not feel the impact in some way of every thought emanating from human consciousness. So as long as we remained unaware of the power we had, we would abuse it unconsciously—to our own disadvantage and possibly to our own destruction.

Everything destructive occurring on our planet flowed from spiritual ignorance—ignorance of the fact that we interact with all living kingdoms. They said that the purpose of the space beings and the nonphysical beings was to help us expand our conscious awareness so that we could radiate from within on a level that was more in keeping with our power and spiritual expression in the human experience.

Over a period of a few days I learned a great deal from Vitko and his related experiences. Whether they were "real" or not seemed irrelevant to me. The message was clear, a spiritual shift in consciousness would benefit humankind.

When Simo and I said goodbye to Vitko, I felt that I should travel to the mountain city of Huarás, where he had been, high in the Cordillera Blanca mountain range. He mapped out where we should go and wished us good luck.

One thing was becoming crystal-clear. Understanding the dimension of outer space which we longed to know would be accomplished in direct ratio to our understanding of our own inner space.

Chapter 25

At 5:30 the following morning Simo and I piled into a van with a woman who, I knew, lived in and ran a government-operated hotel just outside of Huarás. Her name was Suzie. She was German and had married a Peruvian man twenty years her junior. By all reports she was radiantly happy, even though most of her family disapproved.

When I called Suzie (recommended by another friend), she said she had known I was going to call her. She had read *Out on a Limb* the previous Christmas and "knew" she would meet me within a year. There we were, traveling over the isolated desert highways outside of Lima on our way to the Cordillera Blanca, high in the Andes at 22,205 feet.

My easy breathing at sea level was not to last past two hours out of Lima—not that much of a loss anyway because of the pollution.

On the six-hour drive the terrain shifted almost mathematically according to the change in altitude. The lower mountains were sandy, dry, and barren, almost as though a nuclear blast from long ago still stood as a testament of destruction. With each ascending mile the surroundings became more lush and green; the vista more extraordinary in its beauty the higher we climbed.

The mountain road was narrow as it wound its way upward toward the high Andes. Our van seemed to shrink whenever we encountered a vehicle coming from the opposite direction.

We passed mud ruins, potato farms, fields of sugar cane, open acres of cactus, herds of sheep and cattle. And always the life I saw seemed to drift along inside isolated bubbles of casual time all its own. Goal-oriented priorities were laughable to the languid mountain people. A peasant ambled alongside his cow all day long, unconcerned whether he would make it to the market that day or another day.

Women with water vases on their heads walked five miles to the Santa River for their family's water, only to walk another ten to trade a goat for produce. Linear time didn't exist for them. *All* was *now*. You could see it in their attitude: peaceful, unassuming, and unaware of difficulty.

The red pepper trees swayed in the blue sunlight alongside mountain ridges. Yet fields of yellow broom reminded one of Scotland.

When we arrived late in the afternoon at Suzie's mountain hotel in Monterrey we were tired and exhilarated —and I knew I was just exactly where I was supposed to be. I looked out over the vista below me. Curls of smoke spiraled above mountain huts, the snow-covered Cordillera beckoned in the distance, and the high-altitude stars which I knew to be ridiculously large were waiting to come out and greet us.

Why was I there?

I couldn't really answer that myself. I just knew something was going to happen to me and that I should be there to let it.

Suzie gave Simo one small guesthouse. I had another. Suzie and her husband, Jorge, lived in the third.

Jorge was a pleasant young man with dark hair and black pools for eyes, contrasting with Suzie's blond blue-eyed bovineness. They seemed very happy and were swift to understand that I basically wanted to be left alone.

So after unpacking I made my way to the thermal bathhouse, which was a welcome relaxer and I allowed myself to do nothing but simply *be*.

Dinner with the four of us in Suzie's small guesthouse was fresh tomatoes and onions, omelets, and homemade bread. In that altitude a sparse diet is the best. We talked about metaphysics and synchronicity in human lives.

"You can feel when things are meant to be," said Suzie. "You are meant to be here."

She and her husband had seen many spacecraft and of course had heard the stories the mountain peasants told of learning from the occupants of the craft. Suzie said she and her husband had a friend who was a close friend of President Alan Garcia. They said Garcia was a student of metaphysics also and in fact was a Mason; which degree of the Masonic lodge she didn't know.

Sometime that evening after going to bed I began to ruminate on why my spiritual consciousness-raising had begun in Peru. I had been somewhat interested in spiritual matters prior to my trip to this mountainous country, but it was the energy of the Andes that had inspired and moved me in ways that the Himalayas never had.

I remembered again that the Andes were supposed to represent the feminine vibration on the planet earth, and the Himalayas the masculine. Since the feminine vibration was what was finally coming into its own to balance the planet's preparation for the New Age, perhaps I had simply felt the flow of an energy that coincided with my own.

And now it felt as though I was in the Andes again

to realize something more than I ever had before, so that I could *integrate* it into my daily life. And it had something to do with Gerry. In exactly what way I was not certain.

As I tossed about attempting to sleep, the altitude began to get me again; a rumbling nausea accompanied not only by a dizzying headache, but something else. I had the decided feeling that something or someone was trying to communicate with me. I got up and walked around. I lay down and tossed and turned some more. I wouldn't allow myself to relax and receive whatever it was that was trying to reach me.

My night did not go well. But that was for the best, too, because it simply lowered my resistance for what was to occur the following day.

Suzie drove Simo and me around the "Lost Horizon" that we felt we had reached.

Above the Santa Valley, overlooking the village of Mantacatto, I felt I should purchase a piece of land with the intention someday in the future of erecting a spiritual center where people from different areas of the world could come and meditate collectively. It was a strong and positive impulse as I looked out over the craggy white-capped range of the Cordillera Blanca. Again I felt the presence of an energy I couldn't define. Again I couldn't touch it. Gerry never left my mind, not really. And he had always claimed that *I* was persistent!

We left the mountainside and drove by the landslide site of Yungay. I thought of Vitko's prediction screen on the spacecraft. He said he had seen, in those three minutes, the immensity and the swiftness of nature's power. How had the space beings known about it? And why couldn't they have prevented it if they were so interested in saving the human race? In the face of such catastrophic disaster, with all the personal tragedies involved, it was cold comfort at best to believe that the world's collective consciousness was responsible. Just as it was heartbreaking, for those who believe in an exteriorized, loving God, to accept the daily toll of tragedy around them and often in their own personal lives. None of it made sense. Nor could it, until the human race took full responsibility for its own destiny, and included spirituality in that fullness.

After a lunch of wheat-grass soup and fresh vegetables, Suzie drove us into the mountains. An hour into the trek we came across a turquoise lake nestled silent and floating in its own higher kingdom, surrounded by bodyguards of chiseled beauty. The crisp mountain air brushed through my hair. I walked off by myself. I needed to be alone. I felt the haunting energy again, and then, as I looked up I saw the mountain covered in snow that I had seen in one of Vitko's pictures. The "reclining Hindu" people called it because that's what it looked like: a reclining body shrouded in white linen. But in Vitko's picture a spacecraft had hung above the mountain. As I looked at it now I saw only the meditative splendor of its snowy silence—and surely that miracle of beauty was sufficient.

I walked closer to the mountain, pulling an apple from the pocket of my coat.

This was how it had started for me: gazing at a mountain in the Andes some ten years before. Here in these magnificent heights I had first connected to the untapped stirrings inside me that had longed to be recognized. Waking from the dream sleep of unawareness I had realized that I, and each of us, were more than we seemed to be. The realization had happened in the flash of an instant, although I had heard it as a song in my heart for some time. But here I had listened to its lyrical music. And since then it had never left me. It was there to sustain me through the weathers of misfortune and despair, only to accelerate its sweet vibration whenever I respected its existence. It was God and it was me simultaneously. We were intertwined. I could be whatever I wanted to be if I trusted that music, that song, that vibration of God that was *inside* of me.

And now as I munched my apple and raised my arms to the mountain wind I could feel myself make contact with another song energy. I sat down and closed my eyes, relaxing to allow whatever was going to happen to flow through me. A bright light began to form in my mind. It grew and expanded until the image and vision of Gerry appeared above me, yet *inside* my mind. I held tight to what I was "seeing," needing very much to understand what it meant.

Gerry seemed confused and slightly desperate as he hovered in the light. Then he spoke to me.

"I don't understand what has happened," he said. "Where am I?"

I hesitated a moment in my mind before answering. He seemed so real, so separate from me. Then, as though speaking in a thought language, I said, "I think you have gone home."

I could see his face reacting to me so clearly.

"Is this what you were always talking about?" he asked. "Is this what you meant when you said we were souls only living in bodies? And now I have no body?"

I nodded.

"I have been trying to contact you," he went on. "But you were too busy to hear me. I have been around you for so many days."

"I know, Gerry," I said. "I felt you. Why did you do it? Why did you leave now?"

Gerry hovered there as though torn between what he had done and what it would now mean.

"I don't know," he said. "I'm not really certain where I am."

"You are home, Gerry. You are with the light and with that God-energy you didn't believe in."

I felt him absorb what I had said. "I needed to hear that again?" he asked.

"Yes," I said, "I guess so."

"I had no one else who could explain," he said. "I need rest now. I'm so tired."

I watched him in the light of my mind's eye. I realized there was also a light ray emanating from him to me. It became brighter and brighter.

"We are one," he said.

"What do you mean?" I asked.

"I will be with you," he said.

"What do you mean?" I repeated.

Suddenly Gerry began to float away, his light becoming dimmer.

"You have helped me. I will help you. We are one," he said from far away.

Then he was gone. Gone into the mist of my own mind. I looked after him, but he and his light were gone.

I opened my eyes and shook my head. I breathed the cool, crisp mountain air. What had just happened? Had I made it up? Or had Gerry actually, on some other level, in some other dimension, really visited me? His face was so clear, his expression so genuinely confused. Yet if he was dead and only a soul now, why did he have any form at all? Was it because form was the only way I had of recognizing him? Many people who had reported visitations from loved ones who had passed on said that they appeared to them in forms of light or sometimes just bodily forms as they had always been in life. Easily recognizable.

That had never happened to me before now. Perhaps I had never allowed it to happen before. On the other hand, I had never lost anyone I was in love with before.

I got up and stretched again. This was a scene I would like to have included in the show. The point of it would have been that Gerry was a character in my life who proved to me that it is possible to embrace two levels of consciousness at the same time: the earth plane physical level that is so real as it deals out its pain and its difficulties and its joys; and the spiritual level, which in its infinite wisdom is loving enough to guarantee us that *it* is the reality, everything else an illusion. The lesson of each? We create them both.

I didn't say much on the way home. Something had shifted for me. I had learned long ago that the most valuable knowledge is that gained by *experience*. When that happens, everything changes.

I guess I had been as afraid of death as anyone else over the course of my life. The eternal black void of nothingness was indeed frightening, believed in by objective pragmatists who also necessarily believed that physical life was all there was. Death was oblivion, the "natural" way to go. Natural because, as the teaching of relatively recent times had it, what we see with our eyes is what is for real. But that has been changing.

Human beings, a few thousands of years ago, were not as capable of holding a thought or imagining a picture or perceiving some of the concepts that we are capable of today. Their belief in an afterlife rested in primitive deities, earth elementals like wind, sun, and fertility, whose power was physically evident all around them. The source of life, and those things which sustained it, were sacred. If they did not actually recognize the interdependence of all life, they at least respected what they saw as holy on this earth—and let their gods and goddesses take care of the rest.

The concept of an afterlife took on abstract reality when it became codified by the formal religions. Dogma and ritual created both good and bad afterlives—Paradise or Hell—using mankind's urgent need to believe in *some*thing beyond this world as a mechanism through which to amass and exploit power.

Intellectual atheism rejected that kind of power and, as it were, threw out the baby with the bath water, making independence of mind coincidental with an absence of faith.

But actually, the levels of both our psychic and our mental capacities are far greater now than they ever were in the far past. That is a testament to the spiritual and mental progress of the human race. Our minds are more capable today of accepting unusual, unfamiliar, more complex ideas. The advancements in technology attest to that evolution of the human mind. But the inner technology of our unlimited thought has advanced also. And if it is true that we all create our own reality, then the capacity for creative technology is clearly infinite also. The creative technology of perceiving alternative realities is a quantum leap in the progress of mankind.

In the past, death belonged in the province of an exterior, unknowable "God": the mythological garden of paradisiacal afterlife, untouchable and unrealized by mortals who longed to know its promise, its secrets, and, indeed, whether it existed at all.

Lately, more and more people are claiming to have seen the actual "light," the blinding, indescribably loving light that they are certain is "Heaven." "God is light," they say after having had an out-of-body experience. "I died and lived to tell of it," they say. And account follows account of such experiences. The reports are increasing, almost as though the numbers of people experiencing the light are increasing as a testament to the level of receptivity and openness to higher and higher consciousness. The chasm between Heaven and Earth is narrowing, and to no one's surprise.

The *light* is expected now. It had always been there, but more and more we are beginning to recognize that in fact *we* are the light, if only we can bring ourselves to hold that evolved and sophisticated concept. The light is not outside of us. And whenever we recognize that light inside of us, we know we have found the secret to life well kept. We have been a secret to ourselves. That is what has been missing. We have been missing the light from ourselves. *We are the light*.

That night, as I tried to sleep I found myself waiting for something. I wasn't sure what it was. I walked around my room. There was no more feeling of Gerry. I was glad that was resolved. I lay down and closed my eyes. Then I began to feel some strange energy surge through me, similar to what I had felt at Machu Picchu. Then I got a headache and the same nausea followed, except much milder. I opened my eyes. What was happening? I closed my eyes again. Maybe it would all go away.

Instead I felt as though something was trying to communicate to me.

As I lay there with my eyes closed, I felt myself drift off into what the scientists call the alpha state, a narrow band of consciousness somewhere between wakefulness and sleep. I extended no control over what I was feeling or thinking, yet could watch what was happening—a state of being both participant and observer. And then something very strange began to occur.

I saw a huge round gray-colored metal object over my head, as though I were looking through the roof of my guesthouse. It was a giant craft. And to my surprise it wasn't at all beautiful. It was gray and metal. I watched it in awe. Then I began to have flashing feelings coming toward me in another language. I couldn't make out the message. The headache intensified. I knew I wasn't asleep and I knew I wasn't awake. *And* I knew I was really seeing this thing, but I couldn't figure out how. I was not outside, yet I saw it directly over the guesthouse as though the roof were transparent and I was seeing through it.

I wanted to write down my feelings, but I couldn't leave the state of mind I found myself in. I didn't even want to.

Then, as though through feelings, *not* words, I began to get a message. I felt that I was in an apex of time, where there was no measurement of any kind. I felt as though I were at the emotional crossroads of a transformation, where time and matter stood still and there was no judgment, desire, success, or failure. There was only truth and *being*. Then I saw the number 9 form in the center of the visualized crossroads. I didn't know what it meant, although the word *completion* sprang to my mind. As soon as I felt *completion,* the craft disappeared.

In its place was a spectacular ocean of liquid crystal shimmering in front of me. I gazed at it for a while, enchanted, and then felt myself project out over the water. I danced on the waves of undulating, shimmering crystal liquid. It was glorious. I pirouetted, jumped, leaped, and skipped with exuberant joy in and out of the glittering surf.

The implications of dancing on top of the water didn't escape me. In fact, with all my joyful abandonment, I wouldn't have wanted anyone I knew to see me. And then I remembered. . . .

The shift in understanding for people interested in achieving the ultimate in enlightenment was to touch the "Christ" consciousness in themselves and trust it. To know that we were each endowed with such powerful energy that we actually effected a physical force which collectively could alter the course of mankind. The power and reality were not in front of our eyes, not seen, but unseen—within. *We* were responsible for creating everything. Now we needed consciously to align ourselves with the Divine intention of the universe so that our forces could work together.

The image of my dancing on crystal water may have been coming from another time and another place, but the principle of its image was constant and forever. I knew that anything was possible if we desired it.

What we needed now was a new blueprint for human understanding which recognized that we were each

involved with Divine intention, whether we acknowledged it or not. Until now we had identified with reality
as though it existed only objectively, outside ourselves.
The change occurring spoke to a more evolved understanding that the reality of God and Divine intention
existed and began *within* us. Because we understood the
Divine as outside of ourselves, we separated ourselves
from our fellow man and nature. We were now ready to
hold the thought, comprehend the concept, that we and
the God-force were one and the same. Our souls contained the same Divine characteristics as God. We were
made of the same stuff. And so the new and emerging
blueprint for our understanding would be the conscious
internalization of the forces of love, wisdom, responsibility, and power.

As I lay in bed thinking, it hit me that every single
soul on the planet was involved in the process of making
his or her own personal transformation. Or *not* making
it. That was why so many lives were in upheaval. We,
living on the planet, were involved in transition, not
disaster, each of us in our own way, with different lessons to understand and a cleansing to accomplish.

Gerry had accomplished as much as he wanted to
for the time being. Everyone I knew in my life was
involved with his or her own transitions and growth.
And each one of us carried with us a monumental charge
of vibrational energy. It was palpable. You knew a negative vibration as soon as you encountered it, and you
knew that that person had further to go, acting as a
reflector for your own growth, therefore not to be judged.

I was beginning to integrate the forces of the physical and the forces of the nonphysical in my understanding. They coexisted simultaneously in my reality. I was
learning from both. I loved both. I *was* both.

I would continue to play my role in the life I had
written for myself. The world would continue to be my

stage. Some of the characters would exit in a blaze of light; others would enter in the same fashion.

With all its complicated melodrama, high antic comedy, and desperate tragedy, one clear unmistakable truth emerged. The play was the schoolroom in which we understood fully and consciously that we were the Divine intention. It dwelt within us, and the physical effect of that illumination would shine a light on the world that would be profound. The actor and the role were one. The play and the part were one. The God and the human were one. It was truly a Divine Comedy.

ABOUT THE AUTHOR

SHIRLEY MACLAINE was born and raised in Virginia. She began her career as a Broadway dancer and singer, then progressed to featured performer and award-winning actress of television and films. She has traveled extensively on her own all over the world. Her experiences in Africa, India and the Far East formed the basis for her first two books, while her deeply personal investigations into the spiritual realm were the focus of *Out on a Limb* and *Dancing in the Light*. In addition to starring in the miniseries of *Out on a Limb,* Shirley MacLaine wrote the screenplay with Colin Higgins.

BANTAM BOOKS
GRAND SLAM SWEEPSTAKES
Win a new Chevrolet Sprint . . .
It's easy . . . It's fun . . . Here's how to enter:

OFFICIAL ENTRY FORM

Three Bantam book titles on sale this month are hidden in this word puzzle. Identify the books by circling each of these titles in the puzzle. Titles may appear within the puzzle horizontally, vertically, or diagonally . . .

	P	R	O	M	I	S	E	S
Z		A	R		N	U		O
P	L	A	Y	I	N	G		
F	I	L		T	H	E		T
	L		'S		W			O
I	X			M	A	N	Y	
F	L	A	S	H	B	A	C	K

Bantam's titles for September are:

IT'S ALL IN THE PLAYING

FLASHBACK

SO MANY PROMISES

In each of the books listed above there is another entry blank and puzzle . . . another chance to win!

Be on the lookout for Bantam paperback books coming in October: FAVORITE SON, WHITE PALACE INDOCHINE (U.S. only), CHILDREN OF THE SHROUD (Canada only). In each of them, you'll find a new puzzle, entry blank and GRAND SLAM Sweepstakes rules . . . and yet another chance to win another brand-new Chevrolet automobile!

MAIL TO: GRAND SLAM SWEEPSTAKES
Post Office Box 18
New York, New York 10046

Please Print

NAME _____

ADDRESS _____

CITY _____ STATE _____ ZIP _____

OFFICIAL RULES

NO PURCHASE NECESSARY.

To enter identify this month's Bantam Book titles by placing a circle around each word forming each title. There are three titles shown on previous page to be found in this month's puzzle. Mail your entry to: Grand Slam Sweepstakes, P.O. Box 18, New York, N.Y. 10046.

This is a monthly sweepstakes starting February 1, 1988 and ending January 31, 1989. During this sweepstakes period, one automobile winner will be selected each month from all entries that have correctly solved the puzzle. To participate in a particular month's drawing, your entry must be received by the last day of that month. The Grand Slam prize drawing will be held on February 14, 1989 from all entries received during all twelve months of the sweepstakes.

To obtain a free entry blank/puzzle/rules, send a self-addressed stamped envelope to: Winning Titles, P.O. Box 650, Sayreville, N.J. 08872. Residents of Vermont and Washington need not include return postage.

PRIZES: Each month for twelve months a Chevrolet automobile will be awarded with an approximate retail value of $12,000 each.

The Grand Slam Prize Winner will receive 2 Chevrolet automobiles plus $10,000 cash (ARV $34,000).

Winners will be selected under the supervision of Marden-Kane, Inc., an independent judging organization. By entering this sweepstakes each entrant accepts and agrees to be bound by these rules and the decisions of the judges which shall be final and binding. Winners may be required to sign an affidavit of eligibility and release which must be returned within 14 days of receipt. All prizes will be awarded. No substitution or transfer of prizes permitted. Winners will be notified by mail. Odds of winning depend on the total number of eligible entries received.

Sweepstakes open to residents of the U.S. and Canada except employees of Bantam Books, its affiliates, subsidiaries, advertising agencies and Marden-Kane, Inc. Void in the Province of Quebec and wherever else prohibited or restricted by law. Not responsible for lost or misdirected mail or printing errors. Taxes and licensing fees are the sole responsibility of the winners. All cars are standard equipped. Canadian winners will be required to answer a skill testing question.

For a list of winners, send a self-addressed, stamped envelope to: Bantam Winners, P.O. Box 711, Sayreville, N.J. 08872.